HARVARD MIDDLE EASTERN MONOGRAPHS

XII

THE ECONOMY OF MOROCCO
1912–1962

BY

CHARLES F. STEWART

DISTRIBUTED FOR THE

CENTER FOR MIDDLE EASTERN STUDIES

OF HARVARD UNIVERSITY BY

HARVARD UNIVERSITY PRESS

CAMBRIDGE, MASSACHUSETTS

1964

LIBRARY OF CONGRESS CATALOG CARD NUMBER 64-8716

PRINTED IN THE UNITED STATES OF AMERICA

INTRODUCTORY NOTE

This book is directed to the reader who would like to know more about the history of Moroccan affairs — past and current. If the reader is thinking in terms of a general history of twentieth-century Morocco, however, he is warned that the volume represents only a fragment. If his frame is narrowed to Moroccan economic history, then the work would represent only a somewhat larger piece. Thus, from the outset, it should be clear that the author makes no claim to comprehensiveness, even in the economic sphere; indeed, he must leave to the judgment of the reader whether he has reached the more limited goal of identifying and comprehending the really important matters raised during the last fifty years of Moroccan economics.

More than space limitations force a writer to be less than complete. Lack of data is always a problem; and inadequate and often unreliable information, apparently inherent in a colonial situation, is often an even greater one. An awareness of limited competence, which leads to unlimited conscience, certainly plays an additional part. Finally, the researcher must have a "thesis" if his account is to hang together in any meaningful way — and this implies selectivity. The process of selection, of course, requires reading, observing, asking, thinking, accepting, rejecting, and, finally, writing and rewriting. Yet despite all, there always remains the uneasy feeling that another thesis might have done as well or better to explain a complex reality. The thesis set out in the following pages, then, remains only one of many, and as good or bad as the others make it; of this the reader is also warned.

Although one should be wary of writing economic history in terms of stages, the history of twentieth-century Morocco does seem to lend itself to this treatment; it essentially breaks down into three periods, with the breaks marked by two political events — the establishment of the protectorate in 1912 and the re-establishment of independence in 1956. As a matter of form only, the book deals in turn with pre-protectorate Morocco, the forty-four years of French control, and the six years since independence. The periods, however, are tied together by an assumption that parts of the past are still important, that a *tabula rasa* at any point in the course of human events is never all that blank. For example, the economics of the years of French control cannot be really understood without knowing something of the economics of pre-protectorate Morocco. Chapter I is consequently devoted to what hindsight suggests were the factors present in 1912 which continued to be vital during the years of French control, among them land use, tenure, and taxation, the state of the artisan trades, and international treaties. In the four middle chapters, which span the years of French administration, such factors persist and resist mutation. They are the stubborn stuff which become problems faced by the "French Presence," but particular kinds of problems in the light cast by French purposes, actions, and aspirations.

As it turned out, the setting was an ideal one for the apparent propensity of man as administrator to produce other than the effect he intends — that phenomenon which limits the tenure of an administration. For example, settlement in the country for Europeans and sanitation for the Moroccans, both official policies and calculated to please both groups, produced intractable population, unemployment, and social problems. Again, the purposeful development of road and rail "opened up" the country to military conquest and commerce, but it also carried the nationalist idea which, for whatever reasons, proved in the end to be more than a match for the bayonet and the franc. In effect, the commingling of European ideas and techniques in agriculture, industry, transport, and trade with those of the Moroccans assured the reduction in the time span of the protectorate from the long-held French view of infinity to forty-odd years. In the last analysis, since the administrators never understood the logic of the situation they administrated, they never found that proper mixture of policies which would have extended their governance.

The last chapter finds the Moroccans once again managing their own affairs. Many of the problems they face are those unsolved ones which the French themselves inherited; others which the French created. But the problems are now even more acute; further, they are considerably different as they are restated in terms of Moroccan purposes, actions, and aspirations in a world of power politics. In sum, just as the French inherited the legacies of pre-protectorate Moroccans, so the Moroccans inherit the legacies of the protectorate French. These legacies provide the continuity in Moroccan economic history; the discontinuity lies in how they are viewed by those in charge.

There is a final point. As one observes and sympathizes with a Moroccan administration just trying its wings, the mind comes to ponder the source of its mandate. The fundamental question is whether its legitimacy stems from the inherent strength of the nationalist cause, or from the myopia of its predecessor. The question would appear important for Moroccans, and the answer is one that only the Moroccans can give in the years to come.

As the book is principally concerned with economic forces and events, the voices of people are largely mute in the pages that follow. There are many guides for the hand that writes, however, and the contributions of all of them are gratefully acknowledged here.

Above all, one is indebted to the people — famous, infamous, and anonymous — who created and were affected by the matters with which the book deals. The work of Marshal Lyautey, who demonstrated considerable genius within the harsh limits imposed by his mission, cannot be overlooked; neither can the skill, wisdom, gentility, and quiet tenacity of King Mohammed V who led the Moroccans to independence. There are the people of the countryside — the *colon* (French [or European] farmer-settler) with his well-tended fields and black Citroen, and the mountain Berber who wears his poverty with a dignity which should shame the affluent. The French merchant of Casablanca and banker of Paris also play a large role. So does the merchant of Fez. The military — *goumier*, white kepi, and draftee — are present throughout.

Many have contributed much, and many have contributed nothing to the struggle for a better existence in Morocco. Indeed, some were there only for larcenous purpose. It is nevertheless from this panoply of people, motives, and maneuvers that there emerges the story told here of Moroccan economic life during the past fifty years.

More immediately, there are other debts to acknowledge. The occasion allows the great pleasure of recognizing, along with a couple of generations of other students, Professor M. M. Knight of the University of California, as teacher, mentor, and friend. He shared generously his insights and vast store of knowledge of the North African scene.

Among other obligations owing are those to Professor Leon Carl Brown and Dr. Jamil Abun-Nasr, who kindly assumed the task of reading the manuscript and making many useful comments. The encouragement, advice, and understanding of Professor A. J.

Meyer of Harvard University were indispensable. Research fellowships from the Ford Foundation and the Harvard Center for Middle Eastern Studies made it possible to study, think, and travel. Miss Elizabeth Randolph of the Center was extremely helpful with the inevitable administrative matters, while the patience and typing ability of Miss Brenda Sens and Miss Carolyn Cross gave at least legibility to the results.

Most immediately of all, fond recognition is due my wife, who wielded an authoritative pencil with great dexterity. Finally, but far from last, there is Katie, a charming young lady of five years, who more or less respected a closed study door.

My debt to all is very great, because all are partly accountable for what appears hereafter. But since their responsibility is only joint and not several, I am glad to recognize and assume the whole responsibility for all of them.

CHARLES F. STEWART

Graduate School of Business
Columbia University
January, 1963

CONTENTS

LIST OF TABLES

MAPS

THE ECONOMY OF MOROCCO
1912–1962

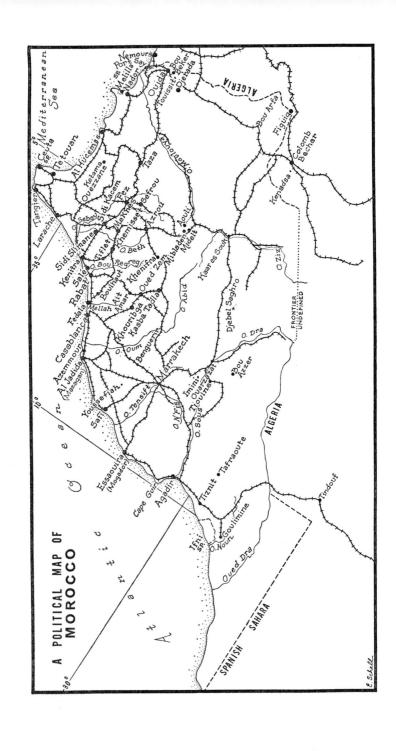

A POLITICAL MAP OF
MOROCCO

Mediterranean Sea

ALGERIA

Nemours
Port Say
Melilla Sp.
Nador
Oujda
Toussit Bou-
Bou
Bekker
Djenada
Bou Arfa
Figuig
Colomb
Bechar

Ceuta Sp.
Tetouan
Al Hucemas
Ketama
Ouezzane
Taza
Kenadsa
Tangier
Larache
Sidi Kacem
Fez
Meknes Sefrou
Sebou
Izhou
Sidi Slimane
Khemisset
Bouli
Kenitra
Tiflet
Mideit
Salé
O. Bou
Regreg
Khenifra
Mibladen
Rabat
Boulhaut
Ait
Amar
Oued Zem
O. Beth
Kaan es Souk
O. Ziz
Fedala
Mellah
Khouribga
Kasba Tadla
Djebel Saghro
O. Moulouya
Casablanca
El Jadida
Azemmour
Benguerir
O. Abid
Bou
Azzer
O. Dra
(Mazagan)
O. Oum
Marrakech
Imini
Ouarzazat
Youssefiah
O. Tensift
Tioutine
Safi
O. N'Fis
O. Sous
ALGERIA
Essaouira
(Mogador)
Cape Ghir
Agadir
Tiznit
Tafraoute
Tirdouf
Ifni Sp.
O. Noun
Goulimine
Oued Dra

FRONTIER
UNDEFINED

Ocean

Atlantic

SPANISH SAHARA

E. Schell.

30°

35°

5°

5°

10°

10°

I

MOROCCO ON THE EVE OF THE PROTECTORATE

The year 1912 marked the end of a long road which western Islam had been traveling for hundreds of years. One by one, the various parts of what had once been a vast and powerful realm had been falling by the wayside. Indeed, the defeat of the kingdom of Granada in 1492, by which the Christians broke the last grip of the Moors in Europe, was no more than another step, albeit a crucial one, in the long, slow decline of Muslim power in the West. Finally, as the nineteenth century drew to a close, Morocco alone of the far-flung empire remained. But its days, too, were numbered; a mere dozen years after the turn into the new century it fell under French protectorate.

It is true that the country had often gained time against this seemingly ineluctable course of events when a strong sultan appeared on the scene. Moulay Ismail, for example, brought security and unity to Morocco and was able to deal with European powers on terms approaching equality during his reign from 1672 to 1727. And for a brief period Moulay Hassan (1873–1894) seemed likely to bring order from internal chaos and to fend off the European powers which found the country a jewel among the lands being swallowed up in the imperial race of the last quarter of the nineteenth century. But such men were too few and far between, and eventually the powers were no longer to be denied: after a rearranging of interests, not without its pains, Sultan Moulay Hafid was presented with a treaty of protectorate on March 30, 1912.

The treaty spelled the end of autonomy for a people who had held the Phoenicians and the Romans to trading posts near the coast and who had maintained their civilization intact in the face of Vandal incursions. It marked the end of independence for a people who had absorbed the Arab invasions of the eighth and eleventh centuries, been Islamized, had formed the vanguard of the jihad (Holy War) in Spain, and had even at one point carried the crusade to Charles Martel at Poitiers. For a brief moment in history, these people had formed the nucleus of an empire which stretched from the Atlantic to Algiers and from the Ebro in Spain to Senegal. Even during the decline, they had been able to turn back the Ottomans and also to contain and then repel the Portuguese from the Atlantic ports and the Spanish from all but a couple of toeholds on the Riff Coast. In fact the British crown lost some of its luster when Berber tribesmen harried His Majesty's garrison into abandoning Tangier in 1684.

The Moroccans were able to expand their empire and later to defend successfully their own shores because they had held a set of ideas and techniques appropriate to the times. They made the fatal mistake of not changing them. The year 1912 was one of protectorate because Morocco had stood still, or at best had merely oscillated between archaic, despotic government and almost complete anarchy. In the meantime, great and profound changes were taking place in nearby Europe.

When General Lyautey, who was the French proconsul of Morocco for an almost unbroken thirteen years, took up his post in the spring of 1912, he was faced with a society based on concepts of the Middle Ages. He was also faced with a definite international mandate which had emerged from the power politics of the period. Lyautey was charged with the *mise en valeur* (literally: bringing under exploitation) of a country old in Islamic tradition but new to the technology of occidental powers centuries in advance. The judgment of his work and that of his successors must necessarily rest in the main upon the raw materials which were at hand.

So before we can proceed to the description and analysis of the economic changes which the French were to bring to Morocco, it is necessary to sketch out in cursory fashion the state of the country on the eve of the protectorate. First, what, in its broad lines, is the geography of the country? [1] What was the state of agriculture and, under this rubric, the condition of land tenure? If we describe the economic life of the fellah, we must for the sake of completeness know something of urban life, i.e., the activities of the handicraft trades and the merchants. Crops once grown and goods once made must be transported, so interior communications must be discussed. Foreign trade should receive its due, for we shall see that it had been increasing before the protectorate, despite the policy of the sultans to limit intercourse with foreigners. The question of foreign trade inevitably brings up

Morocco's treaty position in 1912. The treaties inherited along with the *makhzen* (the Moroccan government) were to plague Lyautey and his successors with the problems which Professor Knight succinctly terms those of "open-door imperialism." [2]

With the broad lines of Moroccan economic activity, vintage 1912, set out, it will then be possible to trace the subsequent course of economic change and to assess its effects on the material well-being and the less tangible but perhaps no less important social well-being of the Moroccan people.

THE GEOGRAPHY

Eastern Arabs refer to Morocco as *Maghreb al Aksa,* the land farthest west; this outpost of Islam holds down the northwest tip of the African Continent. As such, it forms part of the area known as North Africa or Africa Minor, an area separated from the rest of the continent by the world's greatest desert and possessing a geographical and cultural unity which further sets it apart from the countries to the south. But just as there are similarities which link the countries of North Africa together, there are certain differences which give to each its own character. Some of these are in the realm of geography.

When the Italians moved into Libya in 1911, King Victor Emmanuel III was said to have remarked that "we have got the bone of the chop." [3] If there is a loin in the chop which North African geography describes, Morocco is it; only in Morocco's western plains is there significant depth of Mediterranean-type terrain and vegetation. Elsewhere Saharan conditions crowd northward and in some areas almost reach the sea. If the geographical unity of North Africa is found in the repetition of plains and mountains, fertile regions and steppes, the proportions vary among the countries. If, too, the climate and water resources differ among regions, seasons, and years, the extent of the differences varies. And Morocco seems to come out best. That this superior position in natural endowments is only relative, there will be occasion to point out many times in the following pages. Suffice it to say at this point that the French believed in 1912 that Moroccan resources were considerably greater than in their other territories of Algeria and Tunisia. This belief was the economic reason for the protectorate.

Morocco's territorial limits in 1912 (which are also roughly those of today) were determined on three sides by natural barriers, one of which was only partially effective, and on the fourth by an arbitrarily drawn line. The Atlantic and the Mediterranean were definite enough in describing the western and northern boundaries of the country; in the south the Sahara was less satisfactory as it was inhabited by nomads who, in their wanderings, were constantly falling in and out of the orbit of control. The eastern frontier with Algeria was a purely political one, having been partially fixed by the Treaty of Lalla-Marnia in 1845 and completed by a Franco-Moroccan agreement in 1901.

Like its North African neighbors, Morocco is a mélange, geographically as well as in other ways. In an area roughly the size of France, Moroccans are plains people, mountain people, and desert people. Their climate is Mediterranean on the plains and in the Riff, almost Alpine on the Atlantic slopes of the Atlas range, and Saharan on the other side. The mountains which account for this variety are undoubtedly the country's most important single geographic feature. Their economic value lies not so much in themselves, especially in the Morocco of 1912, but in their role as supplier of two factors vital to the economy — water and men.

All told, mountains cover about a third of the country. The principal range, the Atlas, runs from the northeast to the southwest, cutting the country roughly in two. Geographers define it in terms of three chains — from north to south, the Middle, High, and Anti-Atlas.[4] A smaller range, the Riff, forms the country's Mediterranean facade. The Atlas, together with the Riff, describes a large arc opening on the Atlantic; couched within it are the fertile western plains.

This is the section that Lyautey called "useful Morocco" and which the geographer Célérier refers to as the "natural limits." Here the lay of the land, its fertility, and the water regime have combined to create not only the great agricultural area of Morocco but one of the greatest of all North Africa. Composed of the Gharb, Chaouia, Doukkala, Abda, and Chiadma along the coast and the Tadla and Haouz in the interior, the plains extend from Tangier to Essaouira (Mogador), a distance of roughly four hundred miles. Inland, however, a series of steppes cuts off the interior valleys. Broadening in the Doukkala behind Al Jadida (Mazagan) and again in the Gharb near Kenitra (Port Lyautey), the coastal plains reach a depth exceeding fifty miles only in the latter region.[5]

The rivers of the plains look mainly to the Middle Atlas for their nourishment. Its rain and winter snows feed the sources of the Sebou (284 miles), Bou Regreg (111 miles), and Oum ar Rbia (345 miles), which flow into the Atlantic at Mehdia (near Kenitra), Rabat-Salé, and Azemmour, respectively. The Moulouya, which is smaller in flow and about 280 miles in length, also rises in the Middle Atlas and runs in a northeasterly direction to the Mediterranean. The principal river fed by sources in the High Atlas is the Tensift (167 miles); it flows northwest through the oasis of Marrakech and into the Atlantic south of Safi. These and a couple of other rivers have the considerable distinction of flowing throughout the year. (Since Morocco alone of the countries of North Africa has more than one or two such rivers, it is more than likely that its water resources are superior to those of neighboring Algeria and Tunisia.)[6] Countless *oueds* (watercourses) also crease the Atlas slopes, possessing all the characteristics of their counterparts in the rest of North Africa. When they are filled with water after heavy rains or the spring thaws, their flow may be wild and destructive, but it is also ephemeral. For the plains, they serve as a supplementary source of water; but on the southern slopes of the High and Anti-Atlas, their flow is crucial to life.

The *oued* exemplifies the water problem for all Mediterranean countries — too much at one time but mostly not enough over the crop year. Growth of vegetation is inhibited in summer by the lack of water, in winter by the cold, though water is available. It is during the intermediate seasons that effective growth takes place, and if either warm weather or sufficient water is lacking, short crops are in prospect. There must be rain in October at the time of seeding, again in November and December to bring up the grain, and again in March and April to assure the maturity. The trouble is that this schedule more often than not fails to materialize. Summer fog along the Atlantic littoral helps to compensate for lack of water; but summer can also bring locusts and the *chergui* (hot, dry Saharan winds) which in a few hours can wither crops and vines.

As a general proposition, and excluding the Middle and High Atlas regions, where precipitation is heavy, rainfall decreases and average temperatures increase as one moves from north to south and west to east. Thus, Tangier enjoys 800 millimeters (approximately 32 inches) of rain annually, on the average; Casablanca, down the coast, only 400. East of Tangier, the same is true; for the farther along the Riff one goes, the lighter rainfall becomes. Finally, one reaches the arid plateaus that make up eastern Morocco; sheltered from the winds of the west, northwest, and north by the Middle Atlas, Riff, and Iberian Peninsula, this region lacks humidity to compensate for its dearth of rain. (A small but fertile exception to the general aridity of this area is the plain of Triffas, north of Oujda.) Slightly more fortunate is the valley of the Sous, lying well below Casablanca between the open pincers formed by the High and Anti-Atlas. Here, high coastal humidity corrects for the less than 200 millimeters of rain a year. Inland from Tangier, the story is the same. At Meknes, in the north of the plains area, 600 millimeters fall in the average year; Marrakech, to the southwest, registers less than 250. And once the Atlas is crossed, the figures become infinitesimal. So it is that the mountains in their role as reservoir of water have endowed the northwest while disinheriting the southeast.[7]

The mountains are also a supplier of men. The security afforded by impenetrability has made them ideal for pressure of people on resources. Historically, in fact, North Africa's population has been more dense in the mountains than in the lowlands. The result has been at times a flood but always at least a trickle of new blood to the economically interesting regions — in Morocco, the relatively productive countryside of the western plains or the cities which mark their crossroads. This phenomenon of migration from south to north, while occurring throughout Moroccan history, was to present itself in considerable acuity to the French in the years following the establishment of the protectorate.

Though the contour of the mountains turns the face of Lyautey's "useful Morocco" to the west, the Atlantic coast presents an inhospitable front, with few natural harbors. So it is that men and culture have also come to Morocco by the back door, through gaps in the mountain barrier to the east and south. The Arabs, carrying Islam with them, poured in from the east in the eighth and eleventh centuries through the Taza Corridor, between the Riff and the Middle Atlas. Through history, this has been an invasion route into the western plains. Forced open by the Arabs, the corridor remained closed, by stout Moroccan resistance, to the onrushing Ottomans. Four centuries later, it was to be breached by French troops coming from Algeria to join the main force invading Morocco from the Atlantic side.

To the south lie the great routes of the Atlas. Important to

Moroccans since the second century, when the introduction of the camel from Egypt made desert travel not only physically possible but economically profitable, these routes carried caravans laden with slaves, gold, and ostrich feathers to make the fortune of countless generations of merchants in Fez and Marrakech.[8]

The Taza Corridor, the Atlas routes combined with Saharan trails to the Sudan, and the seaways of the Atlantic made Morocco a crossroads of commerce with Europe. The fabulously wealthy Fassi merchants were testimony that the trade was lucrative. But if the mountain passes, the desert, and the Atlantic could be highways for the import and export of goods and culture, they could also be barriers to intercourse with the outside world. Which they were to be depended upon the attitudes of the government, and historically they have been both.

So Morocco has been a purveyor of goods and culture, and so she has lived in splendid isolation protected by mountains, desert, and sea. The nineteenth-century sultans held to the latter policy, as had most of their predecessors. But this time the splendor was destined to dissolve in a defeat at the hands of a new Europe which was not to be denied access to the country. Whatever Moroccan attitudes, the barriers became highways, and goods and culture began to flow in a wave which was to engulf, twist, and transform the old Morocco, leaving islets reminiscent of the Middle Ages, curious dilutions of old and new, and a new economy *à l'européenne*.

THE PEOPLE

Outside of the cities, Morocco was largely a tribal society with all the antagonism embedded in this form of human organization. The permanent political and social organization was the tribe and its fractions, and loyalties were feeble beyond these limits. Yet Morocco was a political entity recognized in international law. The sultan had his representatives in foreign capitals, and there had long been diplomatic representation to the Moroccan court. Bilateral treaties and international agreements both implicitly and explicitly recognized that there was a geographical area called Morocco and that this area was governed by a sultan.

What was the nature of the sultan's control over his subjects? A most important characteristic was his dual role. He was not only the temporal leader of his people; he was also their religious chief, or *imam*. This latter role often accounted for the bulk of the prestige he enjoyed, however small it might at times be. As for his temporal power, it was as large as he could make it through persuasion or force, and thus varied from sultan to sultan. The western plains, with their milieu conducive to sedentary life and their terrain suited to effective military control, contained his traditional supporters. The sedentaries and transhumants of the mountains and the desert nomads, however, had a spotty record of obedience to central authority. A strong sultan was able to extend his authority beyond the plains; a weak one was fortunate to have as much.

The tribes which submitted to the government accepted a *caid* appointed by the sultan as their chief (the appointee might or might not be a member of the tribe over which he ruled). They paid taxes to the sultan's treasury, and they furnished men to fight his battles. But of national feeling there was none. A man was not a Moroccan but an Arab or a Berber. If he was a Berber, he might be Riffian, Beraber, or Chleuh depending on where he lived, his customs, and the dialect he spoke. More fundamentally he was a member of perhaps the Beni M'Guild, the Ait Atta, or the Beni Snassen. If the tribe were large, his allegiance might carry no farther than his fraction; in some cases, it was limited to his subfraction or to his *douar*, where no more than twenty families might live. The family was patriarchal with all the cohesion and discipline that the term implies; indeed the Morocco of 1912 was a patriarchal society at base.

Generally speaking, the Arabs lived on the western plains and the Berbers in the mountains and desert. There were exceptions. Nomadic Arab tribes, for example, were found south of the Atlas; and even in the Sous, the heart of the Chleuh country, small patches were occupied by Arabs. And there were Berber tribes in the plains, most of them Arabized, i.e., their members spoke Arabic, submitted to the sultan's temporal as well as spiritual authority, and, more immediately, accepted the absolute authority of the *caid*. The Berbers were the original inhabitants of the country; the Arabs had first come on a pillaging expedition in the eighth century. A second wave occurred three hundred years later when the Beni Hillal swept over North Africa from Egypt. The legacy from the first invasion had been the Koran and its two corollaries which dominate the Muslim state — civil and religious power vested in the same hands and no fixed rule of succession. The legacy of the second had been a large Arab population. Though the gulf between Arab and Berber was wide in matters of language and culture, a strong bond was provided by Islam. The call to the Holy War received as ready a response in Berber country as among the Arab tribes.

A fundamental feature of Berber society was the *jema'a*, or governing council. Its membership was composed of heads of families, and decisions were taken by majority vote, a governing process unheard of among the Arabs. A leader was elected only in times of emergency and then only for a specified period of time, generally a year. The Berber "republics," as exemplified by the *jema'a*, banded together into confederations whenever the interests of the tribes coincided, but such coalitions were generally short-lived. There was also a conception of balance of power in the organization of factions into two groups in order to maintain a political equilibrium. The laws by which the Berbers governed themselves had been evolved through centuries of usage.[9]

The Arab concept of government was totally different. The *caid*, as the sultan's representative in a tribe, was entitled to absolute and unquestioned authority. Islamic law, the *sharia*, was not customary, but rather derived from the Koran by the learned doctors, the *ulema*. The *caid* dispensed justice in criminal matters, and the *cadi*, or judge, appointed by the sultan as competent in interpreting the law, dealt with cases involving civil status, e.g., succession and inheritance.

The sultan was not always very successful in establishing his form of government in the Berber tribes which fell under his power. The Berbers had maintained the institution of the *jema'a* after their conversion to Islam. Even when a tribe was submitted to the authority of the central government, oftentimes the *caid* and his sheikhs, whose duty it was to administer the fractions of the tribe, were simply superposed on the existing political structure. In such cases, their authority was likely to be nominal, and the internal functioning of the tribe continued much the same as before.

The sultan's absolute authority in the purely spiritual realm was not at all clear-cut, either. While the Berbers had early embraced Islam, they had continued to cling to many of their pagan beliefs and practices, thus producing a brand of Islam that was far from orthodox. They vested the power to interpret matters of religion in their *marabouts* or their sharifs. The *marabouts* represented a step between paganism and pure Islam. They were holy men who possessed supernatural powers in the eyes of the people; and they wielded great influence in the tribes, for good or for evil. So did the Berber sharifs, or alleged descendants of the Prophet. (Many a full-blooded Berber managed to trace his lineage from the Atlas to the Hejaz, a feat which often passed without question.)

Added to differences in language and culture, "maraboutism" was a further divisive factor inhibiting Moroccan unity. That strong antagonism should often spring up between the *marabouts* and the sultan was perhaps inevitable in a society where religion played such a strong role. "When dissident tribes refused to recognize the sultan, they grouped themselves spontaneously around their *marabouts* and sharifs who became chiefs of the Holy War and protectors of the Berber republics." [10]

While the sultan's power was frequently limited by the ineffectualness of his *caids*, sometimes their strength could be a cause of his weakness. When a governor was able to establish a sizable (though not necessarily willing) following, infidelity to his master was many times the next step.[11] To hold the allegiance of his *caids*, the sultan often had to make it worth their while by granting generous shares of the tax revenues. Heading the list of recipients were three powerful families in the High Atlas, the Glaoui, Goundafi, and M'Touggi, who had carved out their territories in the nineteenth century. These domains formed the outposts which protected the plains. Without their presence in the sultan's camp, the plains were highly vulnerable to pillaging expeditions on the part of the dissident tribes. Their support was therefore essential to the peace and security of the country. Lyautey was to realize this fact of Moroccan political life early in his tenure as Resident-General.

Internal wars were interminable in Morocco before 1912, but there is a danger of overestimating their importance. Conflicts among the tribes or against the central government were an integral part of diplomacy; improved position in negotiations, rather than crushing victory over the enemy, was the goal. In terms of people killed and damage done, many of these wars could barely be classed as skirmishes. But the lack of security had its economic effects in a reduced volume of trade and a stultification of capital investment in anything which could not be carried or, in the case of animals, could not be herded to safety. The geography of Morocco imposed physical limitations on the type of economic activity which could be carried on in its various regions; the chronic political instability limited it still further.

In contrast to the mountain and desert country, the lowlands and more particularly the cities were government territory. The rural areas were populated by Arab or Arabized tribes for the most part, tribes which were largely sedentary, devoting themselves to tillage, and which were influenced by their proximity to the cities as well as by that to the mountains. Thus they served to some extent to bridge the gap between city and country (here, the mountain and desert regions) which can be found in almost every country and which was widened in Morocco by the diverse backgrounds of the people. For on the one hand there was a culture derived from Iberian antecedents, on the other, one shaped by Saharan influences. And if the tribes on the plains were something less than enthusiastic about domination by the sultan, they were at least virtually always submissive. The cities, on the other hand, accorded him strong support.

The most important cities in 1912 were Fez, Meknes, and Marrakech; and Tetouan was not far behind.[12] All were inland, and all but Marrakech, which was farther to the south, were heavily influenced in their culture by the Moorish refugees from the Spanish Inquisition. The skilled trades were largely in the hands of the Moors, and music and art bore the stamp of their Andalusian origins. Islam, hardened for the Moors in the crucible of their persecution by the Christians, was as a result quite orthodox and deeply felt in the cities. If the flotsam of the human tide which flowed into Morocco from Spain in the sixteenth century and even earlier manned the corsairs of Barbary, the elite contributed immeasurably to the grandeur and gentility that characterized Fez on the eve of the protectorate and made it the intellectual center of western Islam. The large number of bourgeoisie in the Moroccan cities gave urban life a solidity and stability that was in marked contrast to the turbulence among the tribes in the mountains and the desert.

Economically in the Morocco of 1912, city and country were complementary. The country needed outlets for its grain and animal products; and the city found customers for its handicraft goods and for the imports from Europe which it, as entrepôt, passed along to the rural people. Such imports were rather limited, however, since the Moroccan economy was relatively closed. So it was that the inland cities rather than the ports prospered in commerce, thus accounting for their greater importance at this time.

The picture of the Moroccan people would not be complete without mention of the Jewish element. The origins of the Jews in southern Morocco are relatively obscure. They are purported to have come first with the Phoenicians, and it is said that their numbers were further augmented by the conversion of Berber tribes to the faith. However that may be, it was a rare settlement which did not have a Jewish tinsmith and a rare town which did not contain a *mellah*, the Moroccan equivalent of a ghetto. The inhabitants of the *mellahs* in the cities of the north were for the most part descendants of the Jews expelled from Spain. For during the Inquisition, Morocco gained not only the Moorish artisans who had formed the manufacturing base of the Spanish economy, but also the Jews who had been the financiers. Both groups were a precious addition. The last great infusion of Jews came to Morocco in the sixteenth century from the Leghorn area following the Inquisition there.

The Jewish quarters, surrounded by high walls, were established in the thirteenth century as a protection against the mob. Here, as elsewhere in the world, the Jews lived in constant terror of a pogrom and were compelled to submit to various humiliating restrictions. For example, a Jew was forced to wear a distinctive black robe and hat; he also had to walk barefoot when passing a mosque. And he was forbidden to ride an animal through the streets of the city. But he was useful, too. The jewelry that he made was much sought after in the harems. He was also the moneylender in a country where religion forbade the taking of interest by the bulk of the population. In this function, he was important to the sultans as well as to other government officials; so he sought and received the *demma* (sultan's protection), although it was not always effective. He had another champion in the European diplomatic representation, which made strong protests whenever it felt that a Jew had been wronged.

In addition to the solicitude of the government and the consuls, Moroccan Jews had the assistance of the *Alliance Israélite Universelle* (World Jewish Alliance). This was an organization founded in 1860 and supported financially by European Jewry concerned with the welfare of their brethren in the Islamic states. Especially active in the field of education, it operated thirteen schools with almost 4,500 pupils in Morocco before the protectorate.[13] Classes were conducted in French, and students from the schools formed the vanguard of Moroccans conversant with the

French language and culture. The work of the Alliance, combined with the spirit of mutual aid which motivated Moroccan Jewry to help the less fortunate members of the community, put the Jews in a position to capitalize rapidly on the opportunities which economic changes, under French impetus, were soon to offer.

Before the coming of the French, another foreign contact had served to benefit the Jews. A decline in commerce with Algeria and Gibraltar in the mid-nineteenth century marked the beginning of a sizable emigration to South America on the part of Moroccan Jews, particularly Spanish-speaking ones from Tetouan, Larache, and Tangier. Many of the emigrants, once they had amassed some savings, returned to Morocco to invest them in business; and their contribution to the welfare of the Jewish community was considerable.

The Jews had a good deal of autonomy. Their quarters were self-governed, the administration being responsible to the governor of the city. The inhabitants also had recourse to their own rabbinical courts in civil matters. This practice was similar to the Ottoman millet system, which was established in those areas of the empire where there were large non-Muslim minorities.

The European population of pre-protectorate Morocco was small and largely concentrated along the littoral. The diplomatic corps and the representatives of various European trading firms comprised the bulk of the colony. There were also some missionaries, who confined their proselytizing activities mainly to such cities as Fez and had scarcely penetrated the countryside. The Moroccan government in addition had some European "advisers" at court. The army had French artillery instructors, and munitions manufacture was in the hands of an Italian mission. The English viewpoint was represented by Caid MacLean, who commanded the sultan's guard.

Though the seat of government was at Fez, Rabat, or Marrakech (the sultan and his retinue alternated between the three capitals), the diplomatic corps resided at Tangier by order of the government. The conduct of diplomatic business was consequently a drawn-out affair with slow and uncertain communications between Tangier and the capitals. But the inconvenience was pretty much one-sided, since the sultans wished to confine European influence to the coastal area.

The European traders were concentrated in the ports of Tangier, Larache, Casablanca, and Essaouira. Their interests in the interior were watched over by *semsars* (agents), mostly Jewish Moroccans. The *semsars* were protected under capitulations and were therefore the cause of much controversy between the government and the European powers. Some of the aspects of the protection dispute will be taken up in the section on the treaty position of Morocco.

Diplomats, traders, missionaries, and advisers — none of these groups had substantial permanent interests in Morocco in the form of real property investment up until a few years before the protectorate. But business interests had been growing in the Casablanca area during the five years before 1912. French troops had occupied Casablanca and the Chaouia in this period, thereby reducing the risks of investment. Already Europeans were betting on the future of Morocco, and inflated real property values reflected the optimism. The right of Europeans to acquire real property freely had been granted by the Act of Algeciras in 1906, but it took the presence of the French bayonet, in a country where anarchy often described the politics, to stimulate the abandonment of liquidity for the possibility of a long-term capital gain.

Ethnic groups: Berber, Arab, Jew, and European; religion: Islam, Judaism, Christianity; culture: Saharan, fifteenth-century Andalusian, modern European — all are necessary to the potpourri which described the people of Morocco. These were the qualitative facets; quantitatively, the information on this period is not reliable. Of course there had been no census. The figure for Europeans in 1912 was 3,000 (excluding French troops), probably fairly accurate because the consuls had a record of their nationals. Various writers have attempted to estimate the Moroccan population during that period, and the consensus seems to hover around 3,500,000 persons. Inadequate as this estimate is, there is nothing better available. Unfortunately, the situation was to improve very little after the coming of the protectorate.

AGRICULTURE

A description of the geography and the people of Morocco having been sketched, it remains to see how the people reacted to their environment in the realm of our direct concern, that of the economic. We begin first with agriculture, since the population of pre-protectorate Morocco was overwhelmingly rural. Life was sustained by what the soil would yield. There was minimum recourse on the part of the fellah to city or to foreign sources for the satisfaction of his needs; consequently, the Moroccan economy was relatively closed and definitely real. A good or bad year on the land meant all the difference — a difference between enough to eat and famine. The hazards were many, i.e., drought, floods, locusts, the Saharan winds, tribal fights, and the arbitrary exactions of the *caids*. The presence of any one was serious; two or more in combination were often disastrous.

Moroccan agriculture in 1912 represented a fine adjustment indeed to natural conditions, albeit an archaic one when one thinks of the European technology then available not very many miles away. But precisely because this adjustment was so delicately balanced, the product of centuries of experience in a capricious climate, the impact of the new technology with its accent on the production of cash crops was to be enormous.

LAND TENURE

An immediate problem which the French were to face was that of land tenure. In the absence of any land registration before the protectorate, it is possible to do little more than describe the various types of landholdings and later to watch how the situation evolved after the French took control.

The land in Morocco was held in four, possibly five ways, each of which will be described in turn. They were the *melk*, *habous* (public and private), domanial, and under this heading *guich* lands; finally there were the *arch* (collective) lands. The *melk* lands were those which were privately owned. They were located for the most part in the western plains, since, under Muslim law, land cannot be privately owned unless cultivated, and the cultivable lands were to be found largely in that area. Thus *melk* lands were among the most valuable in the country.[14]

Although the land was privately owned, this is not to say that it was cultivated by the owner. Absentee landlordism, as provided for by the *khammes* (fifth) system, was very much a part of Moroccan agriculture. The tenant supplied the labor on a specified surface, generally a *zouja* (about 12 hectares), in return for a fifth of the crop. (If he supplied other factors, such as seeds or tools, his share would be greater.) In a country where inadequate rainfall and locust invasions were an expectation rather than a surprise to the farmer, the tenant was certain to have years when his one-fifth share would be insufficient to feed his family. In such a case, it was the custom of the landlord to advance the necessary subsistence to his tenant against a pledge of repayment from his share of a future crop.[15] Frequently unable to get out of debt, the tenant was held in virtual slavery by the landlord, bound to the land unless released by his creditor. On the other hand, the landlord could terminate his relationship with the tenant at any time, simply by reimbursing him for the labor he had expended up until that time if the termination happened to take place in the middle of the crop year. The uncertainty of tenure discouraged any capital improvements or use of fertilizers on the part of the tenant, even if his share of the crop left any margin for such investment. Not only was he at the mercy of the landlord; equally as formidable were the *caid* and his exactions, euphemistically known as taxes. Although there were official rates, taxes were levied pretty much according to what the traffic would bear. As one tenant said to de Campon, "Grasshoppers come sometimes, droughts often, and the *caids* always." [16]

Europeans had been granted the right to acquire land in Morocco by the Conference of Madrid in 1880, but *only with the consent of the sultan*. Since such consent was very rarely forthcoming, there was little outright ownership of land by foreigners prior to 1906, when the Act of Algeciras removed the restriction of the sultan's approval. Nevertheless, there was in fact considerable European association with Moroccans in the holding of private lands. Because the protégés of Europeans were exempt from taxation under the capitulations, it was attractive to a Moroccan to enter into such an association and thereby enjoy the privileges of protection. So while land was nominally under Moroccan ownership, it was often at least in part controlled by foreigners, a situation that concerned the Moroccan government to the end of its independent rule. The amount of land Europeans had acquired directly by 1912, most of it in the Chaouia, was estimated by one writer at 80,000 hectares,[17] a figure that available data for subsequent years would suggest is somewhat too high.

Habous lands were the same as *waqf* lands in the Arab countries to the east. Pious Muslims, obliged by the Koran to make charitable contributions, left their lands in trust, with the income to be devoted to charitable or religious purposes. Sometimes the landowner established a private trust at first, for the benefit of his descendants, and the income reverted to the public benefit only when the last of his direct line had died. Others set up public trusts at the outset. In either case, the *habous* lands were managed by trustees who were often inclined to be something less than honest in their administration. Since these tracts had formerly been private land, they were devoted to agricultural pursuits, unless, of course, they were in urban use. And when they were cultivated, it was generally done by tenants under the *khammes* system. As *habous* land was unseizable and inalienable, the French were to encounter considerable difficulty in appropriating it for European colonization without stirring great resentment on the part of the Muslim population.

The domanial lands were those of the government, but for all intents and purposes were owned by the sultan, who *was* the government. There was a distinction made, however, between his private lands and the domanial property. The amount of this land varied with the fortune of the government; most of it was confiscated from rebellious tribes. But as the government had reached a low point in its authority in 1912, so had its landholdings. The bulk of these lands was to be sold almost immediately to French colonists, but their limited extent was to mean a temporary slowing down of settlement on the land by Europeans.

The *guich* lands were domanial lands in a sense, but differed from them in that cultivators had usufruct. These lands, which were located in the fertile areas, were occupied by Arab tribes which, in exchange for the land, offered military service to the government in time of war. The tribes had been settled by Yacoub al Mansour in the twelfth century and, together with the Black Guard, composed of slaves from sub-Saharan Africa and established by Moulay Ismail in the eighteenth century, formed the core of the sultan's military power.

The collective lands were found for the most part in the mountains and on the arid rocky plateaus. In the areas not suited to cultivation, the *melk* type of land tenure was ruled out because of the Islamic legal requirement that private holdings be cultivated. In the small but cultivable valleys of the High Atlas and the Riff, the land was collectively held because Berber tradition had not been penetrated by this Muslim concept. The former terrain was devoted to husbandry, each tribe having carved its own domain through wars or negotiations with neighboring tribes. But the division of land among the tribes was a very unstable one. Tribes in this part of the country were either nomadic or semi-nomadic. As they moved during the course of the year in search of grass and water, a chain reaction was set up. Tribe A might move into the territory of Tribe B, which, because pasturage and water were available to it, would have ordinarily not moved on at that time, but which was forced by this invasion to take over the area occupied by Tribe C. And so it went. The schedule of moves resulted from a *modus vivendi* established by wars or negotiation; in a year when the population had become too great for the resources at hand or when lack of rain resulted in inadequate forage, the precarious equilibrium would be upset, and tribal fights would ensue. Eventually, as both human and animal population became adjusted to the reduced supply of resources, another delicate balance would develop, to be maintained until another crisis presented itself.

Movement in the Middle Atlas, the principal grazing area of Morocco, was both vertical and lateral. Some tribes moved hundreds of miles in an east-westerly direction during the year.[18] The whole system subsumed a relatively stable amount of land available for pasturage. The grazing lands in Morocco before the protectorate spilled over into the zone where cultivation, under propitious conditions, might have been possible. With the protectorate, the cultivated area was to impinge on this zone to the extent that equilibrium among the collective tribal holdings was to be permanently upset.

The cultivable land in the valleys of the High Atlas and the Riff was parceled out among the families by the governing council; each family unit was given the same weight whatever its size. The strips of land were redistributed periodically to ensure that all had the opportunity to cultivate the better soil.

Although land tenure can be categorized into the types just described, there were added complications which must be noted. In the case of *melk* land, ownership of a particular parcel was frequently claimed by several people; and as we have seen, ownership of the collective lands was nebulous, with tribes constantly on the move and with wars and negotiations intermittently adjusting boundaries. A further complicating factor in regard to the *melk* lands was introduced by the Muslim law of inheritance, which demanded an equal division of property among male heirs, with each female entitled to a share half as large as that of a male. In a country with a growing population, there was a concomitant fragmentation of parcels to the point where many owners could not earn even a subsistence living from their property. Along with the population, their numbers were to increase rapidly during the years of French control.

Rural Life and Land Use

The lay of the land, the nature of the soil, the availability of water — all dictated the way of life led by rural Moroccans; and it was a life that ranged from a completely sedentary existence in a *dar* (house) to a completely nomadic one under a goat-hair tent. In between were the semi-nomads, combining characteristics of both the sedentary and the nomad in their pattern of living, and favoring one or the other according to the region they occupied.[19]

More than geography determined the mode of life for Moroccan farmers and forced so many to seek a nomadic existence. The natural environment in a particular region plus market possibilities may have indicated that concentration in, say, tree crops or cereal culture would produce the maximum yield. But the lack of security confronting the farmer would force him to compromise with these economic considerations. In a milieu of war or war threats, the tendency towards nomadism, and the accent on assets that could be moved, was great. The result was an incomplete utilization of resources. On top of this, the archaic techniques represented by a plow dating from Roman times and drawn by donkeys and camels [20] further limited output and thus the area suitable for sedentary life.

The western lowlands formed the main grain-growing area of pre-protectorate Morocco. The people were largely sedentary, either Arabs or Arabized, and submitted to the government. This area was part of the *bled bour*, i.e., land in dry farming. (The pasture lands of the Middle Atlas also fell into this category.) Rainfall was relatively heavy, the Saharan winds more remote, and summer fog supplied additional moisture along the littoral. The amount of rainfall decreased with distance from the coast; and when the borderline was reached between plain and steppe, "grain growing is a lottery where one loses more often than he wins . . ." [21] How much of this in-between zone could be dry-farmed varied according to the rainfall, and reasonable success over a period of years could be assured only by irrigation.

The principal grains grown in the lowlands were hard wheat and barley. The former predominated along the littoral, the latter taking front rank inland, as it could better resist drought. There was no soft wheat cultivation in Morocco before 1912. Olive trees were to be found in the Fez–Meknes area and around Marrakech, but the oil was poor in quality owing to neglect or ignorance of proper care. There were some vineyards in the Doukkala, the

Zerhoun, just north of Meknes, and the valleys of the Riff. Since Islam prohibited alcoholic beverages, however, the vines supplied only table grapes (except some wine grapes pressed by the Jews), and were of minor importance. The plains area also contained a vast cork forest, that of Mamora, lying behind Kenitra.

The extent of sown areas throughout the lowlands varied widely from year to year, even when the government was able to protect the plains effectively. Restricted surfaces always followed a drought, since the seeds were consumed by the hungry fellahin and work animals were weakened by undernourishment. The money-lender was the source of agricultural credit during these critical periods. In the years when grain exports figured in the international accounts it was produce supplied from the latifundia. The tenant farmer did not generally share in the bounty as there were obligations owing to the landlord from previous years.

The narrow but fertile valleys of the High Atlas and the western Riff were fruit country and, in the case of the High Atlas, maize country as well. The collectively-held land was terraced up the mountain slopes; the crops were grown on the thin strips which comprised the steps. This area was *bled seguia*, i.e., land under irrigation. Extensive and complicated irrigation systems captured and distributed the rainwater running in the watercourses. Maintenance of these systems was time-consuming; and one flash flood, not an uncommon occurrence, could wipe out months of labor. Both land and water were apportioned by the Berber governing council. The council also administered the *agadir*, the grain bank of a real economy. Perched on the top of a hill, as far as possible from the reach of pillaging expeditions, the *agadir* was the tribe's warehouse, where reserve stocks, when there were any, were stored against a deficit year.[22]

The High Atlas tribes were largely sedentary, living in clusters of stone houses. Many of them, however, such as the Chleuh who were found on the northern slopes of the western Atlas, had flocks of sheep and goats which summered on the higher slopes. And the Berber federation to the northeast was quite pastoral.

As we have seen, a sedentary life was the corollary to cultivation; conversely, a nomadic existence necessarily resulted from specialization in animal husbandry, since forage and water were insufficient in any single spot. Thus people combining the two types of agriculture were forced to combine the two ways of life. These, then, were the transhumants, and the Middle Atlas was their stronghold. They combined cultivation and animal raising (principally sheep and goats), and thus a sedentary life and nomadism, to varying degrees. The tribes in the Sefrou area, for example, leaned more toward the sedentary life, as their displacements took them to the fertile plains near Meknes. On the other hand, the tribes in the Taza region found themselves on less richly-endowed lands and were oriented toward animal husbandry.

The Middle Atlas also contained the principal forested area of Morocco. The trees of Azrou fed the workshops and hearths of the Fassi. Oak or cedar predominated, depending on the altitude. There was no conservation policy in pre-protectorate Morocco; and cuttings, fires, and flocks had taken a heavy toll. The progressive denuding of forest cover also inhibited the Middle Atlas in its function as a storehouse of water, and the resulting run-off deepened and widened the channels of erosion.

The steppes lying east of the Middle Atlas and south of Oujda along the Algerian frontier were the territory of nomads. Life here revolved around the water points, and their rarity plus the paucity of forage necessitated long displacements. Goats, sheep, and camels supplied a precarious living of milk, butter, meat, and hides. Capital investment or disinvestment followed the weather and was embodied in the size of herds from year to year. There was no selective breeding of animals, but nature had produced a hardy type which alone could survive in so rugged a milieu. The yield in meat was pitifully meager per animal; and since the animals were of small stature, increased yield could be achieved only by multiplication of numbers, with a consequent pressure on forage and water. A drought brought a ruthless decimation of the flocks which was felt over subsequent years until patient rebuilding could restore their numbers. Indeed recovery from a deficit year was a slow, painful process throughout Moroccan rural life, especially because drought was not a phenomenon but a recurring event.

The people of the desert were both sedentary and nomadic. Sedentary life was possible only in the oases, which were fed by the waters flowing from the Atlas or by deep wells. Ribbons of green, startling in contrast to the surrounding country, marked the location of oases along the rivers Ziz and Dra and their confluences. Within these ribbons, irrigation canals outlined a patchwork of hard wheat or barley plots. The date palms found here made their precious contribution of fruit and fuel. The oases were the domain of the *ksour*, fortified enclaves made from the ochre-colored earth of the desert and built aside from all land where water might reach. The "ksourians" were both Berbers and Arabs; many, such as the Haratin along the Dra, bore a strong negroid imprint, since their domains lay along the slave routes from central Africa.

Another inhabitant of the desert was the Touareg. Camel raisers and operators of caravans, these Berber nomads had a further source of income in the people of the oases who had been paying them tribute for ten centuries.[23] The Touareg were, by necessity, a hardy lot; and they did not hesitate to pillage weaker neighbors or to exact money from passing traders in exchange for safe passage. But revenue from the caravans was already drying up by 1912. The slave trade was in full eclipse, as the French had closed Timbuktu, the traditional source of supply. The construction of the railroad from Dakar to St. Louis also siphoned off trade which had formerly moved northward by caravan. Consequently, the camel was losing its importance as a means of transport and as a source of revenue for those who raised them. The decline of the desert economy resulting from the shift of the trade routes was to become even more acute after the protectorate, leaving a large population stranded in an area where the natural endowments are indeed few.[24]

This survey of Moroccan rural life would be incomplete without mention of the valley of the Sous. Here water and pasturage were scarce, especially in the central area, but there was a valuable resource in the argan tree. Low hanging, the argan supplied precious forage for goats and its fruit yielded an oil which substituted for that of the olive in the human diet. The Sous also had the sea, which was rich in fish; in fact, fishing was a major activity in the region.[25] But even before the protectorate, excess population was the chief product of this relatively isolated valley, and the Chleuh, who comprised the bulk of the people living there, were to be found throughout the cities of the north.

Though the Moroccan rural economy was largely a subsistence one, a certain amount of trade was necessary to life. The nomads and the sedentaries complemented each other through trade in grains, fruits, meat, wool, and hides. The cities furnished pottery, cloth, *babouches* (shoes), and metalware from their *fondouks* (wholesale houses) in exchange for agricultural products from the rural areas. The foreigner supplied tea, sugar, candles, cotton cloth, and hardware.

The place of exchange was the *souk*, or market. Generally held once a week in the rural areas, the *souk* was not only a place where trade was carried on; it was also a social and political institution where news was exchanged, revolts were planned, and litigation was settled by the governor. The *souks* were dispersed over the countryside in such fashion that it was generally possible for members of a tribe to reach one through a journey of a half-day or less by donkey. Traders from the cities, both Jewish and Muslim, traveled from one to another, making a continuous circuit. The *semsars* were also on hand, to buy grain for the account of their European principals in the ports. Few markets had permanent buildings; business was transacted in open fields, though sometimes under the covering of a tent.

The volume of trade varied over the year. Business was especially brisk during Muslim holidays and during *moussems* (local religious celebrations). But the yearly total of trade was heavily dependent on the state of the crops. And since the country's whole economic system was based on agriculture, a deficit crop had heavy repercussions on the merchants, the artisans, the European trader, and the government revenues.

Taxation of the Land

As agriculture was the principal occupation of Moroccans, so upon agricultural "wealth" fell the burden of taxation. In an Islamic state, the form that taxation took was ordained by the Koran. The two principal sources of revenues were the *achour* (tax on produce) and the *zekkat* (tax on animals), both paid in kind and both first introduced in Morocco in the twelfth century by Sultan Yacoub al Mansour. The *achour* was the Muslim tithe, the 10 per cent going to the poor to fulfill the duty of giving alms as testimony of love of God and of purification of the soul. The amount was reduced by one-half on produce from irrigated land, since the religion held that a man having to water his land should pay less than one whose land was watered by the rain. At first the tithe was given by the donor directly to the poor, but later the sultan served as intermediary in his capacity as representative of the Prophet and Prince of the Believers. It then became, along with the *zekkat*, a fiscal obligation.

The *zekkat* was a tax of 2.5 per cent levied on the value of animals. Work animals were not included, nor were those which the farmer had held for less than a year. And a specified amount of stock was exempt from the tax. The *zekkat* was also levied on merchandise and precious metals, but this payment remained a moral obligation for the taxpayer. The *achour* and *zekkat* were annual taxes; another tax, the *naiba*, was levied intermittently to furnish the funds necessary to the sultan for his military campaigns. (The *naiba* was not provided for in the religion and so was not really legal.) The burden was a heavy one for the fellahin.

The tax base was narrowed by numerous exemptions. All government employees were *ipso facto* exempt from taxation. Descendants of the Prophet as well as certain holy men were also among the privileged. Non-believers could not pay a Koranic tax; but for the Jews, though not for the Christians, who were excluded from all taxation under the capitulations, the *djeziya* (head tax) served as a substitute. Finally there were the tribes which exempted themselves by force. However, the government did levy a 10 per cent tax on all produce arriving in Marrakech to substitute for revenues uncollectible in Berber country. It also levied taxes on goods going to dissident tribes, the rate of tax varying according to the product.

In addition to these special taxes on produce, the sultans had also introduced regular gate and market taxes, from which the Prophet's descendants, the holy men, and foreigners and their protégés (*dhimmis*) were exempt and thus held a competitive advantage over lesser souls without such immunity.

Attempts at reform of the tax system had been made before the protectorate. In the last quarter of the nineteenth century, Moulay Hassan had amalgamated the *achour* and *zekkat* into a single tax called the *tertib*. Under his plan, exemptions would be discontinued. The European powers, at the Conference of Madrid in 1880, had agreed in principle that their nationals and protégés should be subject to taxation, and an agreement of the diplomatic corps at Tangier in 1881 accepted the principle as long as exempted Moroccans became subject to taxation, too. Moulay Hassan was unable to enforce the new tax; so the old system was maintained until 1901, when Abd al Aziz revived the idea. Under his plan, beasts of burden and fruit trees were to be subject to an absolute rather than percentage payment, while flocks were to be subject to a 5 per cent tax, double the old rate. Everyone was to pay; the minimum holding was abolished. Payment in money was substituted for payment in kind. In the interest of greater public revenues, the privilege of collection was withdrawn from the *caids*. The scheme was ratified by the consuls in 1903 and was thus applicable to foreigners. Like his predecessor, Abd al Aziz met the strong opposition of the *caids*, the descendants of the Prophet, the holy men, and, not least, the employees of his own government. Unlike his predecessor, he made the mistake of abolishing the *achour* and *zekkat* before the new tax was solidly established. As a consequence, the reform not only failed, but revenues were drastically reduced. Abd al Aziz was then forced to turn to foreign sources for funds; and he found a bevy of eager lenders awaiting him.

URBAN LIFE

We have seen that cities had a very necessary role to play in the economy of pre-protectorate Morocco, agricultural though it was. The major urban centers in 1912 did not, however, owe their beginnings to economic need. They had been founded centuries before not as commercial centers but as political capitals. Fez was established by Idriss II in the ninth century, Marrakech by Youssef ben Tachfin in the eleventh century, and Meknes by Moulay Ismail in the seventeenth century. Each became in turn the capital of the country. Later rulers made use of all three capitals[26] and adopted the practice of living a part of the year in each—a necessary step in maintaining the unity of the empire.

Nevertheless, the economic function followed closely on the heels of government decree. The presence of the large retinue of officials, servants, and soldiers that accompanied the ruler on his extended visits to each capital created a heavy demand for local goods and services, and thus was an important impetus to development. In addition, the imperial cities soon proved to have an economic justification quite aside from these influences, one which they earned from their location.

In view of the fact that ports along the Atlantic were almost uniformly poor, and that the country's economy was a relatively closed one, it was only natural that the urban agglomerations situated on the plains, in the shadow of the Middle or High Atlas, were the ones which enjoyed the greatest prosperity, rather than those on the coast. It was just this characteristic, however, that set Moroccan cities apart from their counterparts in the rest of North Africa. To the east, as far as the Nile Valley, the bulk of the urban population was to be found along the sea — in the cities of Oran, Algiers, Tunis, and Tripoli. Tlemcen, in western Algeria, and

Constantine, in the east, were not on the Mediterranean; but they were not far away, and were in any event cities of the second order.

In Morocco, on the other hand, the ports of Tangier, Larache, Mehdia, Rabat-Salé, Casablanca, Al Jadida, Safi, and Essaouira were, before the protectorate, no more than small settlements living from a light volume of foreign trade. Jews and Europeans represented the commercial interests; in fact the Jew in the ports was likely to be more prosperous than his co-religionist in the large cities, and there was no comparison between him and his miserable brothers in the countryside. But whatever prosperity the merchants of the ports enjoyed was subject to the whims of the sultan, the corruption of customs officials, insecurity in the interior, and the dangers of handling cargo in unimproved ports. Harbors afforded little protection from storms; lighterage was the only means of landing and loading cargo. And Agadir, the outlet of the Sous and the nearest to a good natural port in the country, had been closed to European commerce in 1760 by Sultan Mohammed ben Abdallah, and was still closed in 1912. Mehdia, too, had been closed; and siltage made the action permanent.

So it was that Morocco's principal trade routes, while following natural depressions of the country's geography, led not to the sea, but to the plains and their three principal cities. Fez was particularly well located in this respect, which fact, together with the presence of other factors necessary to urban growth, accounted for its pre-eminence.

Célérier divides the favorable conditions for development of Fez into three geographical groupings. The first were those conditions which were strictly local; the second were regional; and the third were national.[27] Locally, and perhaps most important, clean water was available in the Oued Fez throughout the year, and in sufficient quantity to meet the physical needs of the inhabitants and to supply the requirements of industry. Water was used as power to grind grain and crush olives, and the potters used it in producing the ceramics for which Fez was famous. Building materials were available in the surrounding region, which was extremely important in a country where poor transportation facilities made the cost of moving heavy low-valued products prohibitive over all but very short distances. Limestone and gypsum were to be found in abundance, and clay deposits assured a steady supply to the potters. The Sais Plain nearby supplied wheat and barley to feed the city, and olive trees also fared well in the area. To the availability in quantity of water, building materials, and food was added a wood supply. The forests of the Middle Atlas and the Riffian approaches yielded tanbark for the leather trades, cedar and thuya for the cabinetmakers and the carpenters, and charcoal for the smiths and the kitchens of Fez. Hides brought to Fez by the pastoral Berbers of the Middle Atlas supplied the important industry of leatherworking.

While the accessibility of resources promoted the prosperity of Fez on the local and regional levels, it was the accessibility of Fez itself that distinguished it at the national level. Its strategic location earned for it the role of the country's major clearinghouse in the exchange of goods and earned for its merchants the "tribute" they exacted as middlemen at the natural crossroads of commerce. Fez was the destination of the well-traveled caravan route from Black Africa that followed the natural depression of the Oued Ziz, crossed the High Atlas through the Talrhemt Pass, then the arid plateau of the High Moulouya through Midelt, and finally bridged the Middle Atlas to emerge onto the Sais Plain at Sefrou. Then, too, Fez was the first urban center of any size west of the Taza Corridor, which linked Morocco to Algeria. While this route was never as important to Fassi commerce as that from the Sahara, it did play a role in the prosperity of Fez until the French occupation of the province of Oran was completed in 1847. From then on, what trade there was in products from the port of Oran generally went no farther than the region around Oujda on the Algerian-Moroccan frontier. There was considerable commerce, on the other hand, between Fez and the ports of Tangier and Larache, in which transportation costs were less than they were to the east.

The merchants of Fez conducted the bulk of Morocco's commercial relations with other countries, limited as they were. They had overseas representation in Marseille and Genoa, in England and Germany. They exported goods to all the countries of North Africa; there were Fassi merchants in Oran and further along the littoral as far as Algiers. Some even established themselves in Egypt. And to the south, there were thirty Fassi trading posts in Senegal, stretching themselves from Dakar to St. Louis along the railroad built in the 1880's. Incidentally, many of the merchants who had ventured abroad returned to Fez with English, Italian, or French citizenship, thus qualifying for extraterritorial protection, including escape from government control in the important matter of taxation.

There was a long tradition behind the commercial prowess of the traders of Fez; their ancestors had been merchants in Andalusia before their eviction from Spain in the sixteenth century. Along with the merchants came Moorish artisans, as we have seen, bringing to Morocco and particularly to Fez their invaluable skills.

Meknes possessed very much the same characteristics favorable to growth as Fez. It, too, was relatively free from the two shortcomings inhibiting economic development throughout most of the Middle East — lack of water and of wood. And since it was situated less than forty miles to the west, it shared many of the other attributes of Fez described above, including a nucleus of skilled Moors in its population. But it was this very proximity to Fez that accounted in large measure for the secondary role Meknes played in the economy; throughout most of Morocco's history, it was destined to remain, both economically and culturally, in the shadow of its great neighbor.

The growth of Marrakech cannot be attributed to a favorable juncture of local and regional conditions such as existed in Fez and Meknes. It certainly could not be explained by the agricultural resources of the region. The Haouz Plain would have been an unbroken desert except for the efforts of man. Only through an extensive system of *seguias* (open irrigation canals) and a network of ingenious *khettaras* (subterranean canals) and wells was water and thus life brought to this otherwise desolate region. The reasons behind Marrakech's development are rather at the national level, and lie in its role as entrepôt of the south. As Gaignebet puts it, Marrakech was:

The city of the Piedmont . . . point of contact between the plains and plateaus of the west and north, between the valleys and mountains of the south and east, market where are exchanged the cereals of the *meseta*, the fruits of the *Dir*, the animals and wood of the Atlas, where the caravans from the Sahara and the ports load and discharge their goods . . . Marrakech is, above all, a city of *routes*, a great crossroads.[28]

A highly developed social and economic structure had evolved in the major cities of Morocco, one that merits some discussion. What follows will relate largely to Fez, the first city of the land, but is in most cases applicable to Meknes and Marrakech as well.

Professor Coon divides the inhabitants of Fez into four classes: (1) *tajiro* (wholesale merchants); (2) *beqqala* (retail merchants);

(3) master artisans; and (4) journeymen and unskilled laborers. "The merchants of both classes are literate; they can read the Qur'an and other works in classical Arabic. The third class is nearly illiterate, class four completely so." Coon notes the imperfect mobility among the classes when he writes that "the second feeds the first sometimes but only rarely does the third feed the second." [29]

The artisans and other workers were grouped by type of activity into corporations or *hanati*, the largest of which were those for the tanners, shoemakers, and weavers. Membership in these organizations was compulsory. They were guided by the notion of the just price and the principle of quality work. The corporation often accepted collective responsibility for fraud, for bad workmanship, and for injuries suffered on the job. Entry into a corporation was controlled by its leader, called an *amin;* and it was to him that customers carried all complaints against a member. He was elected by the membership for a life term, but served at its pleasure. The *amin* had an assistant, or khalifa, who assumed the duties in his absence.

Above the *amin* in the corporate hierarchy was the *mohtasseb*, an appointee of the sultan and the head of all corporations in a city. His most important function was to set the prices for goods sold by the corporations; he also served as court of appeal from the decisions of the *amin*. The court of final instance, however, was that of the town governor. Nevertheless, the powers of the *mohtasseb* were wide. Eugène Aubin, writing in 1908 of the *mohtasseb* at Fez, noted that:

All economic life in Fez, as well as in the other cities of Morocco, is controlled by a single official, the *mohtasseb*, who is next in importance to the governor and the cadis. This "potentate" possesses the power to imprison his charges . . . he fixes freely the selling prices of the principal consumption goods . . . he supervises the public baths and the management of the corporations . . . he controls the quality of merchandise. His jurisdiction extends over all commercial disputes, which he settles with the advice of experts chosen by the various *souks*. One could imagine what might happen if the *mohtasseb* were inclined toward speculation or extortion.[30]

The importance of the corporations was very great in the imperial cities, less so in the towns, and their influence was practically negligible in the rural areas. A notable exception was the corporation formed by Berber woodcutters in the forests near Azrou. (In Berber territory, the *amin* was chosen by the governing council.)

This group sent roof timbers to Meknes and also policed the forest, and, incidentally, the imperial route from Meknes to the Tafilalet. Later on, when the protectorate was to grant cutting rights in the area to a private French company, there was to be considerable trouble with the corporation, making it necessary to call upon troops to open the road.

Entry into a corporation was not confined to natives of the area in which it was located, and many were composed almost entirely of men who had emigrated from other parts of the country. According to Prosper Ricard, the workers at the public ovens and oil presses of Fez came from the Senhadja and the M'Tir tribes of the Middle Atlas slopes. The Filali, from the Tafilalet, in the southeast of Morocco, were millers and carriers of water, cereals, and charcoal. The Haratin of the Dra were found in all the cities as water carriers. The street porters were tribesmen from the Moulouya and the Guir (around Midelt), and many of the weavers came from Tlemcen, in Algeria. Guardians of wholesale houses were often from Touat, a Saharan oasis, which also supplied laborers to the cities of the north. The more skilled professions, however, such as building crafts, furniture making, and clothing manufacture, were reserved to native urban dwellers — mostly because the special skills required could not be learned in the rural areas.[31]

The Jews in the cities were found in goldsmithing, ironworking, and banking. They monopolized the jewelry trade. And since the Muslim religion prohibited the lending of money at interest, as we have seen, they also controlled the banking business. However, Muslim wholesalers often sold goods on credit to local retailers and to traveling merchants. No interest was charged, but undoubtedly a client paying cash received goods at a lower price.

The *fondouk* was the place where wholesale activities were carried on; in addition, it often served as a shelter for men and beasts. It was from the *fondouk* that the markets in the rural areas were supplied with the items they required from the cities. And it was in this process that the sultan compensated for the loss of revenue from the tribes in revolt by levying taxes on goods destined for the dissident areas.

Although gate and market taxes were also levied locally by the sultan, public services were largely provided by the *habous*, whose place in the land ownership pattern of pre-protectorate Morocco was mentioned on page 18. Education, charity, the city government, and the upkeep of the mosques were all financed by the *habous*. They also met the costs of the religious courts, including the remuneration of the judges. The income to support these activities was derived largely from real estate investment. Almost all property devoted to public purposes was *habous*-owned, including the *hammams* (public baths) and most of the shops in the markets. The water works in Fez, an ingenious distribution system made up of underground canals, also belonged to the *habous*. The power of this institution in the society was indeed far-reaching and profound, and it was to present a thorny problem to the French authorities in their desire to introduce a European system of asset ownership into Moroccan economic life.

All economic activity in Fez revolved around the great mosque; businesses, grouped by trade, clustered around it in a fan-like pattern. That the location of the various specialties in relation to the mosque was uniform and unchanging throughout the cities of the Middle East was noted by Professor Massignon, who also suggested the reason: ". . . since the beginning of Islam, there has been no change in the techniques of the artisans, with the result that the same crafts have continued to exist side by side, fulfilling each other's needs. . . ." [32]

The techniques employed were old, tried, and well adapted to the needs of a closed economy unchanged in its demands upon them for centuries. A minute division of labor resulted in work of the highest order. That this economic and social structure would not prove resilient when Morocco was "opened up" could be expected. To describe its fate, with all our present advantages of hindsight, is to deal with a real problem of economic change — the conversion of old forms to meet new needs.

TRANSPORT

Sultan Abd al Aziz was the only Moroccan who owned an automobile before the protectorate. The country's single railroad was a short line indeed, affording the sultan and his guests a brief tour of the palace grounds. The means of transportation for the rest of the population were animals — donkeys, mules, horses, and camels. Donkeys and mules did double duty as draft animals and as personal conveyances to the market; the horse, which required careful attention and expensive fodder and did not have compensating utility in the matter of earning a living, was reserved for the rich and for the warrior. The camel was the means of "heavy" transportation over long distances.

The raising of camels and the operation of caravans supported the greater part of a whole class of Moroccans — the desert nomads. The camel was unrivalled in land carriage, and he suffered no competition from water transport in interior commerce (the Sebou was the single navigable river in Morocco, and even then for only a few miles); but he was expensive. The British vice-consul at Fez estimated that a merchant paid 146 per cent of the purchase price of dates in getting them from the Tafilalet to the docks at Tangier.[33]

Worn trails linked the cities of Morocco to each other and to the other regions of North Africa and the Sudan. The presence of a bridge was exceptional. During inclement weather, the trails were quagmires, and a caravan was often forced to wait for days beside a watercourse in temporary flood. Added to the perils of the weather were those of banditry. Travel in small groups was impossible on this account; and the formation of a large caravan was often time-consuming, thus adding to freight costs. Communications were equally bad — there were no postal or telegraph services, and news and letters were carried by messengers. Safe delivery was problematical. Together with the slowness and uncertainty of inland transport, poor communications were quite effective in inhibiting trade.

Port facilities were no better — if anything, worse. In a world which had for some years been favored by steam and steel in ocean shipping, the condition of Moroccan ports in 1912 was very poor. The forces of nature were partly responsible. The Atlantic coast supplied little natural protection from the westerly and north-westerly winds; furthermore, those ports lying at the mouths of rivers, e.g., Rabat-Salé on the Bou Regreg and Mehdia on the Sebou, tended to silt up. But the government could also claim a share of the blame. Little was done in the way of port development before the protectorate. A beginning had been made in 1907 on a jetty for Casablanca, the leading port in tonnage from that year on. (It had been opened in 1830 by Sultan Moulay Abd ar Rahman.) But the other ports continued to languish in almost their virgin state. For if the sultans were resigned to giving the ports over to the Europeans, they were also determined to restrict foreign influence by keeping the facilities poor.

Mehdia, the port of Fez and easily accessible by means of the natural depression of the Sebou, had been closed by the government in the hope of preventing Christian penetration into the heart of central Morocco. By 1912, the port had silted up. Larache and Tangier were substituted as outlets to foreign ports for Fez, thereby making trade considerably more difficult and costly. Imports of light high-valued articles such as silk came to Fez by way of Tangier, while bulky products such as sugar, cotton goods, candles, tea, and iron were imported through Larache, one-fourth closer to Fez than Tangier.

The port of Salé was stagnating in 1912, its harbor silted up. At the beginning of the fifteenth century, however, it had been the most important outlet on the coast. Commercial contacts were maintained with Spain, England, and France, and with the Italian city-states of Pisa, Genoa, and Venice. Later on it was a pirate lair for an important contingent of renegades from Spain. For a time it had been strong enough to declare its independence, and thus to deny the sultan his 10 per cent share of the prizes taken by the pirates. But the world trade routes largely shifted beyond the range of the Salé pirates, and European ships grew too large to be captured by their small craft, restricted in size by the lack of deep anchorage. The silting up of the harbor, together with the heavy damage suffered in the Lisbon earthquake of 1755, left Salé an unimportant country town with its back largely turned to the sea.[34]

Al Jadida, to the south of Casablanca, was an important outlet for southern Morocco. The port was originally developed by the Portuguese, who occupied it in 1509–10 as one of the way stations for their commerce with India. Confined by Moroccan hostility to a small radius around the port, the Portuguese finally abandoned it to the Moroccans in 1769. The government in turn closed it, reopened it in 1821 for a Jewish colony from nearby Azemmour, and finally allowed foreign shipping to begin using it in 1882 as a port for the Haouz Plain and for the city of Marrakech. Safi and Essaouira were also possible outlets for this region; but the port of Al Jadida was better than that of Safi, and the route to the former was easier than that to Essaouira. Even at that, Aubin noted that it required four days for a camel to carry his 400-pound load from Marrakech to Al Jadida, a distance of around two hundred kilometers.[35]

The port of Safi was closed to foreign commerce in 1718 but was opened in 1817. However, it was of small importance because of the unsatisfactory state of its harbor. During most of the winter months, cargo handling had to be suspended, and ships were forced to wait for days until a break in the weather permitted the lighters to resume operations.

Essaouira, to the south of Safi, was more fortunate. Begun in 1760 on the ruins of a Portuguese establishment, it was destined to replace Agadir as the outlet of the Sous after the sultan had closed the latter both to punish rebellious tribes in that area and to keep out foreign influence. The Jews had moved from Agadir to Essaouira and, as already stated, at the beginning of the protectorate it had a higher proportion of Jews in its population than any other city in Morocco. Commerce from the Sous, the Oued Noun (the southern border of Ifni), and the Dra; the Saharan oases; and even some of that from the Sudan passed through Essaouira. Before Timbuktu was closed by the French toward the end of the nineteenth century, it was estimated that 500 to 600 camels loaded with ivory, ostrich feathers, and gold dust arrived annually at Essaouira. After this, trade declined and the principal product coming from the interior was sheepskins from the region of Marrakech and the Sous. The Sous also shipped almonds abroad via Essaouira, whose supremacy over Safi is indicated by the tonnage figures for 1907, which Aubin gives as 60,000 for Safi and 250,000 for Essaouira.[36]

Agadir, the southernmost port of Morocco and the natural outlet of the Sous, was constructed by the Portuguese in the fifteenth century to provide a haven for their fishermen exploiting the rich waters off the south Moroccan coast. Eventually, Agadir fell to the sultan in 1541. The closing of the port to European commerce after 1760, however, was not entirely successful in keeping foreigners out of the hinterland. German interests, represented chiefly by the Mannesmann Brothers, installed themselves in the Sous late in the nineteenth century and became interested in agriculture, commerce, and especially minerals.[37] Nevertheless, the closing did prevent the country from using its best natural harbor.

Added to the high costs of interior transport, ocean freight charges were a heavy burden and further served to impair trade in a country where expansion was already severely limited by the lack of effective demand. One writer goes so far as to attribute the stagnation of Morocco to the poor means of transport.[38] Although certainly not the sole factor, there is little doubt that the condition of transportation accounted in significant measure for the state of

Moroccan society and commerce, as an analysis of the effects of the French-supplied modern transportation net will show.

No foreign trade statistics were published by the government before the protectorate; the only figures available are those of the consuls. There would seem to be upward bias in their estimates, perhaps owing to the need to justify the continuation of consular relations with Morocco, and thus their jobs. Nevertheless, it is worth noting some of their observations.[39]

A relatively small number of products were involved in Morocco's foreign trade. In the export account with Europe, cereals, wool, hides, and eggs practically exhausted the list, valuewise. To the rest of North Africa and Senegal, the Moroccans exported *haiks* and *djellabas* (both over-garments commonly worn in the areas), shoes, and silk goods. The principal imports were cloth, sugar, tea, glassware, and hardware. The consumption of tea had become widespread by 1912, placing a certain reliance on the outside world of an otherwise almost wholly self-sufficient rural economy.

The bulk of the foreign commerce in the nineteenth century was carried on with Great Britain. Trafalgar, the Continental Blockade, and, later, the internal upheavals in Europe left Britain with an undisputed lead in trade with Morocco. These were the political factors. On the economic side, British products, especially cottons, were much cheaper than those of French or Spanish manufacture. In the Cobden era, Moroccan exports, notably wool, could enter Britain duty-free. The peak of trade between the two countries was reached in the 1840's, when Britain figured in two-thirds of Morocco's foreign commerce. By the last quarter of the century, however, her share was down to 40 per cent; and she continued to lose ground in the years that followed.

Specifically, Britain was losing to France. Trade relations between France and Morocco were long standing, and they had become important by the time of Louis XIV. In fact, French trade predominated during the seventeenth century and all but a part of the eighteenth. While in the next century France was second to Britain, the two together enjoyed the lion's share of trade with Morocco. At the time when Britain accounted for 40 per cent of the total, France took another 20 per cent. The new century brought a narrowing of the gap between the two countries; in

1901, when Britain's share was 31 million francs, France was close behind with 24 million. For by this time, France had begun in earnest her economic and military penetration of Morocco.

By 1905, it appears that France had once again captured first place among the countries trading with Morocco; at any rate, Boutin reports that her exports to Morocco were larger than Britain's from then on. By 1907, her primary position was clear. In that year, according to Donon, she participated in 45 per cent of the total trade, furnishing 56 per cent of Moroccan imports and taking 32 per cent of the exports. The establishment of the protectorate served, not surprisingly, to increase her lead. In 1913, the first full year of the protectorate, France (and Algeria) claimed 61 per cent of the imports and 53 per cent of the exports, for a 60 per cent share of total Moroccan trade. Britain, on the other hand, saw her commerce sink to less than 17 per cent — just over that amount on the import side, and 12 per cent on exports.[40]

Germany apparently was the third-ranking country in trade relations with Morocco. Her share was small, but seems to have been fairly steady, if the limited data available are any guide. Between 1875 and 1900, she enjoyed 9 per cent of the total commerce; in 1913, just slightly more. It is worth noting, however, that in the latter year no less than a fifth of Moroccan exports went to Germany.

The volume of Morocco's trade with all countries more than doubled between 1903 and 1913; it was 99 million francs in the former year, over 221 million in the latter. But exports accounted for practically none of this increase, for they were just 40 million in 1913, only 3 million more than in 1903. Imports, to the contrary, tripled during this period, climbing from 62 to 181 million.

Thus Morocco's trade deficit, which was 25 million francs in 1903 (and went down somewhat in the years immediately following), climbed to 141 million the first year after the protectorate. The deficit in the early years was financed by loans from French banks to the Moroccan government. Later on, military supplies for the French forces accounted for a substantial portion of the increase in imports, and troop expenditures helped partly to finance the deficit. In addition, the political stability promised by French control encouraged private investments by Frenchmen in Morocco which simultaneously added to and financed the deficit. This pattern of a large passive balance, established at the beginning of the protectorate, was to be characteristic of the Moroccan international accounts throughout the French regime, save for a short period during the Second World War.

The long slow decline of Moroccan power and prestige has been mirrored in its diplomatic history — a story of treaties with economic rights and extraterritorial jurisdiction defined and refined; of most-favored-nation agreements to keep all abreast of the latest concession; of international conferences which writ large the bilateral arrangements that went before; of international loans and control of customs and banking; of distributing the assets of the weak; and, finally, of the delivery of the body politic into the arms of protectorate. If internal disorder and the chronic inability of the government to organize itself effectively were the fundamental causes of decline, the machinations of the powers served to hasten the demise. The Moroccan government, in its last years, could not act; it could only react to threats to its sovereignty pressing in inexorably from London, Paris, and Berlin, and from its own nationals in the Sous and the region of Fez as well. Finally stripped of all financial power by its creditors, caught in a web spun from the rapport of the European powers, imprisoned in imperial Fez by a countryside in revolt, the government had lost all room for maneuver. It could only await the arrival of the French Minister from Tangier, carrying with him a treaty of protectorate.

It is worthwhile to summarize the treaty history of Morocco before 1912 not only because it is important to the beginning of our account of economic change under French auspices, but even more because it was a burden which made its weight felt right up to the very recent past.[41] Its influence on the path that economic change took was profound, as we shall have occasion to see in the pages that follow.

From practically the very beginning, treaties between Morocco and its European trading partners were concerned with two sets of rights — economic (commerce) and extraterritorial (establishment). Put another way, the treaty provisions were guarantees by the Moroccan government of (1) commercial rights as such, and (2) the personal safety of the traders and protection of their possessions. The Moroccan experience was not unique in international economic history, as a review of the history of China or the Ottoman Empire clearly demonstrates. It cannot even be said that extraterritorial rights were always confined to Christian powers in non-Christian lands; the extraterritoriality of the Hanseatic commercial enterprises in England is evidence to the contrary. The common denominator seems to be found rather on the political level, for the relationship results from a bargain between unequals. To achieve an increase in external trade, the weaker partner pays the price of forfeiting control of either land or persons within the geographical limits of his sovereignty. It is also a bargain between political unequals when in the case of economic rights, there is no reciprocity by one of the contracting powers. Most-favored-nation without reciprocity is evidence of an even greater weakness on the part of the lesser power. Indeed, a progressive broadening of territorial and economic rights by treaty revision can only further weaken the effective concession-granting power vis-à-vis the stronger partner. When the latter gains additional strength through factors exogenous to the treaty relationship, the inequality is aggravated. Carried to its logical conclusion, this process means that the economic and political destinies of the weaker power are finally determined unilaterally by the stronger. This point was reached for the Moroccan government the day that the French protectorate was established.

All the major European powers participated in writing the answer to the "Moroccan Question." France and Great Britain were the chief architects, while Germany, because she was a latecomer, was cast in the role of the spoiler. Italy had only recent and relatively minor interests, while Spain had ancient rights, particularly concerning the presidios. Both, however, were only near-great, and thus played no more than a nuisance part; because their influence was small, their price was commensurately low. While the answer was written in the first decade of the twentieth century, its elements had roots deep in the past.

The Beginnings

Moroccan treaty relations with its European neighbors date back at least to the eleventh century, when, according to Donon, the Italian city-state of Pisa first entered into a commercial agreement with Morocco.[42] In a pact in 1358, Pisa also took up the matter of extraterritoriality for the first time. According to the terms of the pact, the security of Pisans and their goods was assured upon the payment of 10 per cent on all merchandise sold in Morocco. Any disputes between the foreigners on Moroccan soil were to be settled by the consuls. In the case of a dispute between a Pisan and a Moroccan, however, the local court would have jurisdiction. Thus was the groundwork laid for Morocco's future treaty relations with foreign powers.

The pattern began to develop more fully in the seventeenth century. France, which had early entered into agreements with Morocco, negotiated three treaties during the century, two in 1631 and another in 1682. Those in the former year granted French merchants freedom to trade upon payment of the 10 per cent import duties (5 per cent was collected on exports), and also gave the French consul jurisdiction in disputes among his nationals. The treaty of 1682 stipulated that disputes between French nationals and Moroccans should be adjudicated by a council of the sultan or by his representative, rather than in the local court. The Netherlands came on the scene the next year, with a treaty setting forth economic and consular rights similar to those contained in the French agreements.

In the eighteenth century, after the time of Moulay Ismail, who cared little for commerce and who had less need of customs revenues than his successors, the list of nations in treaty relationship with Morocco expanded. By the end of the century, France, the Netherlands, Denmark, Spain, Britain, and the United States had all concluded agreements. Most notable, however, were the modifications attached to the definitions of economic rights and extraterritoriality. The most-favored-nation clause, for the benefit of the European powers and without reciprocity, made its first appearance in Morocco in this century, and had become a standard provision of treaties before the century was over. All nations were accorded freedom of commerce and other economic rights, consular jurisdiction in disputes between their nationals, and the right of a special trial in civil disputes between foreigners and Moroccans. In addition, foreigners were freed from internal taxes by the end of the century, and the consuls had gained the right to hear cases even when a Moroccan was involved, if the defendant was a foreigner.

Customs duties were also dealt with during this period. While the principle of a maximum charge of 10 per cent on imports and 5 per cent on exports was long-standing, the sultans were inclined to overlook the principle in practice. (Throughout Moroccan history, the desire for customs receipts, rather than the development of foreign trade per se, motivated the government in its commercial dealings with foreign powers.) The British-Moroccan treaty of 1783 was a reaction against this practice. While Britain had withdrawn from Tangier in 1684, after twenty-two years of occupation, the evacuation did not lessen her interest in Moroccan affairs; and the British capture of Gibraltar in 1704 did much to increase it. Specifically, the 1783 treaty arose over her concern with the food supply of the Gibraltar garrison, which was furnished by the region around Tetouan. According to the terms of the treaty, foodstuffs were to be sent to Gibraltar for one year without payment of export duties, and duties were to be strictly fixed thereafter. A treaty concluded by Spain in 1799 also stipulated fixed export duties, as well as reiterating the maximum import charge of 10 per cent. In addition, a list of 23 "exportable" products was set forth; all others were in effect banned from entering into the export trade.

It was no accident that many of the concessions granted to foreign powers took place during the reign of Sultan Sidi Mohammed (1757–1790). Much of the country was in revolt during his reign, and the sultan needed a large program of pacification. With internal sources of revenue largely dried up, he depended heavily on the yield from customs duties to provide the necessary funds for this as well as for the maintenance of his government. Sidi Mohammed was not the first ruler of Morocco, nor was he to be the last, to be caught between the European powers and the rebellious tribes, both striving to restrict his prerogatives to further their own advantage, and to lose out in the attempt to hold off one while dealing with the other.

THE DEFINITIVE PERIOD

The nineteenth century saw a number of the usual renewals of previous treaties, including one with the United States in 1836, which once again provided for most-favored-nation treatment. But a great deal more happened in the nineteenth century.

In 1856, Great Britain concluded two treaties with Morocco, one of which stands as Morocco's first true commercial agreement, in the modern sense. Up until this time, while questions of commerce and customs had certainly been involved in the agreements, these questions had always been incidental to consular matters. The British commercial treaty provided for complete liberty of import with the exception of certain monopolized products, e.g., firearms and tobacco. A 10 per cent ad valorem duty was to be charged, and specific and fixed duties were agreed upon for exports. In addition, the number of exportable products was raised from 23 to 43. A treaty with Spain in 1861 reproduced the British treaty provisions regarding both imports and exports, and further reiterated the principle of most-favored-nation treatment.

Two more bilateral treaties were concluded with Morocco in the nineteenth century. Germany negotiated an agreement in 1890 which added to the British treaty in two ways: (1) additional products were added to the exportable list; and (2) sizable reductions in duties were granted for all products on the list. A treaty with France in 1892 once again increased the number of exportable items, and in addition provided for a reduction of import duties from 10 to 5 per cent on such items as perfume, gold, and jewelry — items which in most cases France alone was able to provide.

During the nineteenth century, the inequality of bargaining power between Morocco and its "partners" in trade widened beyond all hope of ever achieving a balance. By the time of the Conference of Madrid (1880), the Moroccan delegate was little more than an observer while the future of his country was being hammered out by others at the bargaining table. The drama of Madrid was played against the wide background of the second great period of colonial expansion, a period in which France built the second largest empire in the world.

In 1815, French colonial possessions consisted, for the most part, of a few tropical trading stations vegetating from lack of official interest in Paris. The first move toward empire came in 1830, when French troops were landed in Algeria to carry out a "punitive expedition." The hope was to restore the rapidly fading prestige of Charles X; but although Algeria was invaded in late June, the throne toppled a month later. The initial outlay in French lives and treasure was tremendous; it required seventeen long years of effort to subdue the tribes.

It was during this period that France became interested in Morocco, which adjoined Algeria on the west. During the thirties and early forties, the French were either fighting or negotiating with Abd al Kader, formidable leader of the Holy War against the French in western Algeria; and the latter was being supported by the sultan of Morocco. Finally the sultan's army received a taste of European technology in warfare and went down to defeat at Isly in 1844. Simultaneously, French naval power was demonstrated by Prince de Joinville in the bombardment of Mogador (Essaouira) and Tangier. The outcome of these engagements was the Treaty of Tangier (1844), in which the sultan agreed to refuse asylum to Abd al Kader. This was followed in 1845 by the Treaty of Lalla-Marnia, which set the Algerian-Moroccan frontier in the north but left undefined a vast borderland in the south.

The relatively mild terms of these two treaties did not result from French largesse, but rather from the quiet intervention of the British. Even before the opening of the Suez Canal in 1869, free passage of the Strait of Gibraltar was the chief concern of British diplomacy in Morocco; and after that date, such passage became of course imperative. Lord Palmerston had decided in the early forties that the best method of assuring this would be to adopt a policy of maintaining the status quo, i.e., the independence of the sultan,[43] and the policy was to remain in effect until 1904.

For sixty years, then, British interests and those of the Moroccans coincided, and Britain stood ready to assist whenever the sultan was in difficulty. After the Spanish-Moroccan war in 1860, for example, British bankers supplied the funds to pay the indemnity awarded Spain, in a loan arranged by the Foreign Office. The advice of the British Minister, consequently, was always welcome at the Moroccan court. His consistent counsel was that of caution — to do nothing to provoke the powers. During the reign of Moulay Hassan (1873–1894), the last strong sultan before the protectorate, cooperation between the government and Sir John Drummond Hay, the able Minister at Tangier for many years, was especially efficacious. But however sympathetic the British government was to the continuing independence of the sultan, it eventually developed that Britain had a price for which she could be persuaded to acquiesce in a change of the political status of Morocco.

In the meantime, France's interest in North Africa continued to be heightened. Fifty-one years after her entry into Algeria, she invaded Tunisia, seeking protection for the creditors in what Clemenceau called a "coup de Bourse."[44] Two years later, in 1883, she definitively established a protectorate. Her action of abdicating responsibility for treaties concluded by the Bey prior to the protectorate, thus clearing the way to absorb the economy into the French orbit, brought the word "Tunisification" into the diplomatic vocabulary. By disclaiming previous commercial arrangements and substituting tariff association between Tunisia and herself, France aimed to close the "open door" permanently.

France next turned her eyes toward Morocco. Control of Morocco would eliminate a possible threat from the western flank to the now expanded North African empire; in fact it would round out the empire. France's action of Tunisification was fresh in the minds of her European rivals, however, and she was not to gain control of Morocco so easily, or so completely. Indeed, much of the diplomatic controversy which swirled around Morocco before the establishment of the protectorate stemmed from the memory of Tunisia.

Italy, which had had designs on Tunisia, was bitterly disappointed when it was snatched from her grasp. She therefore watched with particular interest the developments in Morocco, which along with Tripoli was the only "unclaimed" territory remaining on the African Coast. Bismarck Germany encouraged Irredentist France in her colonial expansion with the hope that the loss of Alsace-Lorraine would dim in French memory. Under Wilhelm II, however, Germany entered the colonial race too; as a consequence German support for the French position at Madrid in 1880 was to change to opposition at Algeciras in 1906. Spain, besides playing host to these two international conferences, shared Britain's interest in free passage of the Strait. In addition, she was concerned with the security of her presidios along the Riff shore and of the Canaries off the coast of Atlantic Morocco. Russia's interest in the Conference of Madrid,[45] even though she had no commercial or direct political interest in Morocco, signified that the problem of Morocco had assumed enough importance in European affairs to warrant the attention of the concert of powers. The question of Morocco had become internationalized in the broadest sense.

The Conference of Madrid was the major diplomatic event of the last half of the nineteenth century. The inability of the ministers at Tangier to agree on a limitation of protection extended to Moroccan nationals had caused Britain and Spain to convene this high-level meeting of the powers. The principle of protection, well-established by treaties and by custom and usage, had been abused to such an extent that the sultan, in an interview with Sir John Drummond Hay in 1863, predicted that "if the evils continued to flourish unchecked, his authorities would find themselves in the anomalous position of having to appeal to foreign tribunals established on Moorish soil to govern Moroccan subjects according to foreign laws and usages." [46] The sultan spoke with some cause; abuses of protection undoubtedly played a large role in the disintegration of his authority. The chief complaint from the government was in connection with those protégés who were wealthy farmers. By being protected, they could avoid market and gate taxes. Not only was needed revenue lost to the government, but the protégés had a competitive advantage over their less fortunate neighbors. That protection could also be used for political purposes by a European power with more than commercial ambitions in Morocco was demonstrated by the French grant of protection to the Sharif of Ouezzane, a political enemy of the sultan.

The British and the Spanish, interested in maintaining the independence of the sultan, hoped that the evils of protection would be corrected by the conference. France was less concerned with Moroccan authority, and was backed in her position by Italy and Bismarck Germany. The agreement reached at the Conference represented a compromise between the two positions, but France was to win out shortly thereafter. The agreement on limitation of protection soon broke down, with each nation claiming most-favored-nation treatment.

The Conference of Madrid and the resulting convention went beyond the problem of protection. It was agreed that foreigners and their protégés should be subject to payment of agricultural and gate taxes. As it developed, however, the failure of the sultan to include all of his subjects in the tax rolls kept the provisions from being put into effect. Nevertheless, for their consent to the principle, the Europeans demanded the right to hold real property in Morocco. While this latter provision was also written into the convention, it was qualified by requiring the approval of the sultan for all real estate transactions involving foreigners — approval which, as we have seen, was seldom granted.

The really important thing about the Madrid Convention was that it served to internationalize Morocco's external relations. The fact that the problems of Morocco were now the subject of an international agreement meant not only that the government's time was running out; it also meant that France was not to have the liberty of action in Morocco that she so strongly desired. Indeed, the Madrid Convention was the lineal ancestor of the Algeciras Act in 1906, which contained the international statute that governed, at least formally, France's actions in Morocco until independence in 1956.

During the last quarter of the nineteenth century, Morocco was ably ruled by Sultan Moulay Hassan (until his death in 1894) and then by his Grand Vizier, Si Ahmed ben Moussa, acting as regent for the child heir, Abd al Aziz. Though they most certainly failed in their policy to keep the country from any contact with the Christian world, they were able, by their strong leadership, to postpone the day of reckoning.

THE LAST TWELVE YEARS

Abd al Aziz ascended the throne in 1900, upon the death of the regent, and proved very ineffective as a ruler. Most French writers dismiss him as a gadget-loving buffoon who squandered public funds on his personal folly. His proposed tax reform suggests, however, that Abd al Aziz had at least one moment of real concern for the future of his country.[47]

The failure of Abd al Aziz was due primarily to his lack of interest in following up his ideas for reform and to the resistance of the Moroccan ministers, whose positions were built on unchecked power and privilege. It might also be added that when Abd al Aziz took the throne, negotiations were already under way in the European capitals to dispose definitively of the "Moroccan Question." Soon the sultan could no longer expect support from Britain, the identity of interests having ceased as a result of the Entente Cordiale. The revolt of Bou Hamara in the region of Taza and, finally, the successful coup in 1908 by the sultan's brother, Moulay Hafid, brought the internal chaos which, in the light of agreements concluded by Europeans among themselves, justified direct foreign intervention.

The opening gun had been fired by Delcassé, the French Foreign Minister, in July, 1901, when he argued that Morocco was definitely a geological and economic extension of Oran. His argument would carry far on a map, but not as far as the western plains; and it is certain that Delcassé was not interested per se in the arid eastern plateaus, which were indeed an extension, or in the equally arid eastern slopes of the Middle Atlas, beyond which the argument lost its validity.

Despite the fallacies in Delcassé's reasoning, 1901 was an active year for French diplomacy. The 5 per cent duty conceded for certain French products in the 1892 treaty was generalized to include all products coming overland from Algeria. However, although the 10 per cent rate was maintained in the Atlantic ports, high internal freight charges prevented French products from the east from penetrating farther than the region around Oujda. Another agreement in 1901 delineated that part of the Moroccan-Algerian frontier which the 1845 treaty had left undefined. It further provided for joint policing of the south, i.e., the area around Figuig, and also established the right of French troops to pursue marauders into Morocco. Shortly thereafter, the French army took the Touat oases, over which the sultan had previously laid claim. (When command of the southern area was given to General Lyautey in 1903, military penetration from the south began in earnest, starting with the capture of the oases around Colomb Bechar.)

France also concluded in 1901 the first of a series of agreements which were to give her a free hand politically in Morocco. In secret negotiations with Italy, France conceded the primacy of Italian interests in Tripoli, and Italy in turn recognized that French rights were preponderant in Morocco.[48] Thus disposed of were the objections of one country. Spain was to be next.

The Franco-Spanish agreement in 1902 foresaw the possibility that the day might come when the sultan of Morocco could no longer reign effectively, and the powers would be forced to substitute their own sovereignty. The agreement was in effect an "if and when" partition of the country between France and Spain. As it turned out, the latter came out better in this proposed partition than in the partition that eventually occurred. Tangier and Fez were to be in Spain's orbit (she was destined to get neither); and the southern boundary of the Spanish enclave was placed on the north bank of the Sebou River, thus giving Spain the fertile Gharb, territory which fell to the French when the time came. In addition, Spanish holdings in southern Morocco opposite the Canaries were to be expanded. While the Spanish were eminently satisfied with the terms, they were also worried over the reaction of Britain. Consequently, France turned to the Foreign Office as the next step. She found the British receptive, but not willing to sell their assent cheaply.

The so-called Entente Cordiale dealt with many matters outstanding between France and England; in fact, one writer has argued that agreement was possible simply because there were conflicts at so many points that the bargaining range was very wide.[49] The settlement on Morocco was closely tied to the solution of the rival contentions of Britain and France in Egypt. The result was that France expressed "désintéressement" in Egypt in exchange for a similar pledge from Britain concerning Morocco; and each government promised not to oppose the abolishment of capitulations if the other deemed it necessary.

As for Morocco, Tangier was to be neutralized, and there were to be no fortifications of the coast from Melilla on the Mediterranean to the outlet of the Sebou on the Atlantic. In addition, Britain demanded that her economic rights in Morocco would be maintained for thirty years. For the right of free land access to Morocco by transit across Algeria, she offered the same privileges for French products in Egypt. When France discovered that the Foreign Office wanted the renunciation of French interests in Egypt as well as the neutralization of Tangier, she withdrew her offer to Spain of the territory to the Sebou and also of the city of Fez. So Spain, in an agreement with France signed late in 1904, not only lost Tangier, in accordance with British demands, but saw her share of Morocco further reduced to the Riff territory from the Moulouya River on the east to just south of the port of Larache on the west.

While the rapport was being established by the powers in preparation for the political penetration of Morocco, a step toward economic dominance was being taken by France, or rather by Paris financial interests, at the instance of the *Quai d'Orsay*. Sultan Abd al Aziz, pressed for the means to fund the Moroccan debt, received a 5 per cent loan of 62,500,000 francs in 1904 from a consortium headed by the *Banque de Paris et des Pays-Bas*. The loan was secured by customs receipts from both imports and exports, two-thirds of the daily revenue to be paid by the *Oumana* (Moroccan customs) to the *Service du Contrôle de la Dette*. As Donon pointed out, the French agents who supervised the debt service were carefully selected, which underlined the fact that their function was to be more political than financial.[50] We shall see shortly how control over public finances was extended, and what the political overtones were.

Moroccan anxiety over the rumored agreements between France and Britain and between France and Spain (they were not made public until 1911) was shared by Germany. It will be remembered that under the guidance of Wilhelm II, Germany had also entered the colonial race. Her commercial interests in Morocco were small, but she resented the failure of the French to consult with her. Final implementation of French designs, after the preliminaries had been disposed of by the purchased acquiescence of Britain,

Spain, and Italy, was set back seven years by the Kaiser's speech at Tangier in 1905. Moreover, the conditions under which France could operate were drastically changed by the Act of Algeciras in 1906, which was a direct result of this speech. The Kaiser had inserted himself, if only briefly, into the role of defender of the status quo in Morocco, vacated by Britain in 1904.

At the Conference of Algeciras, Morocco once more became the focus of attention of the concert of powers. France had staunch allies at Algeciras in Great Britain, Italy, and Spain; and the United States was a tacit supporter. Germany fought almost alone, but despite the inequality of the struggle, the results of the conference were hardly favorable to France. The "open door" was confirmed in the preamble of the final agreement, and again in Article 105, when the principle of "economic liberty without any inequality" was proclaimed. It was made clear, too, that the principle was meant to extend to all business transacted, not merely to trade. For example, Article 105 provided that all public works projects be submitted to bids.

France could not argue, as she had in Tunisia, that the protecting power was not bound by prior agreements; Article 123 stated that the provisions of previous bilateral treaties were confirmed unless they conflicted with the Act of Algeciras. In this way, the general 10 per cent duty on imports, as provided in the British and Spanish treaties of 1856 and 1861, respectively, was maintained. So, too, was the 5 per cent rate on gold, jewelry, perfume, and liquors granted in the French treaty of 1892, and the like rate on all imports coming from Algeria agreed to in the Franco-Moroccan accord of 1901. On the other hand, the Act of Algeciras explicitly provided in Article 66 for a 2.5 per cent surtax on imports, with the income earmarked for port improvement and inland transportation.

The political primacy of France and Spain in Morocco was recognized in granting the police power in the eight ports open to commerce (and in an area of six miles around each one) to those two nations. The police afforded the necessary security to stimulate capital investment in the ports. (Article 60 allowed Europeans to acquire property without the permission of the sultan, thus removing the proviso of the Treaty of Madrid.) The improvements in the ports promised by the fund fed by the 2.5 per cent import surtax were additional stimuli to capital investment by Europeans.

Finance also received attention at Algeciras. The act provided for the creation of a *Banque d'Etat*, with equal shares of capital being assigned to the signatory powers. Two shares were also granted to the consortium of French banks participating in the 1904 loan. The privilege of issuing notes was reserved to the bank, and it also acted as treasurer to the Moroccan government.

In view of the fact that four of the signatory powers of the act (France, Great Britain, Spain, and Italy) were already committed to a quite different course than the one which it charted, it is not surprising that violations, both of the letter and of the spirit, occurred almost before the ink was dry. In 1907, a Frenchman, Dr. Mauchamp, was murdered in Marrakech; Oujda paid the penalty by being taken in retaliation by French troops from Algeria. The region of the Beni Snassen to the north of Oujda was also occupied. These acts were clearly an infringement on the independence of the sultan and the "integrity of his realm," both solemnly proclaimed at Algeciras just one year before. In July, 1907, the massacre of seven Europeans working on the jetty at Casablanca provoked the landing of a French force to protect the lives and property of its nationals. Soon after, the beachhead at Casablanca was expanded to the occupation of the Chaouia.

Behind the troops at Casablanca and Oujda came the French civilians — traders, merchants, and speculators. These two areas, then, began to receive their leaven of Europeans five years before the protectorate was established. On the financial side, 1907 saw the agents of the bankers take positions next to the Moroccan customs officials to assure that there was no embezzlement of funds.

The French actions in 1907 brought reactions in the interior of Morocco and also in Germany. On the local scene, there were revolts against the sultan as the man allegedly responsible for the European penetration. The one hatched at Marrakech by the sultan's brother, Moulay Hafid, with the support of the Glaoua chiefs, bore fruit when the pretender's followers defeated the troops of Abd al Aziz. Moulay Hafid became sultan in 1908 and disposed of Bou Hamara, who had proclaimed his right to the throne from a stronghold in the Taza area, the next year.

As for the Germans, they saw in the French actions a violation of the Act of Algeciras. They proceeded to compose their differences with the French temporarily by concluding a treaty in 1909, in which Germany conceded the preponderant political interest of France in Morocco. In return, the "open door" was reconfirmed, and at the same time the two countries agreed on a sharing of the public works contracts. The treaty proved to be short-lived; the two parties soon fell out over its interpretation. The Germans argued that the agreement covered the operation of public works as well as their construction, while the French maintained that only the latter was included.

The *Service du Contrôle de la Dette* took over direct control of the customs in 1910, replacing the Moroccans. In return for this concession and for the pledge of all public revenues as security, the bankers agreed to an additional loan of just over 100 million francs. The sultan had finally lost control of all revenues.

The penetration of the Europeans into the country at an increasing pace did not go unnoticed in the rural areas. By 1911, Moulay Hafid found himself caught in the same vise as his predecessors — between the European powers and the tribes. Besieged by the latter in Fez, he was compelled to call for the assistance of the French. An expedition dispatched from the Chaouia succeeded in raising not only the siege but also further protests from Germany. The latter saw the Fez incident as the final move by France to annex Morocco. Its answer was hardly diplomatic, appearing as it did in the form of a gunboat off Agadir. Once again France was forced to the bargaining table.

In the accord of 1911, the Germans accepted the principle of the French protectorate in exchange for a slice of the French Congo (about 100,000 square miles) and a reiteration of the guarantee of economic equality in Morocco. This equality was defined as extending to non-signatories of the Act of Algeciras, to all kinds of business, and to domestic taxes and transport rates. There were to be neither export nor production taxes on iron ore. Public works contracts would be let only by bids. Military railroads could be built to aid the pacification, but they had to be narrow gauge and could not be used to carry either civilians or commercial freight, even without charge. It was also agreed that the first commercial railroad constructed in Morocco would run from Tangier to Fez.

After the Franco-German accord of 1911, France did not delay long in taking possession of the political freedom so dearly bought. On March 30, 1912, the Treaty of Fez was signed. Under the treaty, France agreed to respect the independence of the sultan and the integrity of his realm. France also undertook to introduce such reforms as she deemed necessary to the well-being of the Moroccan people. Foreign affairs, national defense, and finance were to be controlled by the French Resident-General as the representative to the sultan. On these principles and provisions rested the French protectorate over Morocco.

Spain received her zone of influence by virtue of the Franco-Spanish treaty of November 27, 1912, which gave to Spain a sub-protectorate over the Riff country. Article 13 assured respect for the provisions of the Act of Algeciras. There was also a provision for customs unity of the two zones; no changes in customs matters were to be taken by the authorities in one without the approval of those in the other. The sultan's authority was to remain complete over both zones, but was delegated in the Spanish area to a khalifa residing at Tetouan. The status of Tangier was not to be determined until 1923, when it was internationalized. The sultan's authority there was to be exercised by a *mendoub* (delegate).

So the territory of Morocco was divided three ways — between France, Spain, and an international administration. But the lion's share, both in terms of territory and resources, natural and human, went to France; consequently most of what follows will be concerned with the French zone. It is here that the possibilities and the realizations of economic development were greatest, so it is here too that we can best describe and analyze economic changes as they have appeared in Morocco. In the final chapter, however, which is concerned with the years since independence, the problems of reintegration of the former Spanish zone and Tangier with the much larger area to the south will be discussed.

II

PACIFICATION, POPULATION, AND PLURAL SOCIETY

Economic change does not take place in a vacuum; political and social factors are ever present, ever altering its course. These factors are especially important where a particular type of economic organization is introduced into an essentially alien milieu, as happened in Morocco under French direction. Indeed, a consideration of political and social factors is essential to an understanding of the economic evolution that occurred in the country after 1912.

Morocco is not unique in having had its economic development imposed and guided by outsiders.[1] Nor is it unusual because long, costly, and sustained military effort was needed to bring the measure of order essential to meaningful economic development. Certainly the rapid population growth in Morocco during the protectorate was a phenomenon of the world in general and not of this country in particular. The qualitative aspect of Morocco's population increase — the growth of the plural society — can be found elsewhere, too, notably in certain countries of Southeast Asia. Morocco is unique, however, in that it has had all of these things in a particular combination.

The military-political aspects of French control, the population increase, and the growth of the plural society all seem to warrant some attention before beginning to discuss the course of economic change in Morocco over the protectorate years. By spelling out the evolution of these factors now, their implications for economic change should be more meaningful to the reader later on.

THE MILITARY OPERATIONS

Economic developments in Morocco during the early years of the protectorate must be arrayed against a background of two military efforts in which the French were engaged: the war in Europe and the pacification campaign in Morocco itself. The unique role played by Marshal Lyautey during these years must also be given some attention.

When Lyautey took up his post as Resident-General in April, 1912, the French Army held the Chaouia, Rabat and its environs, the region of the Upper Moulouya and Oujda, and the south-eastern oases. The Fez area was in revolt, while in the south, a new pretender to the throne, Al Hiba, threatened to prevent French occupation of Marrakech. The immediate task of Lyautey was to stabilize the situation. The relief of Fez was quickly accomplished, and Colonel Mangin entered Marrakech soon after. The powerful families of the High Atlas, promised autonomy in their regions by the French, drove Al Hiba from his retreat in the Sous into the desert. As a result, Agadir fell to French forces in 1913.

The year 1914 saw the pacification of the bulk of the western plains. In the east Taza was taken, thereby assuring communications with Algeria. The Zaian region around Khenifra was also pacified, permitting the establishment of communications with Marrakech for both Rabat and Fez. The front now ran almost on a line from Agadir to Oujda, roughly the limits of the dry-farming areas.

Two months after the capture of Khenifra, France was fighting for her life in Europe. Ordered to send the bulk of his forces home and to withdraw the remainder to the coast, the Resident-General complied with the former directive and had the latter rescinded. Depleted ranks were filled with overage reserves. By judicious use of his troops, e.g., mobile columns which could be rushed to trouble spots, Lyautey not only held the ground already taken, but substantially extended French control. Included in his operations were the capture of Tiznit in 1917 and the pacification of the Sous Valley, which was completed in 1919. In addition, the route from Meknes across the Middle Atlas to the Tafilalet was opened up during the war years, thus providing a springboard from which to launch later campaigns in the southeast.

The mountains and the bulk of the land beyond — the traditional areas of revolt — remained to be subdued in the post-war years. In 1922, one-third of the country was still outside of French control. Even though the French were able to bring all modern weapons, including aircraft, to bear, the campaign was to last twelve more years. It was a campaign of no quarter at times, reminiscent of the Algerian operations a hundred years before. Pacified in turn were the Middle Atlas (1931), the Tafilalet (1932), the Djebel Saghro (1933), and finally the Anti-Atlas and the far south in 1934.

The most ominous threat to French domination, however, came from the Riff. The struggle between Abd al Krim and the Spanish spilled over into the French zone in 1925, when both Taza and Fez and thus the vital communications link with Algeria were threatened by the Riffians. This development resulted in heavy troop reinforcements from France and the final subjugation of the Riffians by combined French-Spanish military action in the spring of 1926. It also resulted in the resignation of Resident-General Lyautey and his replacement by Senator Steeg.

Although Lyautey was largely concerned during his tenure in Morocco with extending French control throughout the country, he was able to accomplish a measurable amount of economic progress. The security resulting from the pacification was enough in itself to bring increased production and trade without altering techniques. Too, the presence of French troops in Morocco helped create effective demand for this increased production. Not so incidentally, it also placed a heavy burden on the French taxpayer. While the protectorate enjoyed budget autonomy from the beginning, the expenditures for Moroccan national defense were carried by the French budget — and the pacification was part of this defense.

It has been estimated that from 1907, when Casablanca was occupied, until 1913 the French Parliament authorized 479 million francs (roughly $95 million) for supplementary expenses of troops in Morocco. These appropriations were in addition to regular ones required to keep the soldiers if they had remained garrisoned in France. Together, the two appropriations during the six-year period totaled $237 million. Expenditures for troop maintenance continued to loom large throughout the protectorate years, and thus served as an important demand factor in the economy and as an important source of foreign exchange to help meet the chronic deficit on trade account. In fact, according to Knight, total military expenses of France in Morocco from 1907 to 1927 were roughly equal to the total French capital existing in the country in the latter year.[2]

Needless to say, calculations of returns on investment would have been considerably lower had troop expenditures, which really made the investments safe, also been capitalized. Instead, returns to European investors in Morocco looked good, because military costs were charged as a current expense to the taxpayers in France.

The World War hampered Lyautey's economic plans in that it brought inevitable shortages of capital goods. Nevertheless, he was able to turn a minimum of such goods into the beginnings of the transportation network antecedent to full colonization. Furthermore, some of the economic evolution of the early years was directly attributable to the struggle in Europe. The heavy demand for farm products in France, with much of its agricultural land laid waste, was an impetus, and a strong one, to increased production. Indeed, Morocco's participation in foreign trade expanded noticeably during the war years. In response to French demand, both sown area and prices increased in the country, and both were reflected in the international accounts. In the four years after 1914, exports rose from 31 million francs to 114 million. At the same time, imports were climbing from 133 million francs to 314 million.[3] From the very outset, a pattern of large passive balances was established. Further characteristics were a large money inflow — much of it for troop maintenance as already noted — and a dependence on France as a high-price market for exports.

The war also helped to alleviate Morocco's population pressures for a time. As we have seen, people from the south of Morocco had been emigrating to the cities in the north and even to Algeria before the protectorate. With the arrival of the French, employment possibilities were broadened to include the factories, fields, and mines of France. And with the war, the French actively recruited Moroccans for service as soldiers as well as workers. Bernard estimated the number of Moroccans sent to the western front at over 40,000.[4] In addition, 35,000 workers emigrated to augment the labor force in the coal mines of Pas-de-Calais, the fields of the Midi, and the factories of Paris, Lyon, and Lille.[5]

Some of the workers came from tribes still in revolt, but mostly they originated from around Essaouira and Marrakech, areas then pacified. Lyautey was able to guarantee full employment in the other pacified areas, due in part to the demands created by the war. Indeed, he proscribed recruitment in these areas in a note written early in 1918. Thus Lyautey could put off painful structural adjustments in the country's economy until after the war. With the exception of 1913, when there was a famine, the years to 1920 were prosperous ones for Morocco.

As it is the economy of Morocco which is our primary concern here, so it was with Lyautey. An admirer of his English colonial predecessors, he translated Rhodes' maxim that "rails cost less than bullets and carry farther" into "un chantier vaut un bataillon." The imprint of Lyautey's ideas has been indelible on the face of Morocco — from the plan of the cities to the pockets in the *djellabas* worn by Moroccan ladies. The *démarrage* (literally: unmooring) bore his personal stamp; the major decisions and many of the minor ones were his; and all of them reflected his colonial experience and philosophy. On the economic as well as the military front, Lyautey advanced where he could and otherwise made plans for the future. During his thirteen-year tenure, he laid the foundations for the successes and failures of French policy in Morocco.

Thanks to Lyautey, the scorched earth and *refoulement* (literally: forcing back) that had characterized early French policy in Algeria were largely passed by in Morocco in favor of conjoint political and economic action, with force as a last resort. Nevertheless, Lyautey's public pronouncements constantly remind us (and the *colons*) that there was not a grain of wheat in Morocco which had not been fertilized by the blood of a French soldier.[6]

French bloodshed did not cease with the end of the pacification. But after 1934, dissidence took a somewhat different form in political protest, which was followed by violence when the protest went unanswered. A new spirit had arisen in Morocco; after centuries of tribal loyalties, the people were finding a national conscience and a desire for self-determination as a nation.[7] The implications of this new political spirit for the economy, which were many, will be dealt with in succeeding pages. The existence of the spirit, and the fact that it meant continued French expense for troop maintenance in Morocco, are all that need to be noted here. The "French peace" was an uneasy one, one ultimately kept — as long as it was kept — only by the bayonet.

THE DEMOGRAPHY

The completion of the pacification in 1934 meant, theoretically at least, that all the natural resources of the country could then enter into interregional exchange or into foreign trade. (The pacification actually created certain of these resources in the sense that it made possible exchanges of things which had had no value within the areas in dissidence. Minerals in the Atlas are an example; only the possibility of an effective demand from the outside gave the ores of the mountains their value.) As for human resources, the pacification meant that a measure of interregional specialization could take place and also that the resources might move where rewards promised to be greater.

There can be no doubt that the human resources of Morocco grew numerically, both by natural increase and by immigration, during the protectorate. The growth of the Muslim population was all natural; in fact, a slight reduction must be made for emigration. The bulk of the emigrants were in Algeria and France, where their numbers were estimated at 50,000.[8] The natural increase, however, far outpaced the emigration that occurred. The base for this increase was a high fecundity, which had always existed in the society. While economy had largely eliminated simultaneous polygamy, easy divorce made possible its replacement by what Gautier has called "successive" polygamy.[9] Up until the protectorate, however, the propensity for high reproduction had been largely counterbalanced by a high mortality rate. It was the French who upset the balance by introducing conditions favorable to a lowering of the death rate. Security itself was a major factor. Others were the numerous medical and sanitary measures introduced by the protectorate government.

The Jewish segment of the Moroccan population was also subject to natural increase. In this case, however, the numbers were proportionally reduced by emigration; it has been estimated that 8 per cent of the Jews had moved to Israel by 1952.[10] As for the Europeans living in Morocco, their ranks swelled steadily during the protectorate, through natural increase and particularly through immigration.

Unfortunately, it is difficult to describe Morocco's population growth in more specific terms with any degree of certitude. The figures are very loose for many reasons, one of which lies in the nature of an Islamic society which basically resents probing by outsiders into family affairs. The French, too, must take some of the blame for the dubious quality of the data; there were serious defects in matters of both technique and personnel in the census operations. Furthermore, nothing but the roughest of estimates was possible in the large areas still outside government control in the early years of the protectorate.

While the difficulties of census-taking applied principally to the Muslim population, this group was by far in the majority. Consequently the aggregates were little affected by the accurate

TABLE 1. CIVILIAN POPULATION OF THE FRENCH ZONE OF MOROCCO, 1921–1952

ETHNIC GROUP	POPULATION (in 000)					AVERAGE ANNUAL INCREASE (in %)			
	1921	1926	1931	1936	1951-52	1921-26	1926-31	1931-36	1936-51-52**
Muslims	4,162	4,682	5,068	5,881	7,442	2.2	1.6	3.0	1.5
Jews	91	107	125	162	199	3.2	3.4	5.2	1.4
Europeans*	81	105	172	202	363	4.2	10.0	3.2	3.9
Total	4,334	4,894	5,365	6,245	8,004	2.4	1.8	3.0	1.6

*Includes Algerian Muslims, who have a form of French citizenship, and the relatively small group of non-Moroccans who are not citizens of a European country.

**The census of the Jewish and European segments of the population was taken in 1951, that of the Muslims in 1952. The individual annual increases are figured accordingly, and the annual increase for the total population is based on a period of 15.5 years.

Source: *Annuaire statistique de la zone française du Maroc, 1952*, Gouvernement Chérifien, Service Central des Statistiques (Rabat, 1952), p. 12 for the basic population data. The rates of increase were calculated by the author.

counts of Europeans which resulted from a well-defined civil status, or the probably equally accurate counts of the Jewish population furnished by the rabbis. In the case of Europeans, however, there may have been an inclination to understate their numbers in order to show that "protected" Morocco had not been made over into a land for Frenchmen.

With these limitations in mind, we can now turn to an examination of the available demographic data. The first census was taken in 1921 and was followed by others in 1926 and 1931. All three suffered from poor enumerating techniques and from the weakness of estimates made for the unsubdued areas. A census in 1936 was the first to cover the whole of the French zone, but the methods of doing so were highly dubious; for example, tent counts and a multiplier were substituted for head counts. The first postwar census of 1947 was not reliable either, as it consisted of a count of ration cards — a procedure which undoubtedly resulted in overestimation of the population. The 1952 census, the last the French took, is undoubtedly the most reliable of all those taken during the protectorate years, but it too should probably be treated with a certain amount of skepticism.

Table 1 summarizes the results of these various enumerations, with the exception of that of 1947. The figures relate only to the civilian population, and thereby exclude the sizable group of Europeans on military duty in Morocco as well as Moroccan troops serving under the French. As can be seen from the table, the population of Morocco was found to be slightly in excess of eight million in 1951–52, an increase of 85 per cent over the first census in 1921. Even with a liberal allowance for under-enumeration in the earlier year, the growth was undeniably tremendous. While there appears not to have been any very clear pattern in the rate of growth, this may be attributable to defects in the figures as much as to anything else, at least as far as the Muslim population is concerned. Thus, according to the censuses, the Muslims increased more rapidly in the years from 1931 to 1936. In fact, however, the average annual rate of 3 per cent recorded during these years is undoubtedly too high for the period, as a result of an underestimation in the former year and an overestimation in the latter. The yearly rate of 1.5 per cent indicated by the 1951–52 census is certainly a more realistic one, although in this case the rate is probably something of an understatement, in view of the nature of the 1936 enumeration.

The very sizable increase of more than 75 per cent registered by the Muslims since 1921 is far outweighed by the percentage increases that occurred in the two minority groups. Since the figure for the Muslims is probably based on an underestimation in 1921, the balance actually shifted toward the Jews and the Europeans to an even greater extent than the figures show. The Muslims, however, continued to weigh down the scale by virtue of their sheer numbers, so that while they represented at least 96 of every 100 people in the country thirty-five years ago, they accounted for only around three less in 1951–52.

The Jews, as can be seen, more than doubled in number after 1921. Their rate of increase was greater than that of the Muslims in every period save the last, which saw an outflow to Israel, estimated by the *Service Central des Statistiques* at 15,000 in the years from 1948 through 1950.[11] Despite emigration, however, it appears that the Jews held their own numerically under the French; in fact, their proportion of the population actually increased slightly, from 2.1 per cent in the first census to 2.5 per cent in the last.

While it is true that Morocco was not made over into a land for Frenchmen from the standpoint of numbers, the Europeans, most of whom were French, clearly led the way, percentagewise, in the population growth, with a 350 per cent increase in the years from 1921. Thus, while representing only 1.9 per cent of the total population according to the census of 1921, Europeans accounted for 4.5 per cent in 1951–52. On a yearly basis, the greatest portion of this growth occurred during the period from 1926 to 1931, when immigration was stimulated by a favorable business climate resulting in large part from official encouragement of French settlement. The large drop-off in the years immediately following (1931–36) can be attributed to the world economic crisis. By 1931, however, the Europeans had supplanted the Jews as the more numerous minority group, a position they continued to maintain.

The enormous growth that occurred in Morocco during the years of the protectorate was characterized not only by a shift in the relative proportions of the three segments of the population, it was also marked by a shift in the geographical distribution. As might be expected, the urban areas in general increased at a more rapid rate than the country as a whole. Furthermore, it was the coastal cities in particular which prospered numerically under French control. The most striking example is offered by Casablanca, which was transformed from a small town of perhaps 20,000 or so inhabitants in 1912 into a sprawling metropolis of 682,000 people according to the census of 1951–52, or almost 9 per cent of the country's total population.

Nevertheless, Morocco still remained overwhelmingly rural in the political sense of the word, as the distribution of the population in 1951–52 by place of residence in Table 2 shows. As can be seen, only 23 per cent of the people were living in the 19 cities. It can also be seen that it was the Muslims, not the Europeans or the Jews, who were responsible for the heavily rural nature of the country. Four-fifths of each minority group were found in the urban areas, and no less than 37 per cent were in Casablanca alone. Nevertheless, the minority groups were sufficiently less sizable so that, even taken together, they were far outnumbered by the Muslims in every city — this despite the fact that 82 per cent of the Muslims resided in the rural areas.

Table 3 summarizes data developed in the 1951–52 census relating to the number of people engaged in various types of economic activity. While the data should be regarded as only very approximate, they are nonetheless of considerable interest. They clearly show that the country remained overwhelmingly rural in the economic as well as the political sense. Once again, it was the Muslims who made it so; 70 per cent of them were reported as engaged in agriculture. The Jews, on the other hand, leaned heavily toward the urban pursuits of handicrafts, manufacturing, and commerce. As for the foreigners living in Morocco, over a quarter of them were in manufacturing and almost as many were in the civil service and other "white collar" occupations or the professions, a category that claimed only 2 per cent of the Muslim population.

A population pyramid for the Muslim population was constructed for the first time as part of the 1951–52 census. On the basis of a sample of 547,000 persons, it was estimated that close to a third of the total population was less than ten years of age. Thus the Muslims were an extremely young people, a people with a vastly increased life expectancy, and with no immediate prospects of an effective check on their numbers through voluntary limitation of births.[12] The view was widely held that they were increasing by a rate of at least 2 per cent a year — a rate which would double the population in thirty-five years. The economic implications of growth of this magnitude are tremendous.[13]

TABLE 2. DISTRIBUTION OF THE CIVILIAN POPULATION OF THE FRENCH ZONE OF MOROCCO BY PLACE OF RESIDENCE, 1951–52
(in 000)

AREA	MUSLIMS		JEWS		EUROPEANS*		TOTAL POPULATION	
	No.	%	No.	%	No.	%	No.	%
All municipalities	1,376	18.5	159	79.9	288	79.3	1,823	22.8
Casablanca	472		75		135		682	
Marrakech	187		16		12		215	
Fez	150		13		16		179	
Rabat	105		10		41		156	
Meknes	107		12		21		140	
Oujda	51		3		27		81	
Safi	50		3		4		57	
Port Lyautey (Kenitra)	44		3		9		56	
Others (11)	210		24		23		257	
Rural Areas	6,066	81.5	40	20.1	75	20.7	6,181	77.2
Totals	7,442	100.0	199	100.0	363	100.0	8,004	100.0

*See first footnote, Table 1.

Source: Annuaire statistique de la zone française du Maroc, 1952, Gouvernement Chérifien, Service Central des Statistiques (Rabat, 1952), p. 13.

TABLE 3. DISTRIBUTION OF THE WORKING POPULATION OF THE FRENCH ZONE OF MOROCCO BY OCCUPATION, 1951–52

OCCUPATION	MUSLIMS		JEWS		EUROPEANS*		TOTAL POPULATION	
	No.	%	No.	%	No.	%	No.	%
Fishing, forestry	8,445	.3	113	.2	1,150	.8	9,708	.3
Agriculture	2,055,155	70.8	476	.9	8,382	6.2	2,064,013	66.8
Mining, quarrying	18,795	.6	47	.1	2,366	1.7	21,208	.7
Handicrafts, manufacturing	286,275	10.0	25,693	47.9	36,517	26.9	348,485	11.3
Transportation, port administration, stevedoring	241,330	8.3	2,347	4.4	10,745	7.9	254,422	8.2
Commerce	106,560	3.7	12,400	23.1	15,261	11.2	134,221	4.3
Personal services, health	68,685	2.4	4,506	8.4	8,958	6.6	82,149	2.7
Administration, liberal professions	60,900	2.1	4,143	7.7	35,412	26.1	100,455	3.3
Guards, watchmen	26,320	.9	55	.1	10,251	7.6	36,626	1.2
Not classified	26,990	.9	3,905	7.2	6,714	5.0	37,609	1.2
Totals	2,899,455	100.0	53,685	100.0	135,756	100.0	3,088,896	100.0

*See first footnote, Table 1.

Source: La conjoncture économique marocaine, année 1954, Gouvernement Chérifien, Service Central des Statistiques (Rabat, 1954), p. vii for the data on the Muslims and Annuaire statistique de la zone française du Maroc, 1952, Gouvernement Chérifien, Service Central des Statistiques (Rabat, 1952), pp. 26, 27 for the data on the Jews and Europeans.

THE GROWTH OF THE PLURAL SOCIETY

We have seen how greatly the human resources of Morocco grew after the coming of the French. The crucial point as far as the economist is concerned, however, is not so much the extent to which these resources became more numerous as the extent to which their skills and material well-being increased. It is because of these that one of the principal characteristics of the population increase, i.e., the growth of the plural society, needs some further discussion.

The plural society is a sociological concept, but its implications for economics are many. In Morocco, as elsewhere, its existence invariably served to restrict particularly the occupational mobility of labor, thereby preventing good allocation of resources as well. Thus the qualitative aspect of Morocco's population growth in the years of the protectorate exerted by and large a negative influence on the increase in productivity during these years.

Plural society in Morocco was typical of that found in most exploitation colonies in that the ruling group was composed of nationals of a North Atlantic nation who were in the minority and who had a different culture, language, and religion from the majority. It was atypical, however, in the sense that there was a small coterie of foreign officials, plantation overseers, and traders forming an island in the midst of a sea of natives. The minority in Morocco was still very much in the minority, but at the same time it had penetrated much deeper than had traditionally been the case.[14] Although the penetration was not as extreme as in Algeria, where there was a proletariat of Europeans, nevertheless there developed in Morocco a *petite bourgeoisie* of immigrants, who had to be considered in every instance where relations between the elements of the plural society were regulated. Because the minority had political control and because the above group was part of the minority, the interests of the native majority, from whose level the *petite bourgeoisie* was only slightly removed, was apt to be given less attention than they might otherwise have received. The situation was further complicated by the existence of a minor subdivision of the native group — the Jews — which received the favors of the ruling minority. Neither group was thereby endeared to the Muslim masses, which outnumbered both by an overwhelming majority.

In any exploitation colony, a disposition to protest on the part of the majority jeopardizes the precarious position of the directors of the society, who find themselves sitting on a powder keg but who also find that to give a little takes profit from the game — profit that they are loath to surrender. In Morocco, the majority constituted a threat not only to those who controlled commerce and industry but to the holders of petty interests as well. Furthermore, the political control of the dominating minority maintained economic privilege not only for itself but also for a select native minority.

Before the protectorate, the European minority was so small and had so little political power that problems concerning relations between it and the Muslim majority were relatively minor. The real problems arose with the shift of political control. In addition, what had been an insignificant minority became a significant one, with a sizable stake in Morocco and with an increasing tendency to identify itself with the future of this country rather than that of the country from which it came.

In most cases, the country of origin for the foreign population was France; but other peoples of the northern rim of the Mediterranean basin were also to be found — notably Spaniards, Italians, Gibraltarians, Maltese, and Portuguese. As a general proposition, the French were the investors and the entrepreneurs, while the others were the overseers on farms and the foremen in factories. There was no serious conflict of interests between the groups, as the economic future of the little people depended on the perpetuation of the power and control of the big ones.[15] For those at the bottom of the economic and social ladder, there was a tendency to develop a "poor-white-trash" complex vis-à-vis the Muslims, as the latter were a potential threat to their small domain.

On the whole, the Europeans were utterly oblivious to the problems of the vast proletariat whose docile acceptance was required for the continuance of their hegemony. This was especially true of those who formed the postwar influx of immigrants. Even most of those who knew the Moroccans from long experience, the European farmers and some of the Native Affairs officers, were not likely to let any instincts of paternalism interfere seriously with the pursuit of their immediate personal interests; the divergence between these interests and those of the Muslims was simply too great.

Incompatibility of interests was less pronounced between the two minority groups. Precisely because the Jews were a minority, they did not constitute the threat to the Europeans that the Muslims did. Indeed, much of the policy under the protectorate was to favor the Jews and thus to foster the differences existing between them and the rest of the Moroccan population. Not citizens but protégés (*dhimmis*) before the protectorate, the Jews retained the same status afterwards[16] but with much wider opportunities. They played an economic role out of proportion to their numbers.

Although big business was initially reserved to the Europeans, the Jews found a place in smaller business. Small affairs, by judicious management, often have the tendency to become large affairs; and many Jews became leaders in Moroccan commerce and finance. Lesser businessmen of the Jewish community formed a bridge between the French and the Muslims. Speaking Arabic and wise to the ways of the markets, yet conversant with Western-type methods of doing business, these men made their profits as the middlemen. Yet others, Jews whose fathers wore the black caftan symbolic of the humble status to which these people were formerly relegated, became minor civil servants, bank clerks, and employees in the business houses.

The Jews displayed a remarkable mobility, spatially as well as occupationally. Casablanca, the business capital of Morocco, was the chief pole of attraction for them — at the expense of the oases, which had ceased to play their traditional role of entrepôt on the caravan routes. The shift of emphasis in commerce from the interior cities to the ports also brought a corresponding shift in the Jewish population; in addition, there were many who abandoned the ghetto for the European quarter of the town.

Thus the Jews built for themselves a position based on continuing French control, and thus they came to identify their interests with those of the French. The fusion, however, was not complete. Equal rewards for equal effort was not the rule; a Jewish clerk was paid less for the same work than a European but more than a Muslim. Nor was Vichyism entirely eradicated from the thinking of the European segment of the population. As satellites, the Jews moved in the direction of the Europeans without enjoying completely the prerogatives connected with membership in that group.

On a numerical basis, the Muslim population was the segment of the plural society which should have received the most attention. The Muslims were not only the principal producers and consumers; they were until 1955 the only citizens of Morocco (although without many of the rights and privileges usually associated with citizenship). Yet they were not the animators of the economy; the impetus was supplied rather by the Jewish and even more by the European minority. The growth of the plural society operated against the Muslims, not only limiting their opportunities for advancement but in many cases actually pushing them farther down the economic ladder. Only an infinitesimal portion of this most numerous segment of the population was able to achieve an increase in status comparable to that recorded by the Jews under French control although, like the Jews, they were able to wield considerable influence.

In one way, the coming of the French actually served to lessen the plurality of the Moroccan society. Thanks to the security brought to the country and to the increasing contacts between the elements of the Muslim population that resulted, the old Arab-Berber division sharply faded, despite French efforts to maintain this division as one way of maintaining their position.[17] Thus the Muslim became more and more homogeneous culturally. He also became increasingly homogeneous economically, as more and more people from the countryside arrived to swell the ranks of the urban proletariat. Finally, he became more and more dangerous to the minority in power; the *déracinés* (literally: uprooted ones) in particular proved to be political dynamite, exposed as they were to the material benefits enjoyed by the controlling minority yet denied a share in these benefits by the workings of the plural society as it developed during the years of the protectorate.

An important influence on economic change, then, was the existence of three well-defined social groups, the first in control of the government and in charge of the allocation of resources and the distribution of the dividends, the second tending to identify itself more and more with the first but not assimilating itself completely with it, and the third and most numerous being the "hewers of wood and drawers of water."

More specifically, as will be seen later in greater detail, the growth of the plural society resulted in a dual economy composed of modern and traditional sectors. Modern enterprise was largely European owned and operated, whether in agriculture, industry, trade, or transport. Accommodation of modern enterprise on Moroccan soil required both space and markets and, since both were limited, the traditional sectors were compelled to yield. Thus, a European agriculture based on cash crops for export required the very best land in a country which was on the margin of the grain-growing areas of the world; this meant that the fellahin had to move farther out on the fringes. In industry, the growth of textile manufacturing meant that the artisans were forced to give up markets, proving once again that man is no match for the machine. At the same time, industries grew (breweries, wineries, and canneries) which either served only those in the modern sector or sent their products abroad. Foreign trade was largely monopolized by the Europeans, as were the railroads and bus lines.

Under these conditions, it is little wonder that the traditional sectors disintegrated or, at best, stagnated. Meaningful economic development involves not only the creation of new organizational forms but, if full costs are incurred, the subsidization of the demise of old ones. Just as troop expenditures were never capitalized, neither was the misery of Moroccans in agriculture and the artisan trades. The balance sheets of the modern sector looked good thereby, but the failure to include all costs meant in effect that relatively few statements would be issued.

In summary, French troops brought security and purchasing power supplied by French taxpayers to Morocco, both powerful forces for rapid economic change. Population growth and the rules of the plural society meant distorted development and massive problems of correction which remain for an independent Morocco to solve. The following chapters, in essence, trace the evolution of these problems.

III

THE EVOLUTION OF AGRICULTURE

The coming of the French brought about a dualism in the Moroccan economy, and the rules of the plural society served in large measure to maintain it during the protectorate. The goat-hair tent and the villa in living quarters, the six-by-eight cubicle and the *Galeries Lafayette* in commerce, the ancient oil press and the modern factory in industry, the plodding donkey and the sleek American car in transport — all were manifestations of different functions by the various segments of the plural society in Moroccan economic life.[1]

Nowhere was the dual economy more evident than in agriculture. Prior to the protectorate, Moroccan agriculture was native agriculture. Association of Moroccans with Europeans did nothing to change methods but was simply a device to avoid taxation. With the settlement of French farmers on the land, however, a new type of agriculture developed alongside the old, one which differed from it by virtue of the size of holdings, their location, the techniques employed, the kinds of crops grown, and the availability of credit and marketing facilities. This is not to say that native and European agriculture in Morocco were mutually exclusive; indeed a major preoccupation in this chapter will be with the interactions of the one upon the other. Nevertheless the differences were more than enough to warrant a discussion of agriculture in terms of its dual nature.

LAND TENURE

The establishment of the protectorate served to intensify the already growing European interest in securing land in Morocco. Ownership, however, was highly precarious under Islamic law, and the absence of registration made searches of title impossible. On the one hand, there were French buyers eager to acquire land, but at prices far lower than what would be expected under a new regime devoted to establishing security and to developing a modern transportation net. On the other hand, the entry of French buyers into the market for land increased not only prices but also the temptation to fraud on the part of the local population. Moroccans could be seen feverishly turning furrows in order to establish a private claim to land formerly devoted to pasturage in common. In addition, the same land was often sold to different buyers, or a single buyer was forced to purchase the same parcel several times in order to settle conflicting ownership claims. From the French viewpoint, therefore, it was necessary to bring land under the control of a Western system of asset ownership. Registration was the logical first step to take.

Dahirs of 1913 and 1915 instituted a Torrens-type system of land registration.[2] If an owner desired to register his land, he had to produce a title which was cleared by publication. All expenses incurred for the registration were paid by the applicant. Thus even if the Moroccans could be made to see the advantages of registration, the expense involved was often a deterrent. While registration was optional, those who declined did not necessarily remain unaffected by the system. If another contested the unregistered claim of a Moroccan to his parcel, the defendant was compelled to share in the expenses of the tribunal which settled the case. Many contests went by default when the defendant either was unaware of the challenge or could not afford a defense.[3]

A 1914 decree distinguished alienable from inalienable lands. *Habous, guich,* and collective lands — in other words, all lands save *melk* (privately owned) and domanial (government owned) — were declared inalienable in the sense that conveyance could take place only with the approval of the local governors and judges. Lyautey thereby apparently hoped to avoid the mistakes of Algeria, where thousands of hectares were sequestered without indemnity in the early years of the occupation.[4] It is true that there were no large free grants of land to Europeans such as had occurred in Algeria, especially during the Second Empire. As it turned out, however, the 1914 decree actually set the stage for eventual expropriation.

Domanial lands, over which the French took immediate control by virtue of the protectorate agreement, were sold to the *colons.* Thus the private colonization resulting from the purchase of *melk* land by individual Europeans was supplemented by official colonization very early in the game. However, land for both types of colonization soon became scarce. *Melk* land for sale at bargain prices was hard to find by the end of the First World War. Domanial lands, not extensive at the beginning of the protectorate, had been greatly reduced. Much of the remainder was unsuited to European settlement — especially if better lands locked up by the 1914 decree could somehow be made available.

The key was contained in a decree of 1919, which was designed to relieve the upward pressure on land prices, aggravated by the postwar influx of immigrants, by increasing the supply. Under the law, the collective lands became the property of the occupying groups subject to the clearing of titles.[5] The principle of inalienability was also reconfirmed, thus freezing the occupying group to its land. These provisions served as preliminary steps to the taking of collective lands for official colonization, since other provisions made it clear that these lands were inalienable only in so far as private transactions were concerned. A *Tutelle Administrative des Collectivités Indigènes*, headed by the Director of Native Affairs, was established by the law for the purpose of ascertaining the land requirements of the tribes under its jurisdiction (in other words, all those that were "pacified") in order to determine the amount of "superfluous" land available for seizure by the government and subsequent sale to Europeans. A tribe, part of whose lands were chosen for colonization, was to be compensated at a price determined by the government and was then to be resettled on its remaining territory. There were also arrangements whereby the collectivity might be broken up and the land distributed among its members.

The criteria for the determination of "superfluity" of tribal lands are not clear. There is, however, one piece of evidence of French thinking in the matter of the size of holdings, in the form of an official publication during the period that expropriation of collective lands was being actively pursued. According to the author, a Moroccan "tent" needed 12 hectares of good land, 15 hectares if the land were average, and 20 hectares if it were mediocre. Six pages later, the writer sets out his conception of the ideal size for *colons'* parcels as 400 hectares or above for the large farmer, 100 to 150 hectares for the medium-sized farmer, and 2 to 40 hectares for the small truck farmer settled along the coast near the markets of the rapidly-burgeoning cities.[6]

Consciously or unconsciously, the French, by reducing the amount of land available to Moroccans, made a difference in the type of agriculture that the latter could carry on. Presumably an extensive type of agriculture was used as evidence of excess lands, especially if the lands were fertile; but it certainly did not follow that the tribesmen could automatically adjust their agricultural programs to an intensive, capital-using type. The proceeds from seized lands were of little help. In most instances, prices were so low that they could little more than compensate for one year's revenue from the lost lands. In at least one instance, a tribe received no compensation at all.[7] The inability of the tribesmen to adjust technically to the new circumstances of reduced land area meant, in effect, that the dualism in agriculture between Moroccan and European was even more pronounced than it would have been otherwise.

After so disposing of collective lands, the next step for the authorities was to provide for the seizure of *guich* and *habous* lands. The *guich* lands, it will be remembered, were settled by Arab tribes which were obligated to give military service in exchange for using the land. After the protectorate, national defense was the responsibility of the French army, so *guich* lands were ripe for expropriation. The *habous* lands, held in trust for religious purposes, were also made seizable by the government, although public opinion caused the French to move somewhat more slowly here than they undoubtedly would have liked. The proceeds from the sales were to be invested elsewhere; but since trust lands were among the most fertile in the country, alternative investment opportunities were not likely to be as attractive even if the compensation for the land approached its real value.

Melk land was also eventually brought under the control of the government; it was provided that such property could be seized if needed as a public utility. Included in the definition of public utility was land within the "perimeters of colonization." Compensation was once again determined by the government. If the owner desired payment in kind rather than cash, then land was found for him outside the perimeters. The French also attached the *merdjas* (swamplands especially prevalent in the Gharb and in the valley of the Sebou) to the public domain. Later on most of the swamps were drained and sold to Europeans.

A problem related to the availability of land was that of the water supply. In a country where rainfall is irregular and often inadequate, the French felt the need to regulate water usage. Heretofore, the governing council had apportioned water in Berber country and the farmer had helped himself in Arab territory. Under the protectorate, however, the water supply was incorporated into the state domain, and usage rights were strictly regulated. In any event, the Europeans were favored in their administration.

Thus did the protectorate government provide for the French farmers who migrated to Morocco after 1912. All types of land-holdings were brought under the control of the French authorities, enabling them to move in any direction in order to settle Europeans. Thus too was the stage set for abuses which made those by the Moroccans in the early days of the protectorate seem petty by comparison.[8]

SPACE FOR EUROPEANS

It was a happy circumstance for the French that the area of Morocco most ideally suited to European settlement — the relatively flat and well-watered territory along the coast — was also one ideally suited to military conquest. As we saw in the last chapter, Lyautey's "useful Morocco" was subjugated by 1914. The Atlas Mountains and the desert were in dissidence for the most part, but were in any event not suited to European settlement. Thus the tribes in these regions had no worry about dispossession under the "arsenal of *dahirs*" [9] just described.

It was not so for their countrymen to the northwest. The Chaouia naturally received the first dose of colonization, since the French had been occupying the region since 1907. The pre-protectorate holdings, however, were both recent and relatively few. Furthermore, much of the land was held for speculation and was not actually under cultivation. After the establishment of the protectorate, European holdings not only became actively cultivated in the Chaouia, but quickly spread northward into the rich Gharb.

To the south, the Doukkala, although fertile and fairly well-watered, was largely eliminated as a possibility for European colonization owing to the relatively heavy density of the tribes in the region. Farther south, the Sous was also eliminated to a large extent; there was not only a heavy population density but also inadequate rainfall. Those *colons* who did settle in this region clustered around the relatively few water points.

In 1913, the year after the protectorate was established, there were approximately 73,000 hectares (roughly 180,000 acres) under cultivation by Europeans.[10] Three-quarters of this land was located in western Morocco, and the remainder was around Oujda,

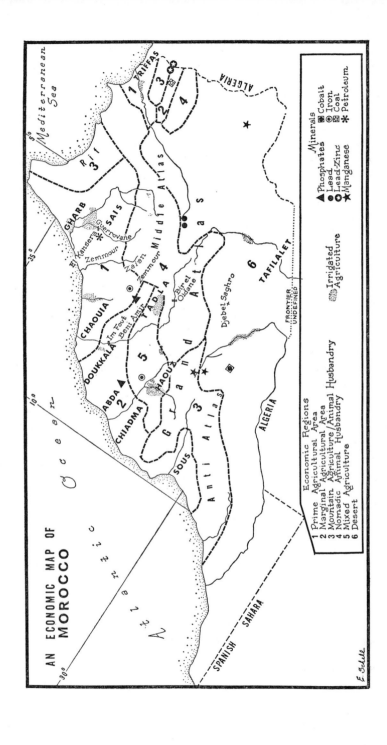

AN ECONOMIC MAP OF MOROCCO

Mediterranean Sea

ALGERIA

Minerals
▲ Phosphates
● Lead
◐ Lead-Zinc
★ Manganese
⬢ Cobalt
⊞ Iron
◉ Coal
✳ Petroleum.

Economic Regions
1 Prime Agricultural Area
2 Marginal Agricultural Area
3 Mountain Agriculture/Animal Husbandry
4 Nomadic Animal Husbandry
5 Mixed Agriculture
6 Desert

⬚ Irrigated Agriculture

TRIFFAS

Rif

GHARB

SAIS

El Kansera
G. Guennovane ✳
Zemmour
Nsfen
Zemmour

Middle Atlas

CHAOUIA

Im Fout
Beni Amir
Bir el Oddane

TADLA

Grand Atlas

DOUKKALA

ABDA

CHIADMA

HAOUZ

Djebel Saghro

Anti Atlas

SOUS

TAFILALET

FRONTIER UNDEFINED

ALGERIA

O c e a n

Z i z

SPANISH SAHARA

E. Schle

next to Algeria. All of it had been settled by private colonization, which continued to increase rapidly in the following years. However, Lyautey held a fairly tight rein on official colonization at first, limiting it, as we have seen, to domanial lands until 1919. In the years from 1916 to 1918, the protectorate granted around 8,000 hectares to European settlers.[11] In keeping with the Lyautey policy of large-scale farming rather than *petite* colonization, no single grant was less than 150 hectares (370 acres).

The real extension of official colonization began shortly after the war and reached its peak in the period from 1926 to 1932. These years also marked a shift in policy which continued until independence. From 1918 to 1923, official colonization accounted for 71,500 hectares, divided into 449 parcels. Of this amount, 12,000 hectares were distributed in 17 parcels to large-scale farmers (those in the 400- to 3,000-hectare class), 57,000 hectares in 226 parcels to *colons* in the medium class (150 to 400 hectares). The remaining 2,500 hectares were delivered in 206 parcels of 20 hectares or less.[12] By 1932, land distributed through official colonization totaled around 200,000 hectares, which, when added to the private colonization that had taken place up to that time, gave the Europeans 675,000 hectares of land in Morocco.

By 1953, European holdings amounted to approximately one million hectares (or roughly 2,500,000 acres), distributed among 5,900 farms.[13] Private colonists numbered slightly over 4,000 and held 700,000 hectares, while half as many official colonists held the remaining 300,000 hectares. Nine hundred farmers, or 15 per cent of the total, held 60 per cent of this land in parcels of 300 or more hectares. Conversely, more than 5,000 farmers held the remaining 40 per cent in parcels under 300 hectares in size. The importance of the small farmer is demonstrated by the fact that 31 per cent of all the settlers were farming less than 10 hectares each.

The one million hectares owned by Europeans in 1953 represented only 6.5 per cent of the farm and range land in Morocco. European holdings included, however, 10 per cent of the total crop land, 23 per cent of the orchards and vineyards, and only 4 per cent of the fallow and range land. The significance of these figures becomes apparent when it is noted that the Europeans accounted for only slightly more than one per cent of the rural population. In terms of value of output, an estimate for 1956 put the contribution of the modern agricultural sector at 25 per cent of the gross value of all crops, 80 per cent of the wine and citrus fruits, roughly 33 per cent of vegetables and legumes, and 15 per cent of the cereals.[14]

The above data relate to outright ownership only; to know the proportions of the various types of land actually farmed by Europeans, it would be necessary to add information relating to rentals of land — information which was not available during the protectorate. A suggestion of the way it might affect the preceding percentages, however, is found in the experience under decrees of 1926, 1931, and 1941 permitting *colons* to rent collective lands not expropriated under the *dahir* of 1919. (Previous to 1926, rentals were restricted to lands in private ownership.) While the protectorate did not release the figures on the amount of land thus secured by Europeans, we do have the opinion of a well-informed, but by request anonymous, source in Morocco. It was his view that the lands that were rented by Europeans from collectivities under the authority of the decrees just about equaled in amount the lands rented by collectivities from Europeans. He went on to point out, however, that it was a different story in terms of the quality of the land; the *colon*, by and large, was renting bottom land, while the collectivity was renting hillsides and rocky areas. Since many of the rental agreements extended in perpetuity, it would appear that the Europeans were farming an even greater proportion of the cultivable land in Morocco than the figures on land ownership indicated.[15]

In addition to outright ownership and the rental of land, Europeans continued the practice of associating with Moroccans in various farming ventures. One method of association was the *bel khobza*, whereby the native proprietor furnished the land and the European partner supplied the labor, seed, and other materials. The returns were divided according to the quality of the land, i.e., the better the land, the greater the landowner's share of the profits. Another type of contract was known as the *ben nous*. One party contributed the land, the other perhaps the animals or the labor. The remaining expenses were shared equally, as were the returns. Yet another form of association, the *m'saroa*, was found in the growing of fruit, especially olives. In this case, the Moroccan planted the European's land and cared for the trees from eight to ten years. At the end of this period, the land was divided equally between the associates. In animal husbandry, a European may have bought cattle and entrusted them to a Moroccan to raise. When they were sold, the proceeds were divided equally. The *khammes* system was also maintained during the protectorate. While this type of contract remained almost exclusively one between Moroccans, Europeans occasionally associated with Moroccans in this manner. All these and other contractual relationships existing in Moroccan agriculture served to alter somewhat the land tenure situation.

SPACE FOR THE FELLAH

The settlement of Europeans on the land obviously reduced the amount available to Moroccans. Such a move was considered justified on the grounds that, by example, the techniques of the *colon* would be absorbed by the fellah, who could then presumably produce more on his reduced holdings than he had been able to on more land theretofore. By placing Europeans around the countryside, then, the French would improve the lot of the Moroccans — thus carrying out one of the principles of the protectorate.

Two things proved to be wrong with such reasoning, however. The million hectares given over to colonization were among the best in the country, and substantial improvements by the Europeans made them even more productive. Thus the heart of agricultural Morocco was cut out for Europeans, and the Moroccan found the quality of his land being reduced even more sharply than its quantity. Modern methods could not make a small plot of rocky hillside more productive than rich and more extensive bottom lands farmed under the tried and true, if primitive, techniques evolved through the centuries. Furthermore, the establishment of the "perimeters of colonization," where only European farms were allowed, largely prevented any peeks over the French shoulder. (Even when this was possible, it did not mean that the Moroccan had the wherewithal to emulate the European methods.) Rather, as Page pointed out, "the geographic distribution . . . indicates much more a juxtaposition than an interpenetration of the two economies." [16] Dualism, then, had its geographical, as well as its technical, aspect.

At the same time that the Moroccans were being relegated to the marginal farmlands, they were experiencing heavy population growth. Furthermore, the conversion of much collective land to private ownership helped to alienate surfaces, if not to Europeans then to large Moroccan landholders. The pressures resulting from all of these developments forced many Moroccans either to work for Europeans or to migrate to the cities. Thus a large proletariat developed, part of it rural, forced to tend someone else's land in an effort to subsist, and part of it urban, flocking to the sprawling *bidonvilles* ("tin-can towns") that edged all the major cities.[17]

There is much available evidence on which to draw for examples of what meeting the "needs" of European colonization meant to the Moroccans. One author, writing in 1938, cited the case of the region of the Gharb around Sidi Slimane, an area comprising 35,000 to 40,000 hectares which were irrigable from the Al Kansera barrage on the Oued Beth. Half of this land was owned by 700 Europeans, while the remainder was held either collectively or privately by "an extremely numerous proletariat" which, left with lands too small and unproductive, was forced to hire itself out as farm labor.[18]

Olivier, writing a year earlier of the region of Meknes, to the southeast, stated that *colons* occupied 24,000 hectares of the best lands of the Guerrouane, leaving 49,000 hectares for the tribe. The author noted, however, that one-fifth of the tribal land was unsuited to any type of agriculture. Thus the 4,670 families of the tribe (24,500 people) had only a little more than 8 hectares of land each. Olivier added that even the low average did not denote the real problem, since many families had no land at all. While the landless could normally find work on the European farms, the economic crisis then in progress had reduced this rural proletariat to destitution.[19]

The plight of another tribe in the region of Meknes, the Ait Youssi, has also been described. Transhumant, this tribe had long descended from its headquarters around Sefrou to the plain of Meknes, where it cultivated the land and wintered its flocks. After the settlement of Europeans on this land, the tribe had no place to migrate. The balance between cultivation and animal husbandry that it had depended upon to survive was permanently upset, and even the latter activity was seriously limited. Heavy winter snows in the Middle Atlas caused this tribe to lose up to 50 per cent of its flocks.[20]

Yet another example of what the coming of the French meant to the Moroccans is provided by the experience of a fraction of the Beni Oura, a tribe located northeast of Casablanca near Boulhaut. The western and best part of the fraction's land was quickly taken up by European colonization. In 1922, the remaining land, 1,000 hectares, was divided equally among the families of the fraction. By 1951, five families held, all together, 550 of these hectares, and twenty-five families held another 350. The remaining 100 hectares were divided into uneconomic 2- or 3-hectare parcels. Thus, once again was a rural proletariat forced into being.[21]

The total amount of farm and range land held by Moroccans in 1953 was estimated at around 14,400,000 hectares (a little less than 36 million acres), just about half of which was cultivable. Europeans, on the other hand, were able to cultivate two-thirds of their holdings. Moroccan-owned land was divided among 800,000 to 900,000 farms.[22] If we take 850,000 as an approximation, then the average Moroccan farm consisted of 17 hectares, 8 of which could be cultivated. The corresponding figures for the Europeans were 170 and 112. On a per capita basis, each of the 6,000,000 Moroccans living in the rural area had 2.4 hectares of land, contrasted with the European's 13 hectares. These figures, of course, take no account of wide differences in the quality of Moroccan farmland, or of the way in which these differences served further to distinguish the average Moroccan farm from that of the European.

Unfortunately, no information was published on the distribution of Moroccan holdings by size. According to numerous authorities, however, there were thousands of holdings of less than 5 hectares. Furthermore, it was estimated that 60 per cent of the rural population was either farm labor or *khammes*, and thus not tied by ownership to the land.[23]

Although it was evident by the late twenties that a large floating population was developing in Morocco, it was not until 1945 that the authorities took official recognition of the situation. A *dahir* that year established a *bien de famille*, or family patrimony, of 8 hectares — a minimum amount of land for each rural family which could be neither alienated nor seized, nor even rented. It is interesting to note that this figure is 4 hectares less than the amount recommended by Bondis in 1928 for a Moroccan family settled on good land, and 12 hectares less than that for a family on mediocre land.

By the law of 1945, the French apparently hoped to keep the Moroccans on the land and out of the cities' *bidonvilles*. In fact, however, the *bien de famille* was both too little and too late for most Moroccan families. It was a futile gesture in the face of a secular detribalization of Moroccan rural society, a detribalization which population growth and official land policy had set in motion.

THE REVIVAL OF THE TERTIB

With around two-thirds of its population engaged in farming, the protectorate government depended heavily on agricultural levies to raise revenues. The *tertib* — the tax which both Moulay Hassan and Abd al Aziz had tried to impose without success[24] — was reintroduced by *dahir* in 1913. (Actually it had been applied in the Chaouia the year before.) The *tertib* was simply a combination of the old *achour* and *zekkat*, payable now in money rather than in kind. However, it had the advantage of being all things to all segments of the plural society. For the Muslims, "tertib" was just a new name for the old Koranic taxes; nevertheless, the name change was sufficient to make the tax applicable to Europeans, who, as non-believers, could not pay a Koranic tax. It was thus applicable to the handful of Jewish farmers in Morocco, too.

The *tertib* was not a tax on the land but a tax on the revenue from the land; more precisely, Jouannet described it as "a tax on the anticipated revenue which in turn is a function of the presumed yield of the crops." [25] Both yields and revenues were estimated in advance, with the tax due at harvest time. The amount of the tax varied directly with year-to-year fluctuations of crop yields and market prices. The size of the tax bill then was not a function of the budget requirements of the governmental unit, as with real estate taxes in the United States, but depended instead on the fortunes of agriculture from one year to the next. The *tertib* was in effect an income tax, based on *gross* rather than on net revenues. No allowance was made for varying costs except as there were certain rebates on the tax which allegedly helped to compensate for cost differences among the farmers. The conditions which had to be met for rebates will be discussed below.

As the first step in the administration of the *tertib*, the taxpayer was required to make a declaration of his taxable resources, i.e., the amount of land in various types of crops and the number of animals and producing trees and vines in his possession. The Moroccan had to make this declaration orally before a commission composed of the *caid*, the *sheikh*, and *adel* (notary), the notables of the tribe, a French tax collector, and the representative of either the civil or the military authority, depending on the type of control in the area where the tax was being collected. The declaration was subject to verification. The European farmer made his declaration in writing to French authorities only, and the contents were kept secret. His declaration also might be verified but seldom was, according to reliable sources in Morocco.

For a cereal crop, once the surface and type were established, the commission proceeded to assign it to one of several categories of anticipated yield per hectare.[26] An average price per quintal for each category of yield was then estimated. To the product of this average price and the *average* yield of the category to which the crop had been assigned (less one quintal as an allowance for the seed), a 5 per cent rate was applied to determine the tax liability per hectare.

For truck crops, an absolute amount of tax was levied per hectare, the amount depending on the size of the holding and whether or not it was irrigated. Livestock was also subject to an absolute tax, levied per head. Orchards and vineyards formerly were taxed on a per-tree or per-vine basis, but in 1939 a tax on anticipated yields similar to that for cereal crops was instituted.[27]

In the early years of the protectorate, the *tertib* and customs duties, the latter also being very sensitive to the fortunes of agriculture, supplied the bulk of government revenues. The *tertib* alone yielded 2,243,000 francs in 1912, when it was applied only in the Chaouia. The extension of the taxable area by the pacification, better assessment and collection procedures, and a rise in grain prices all helped to push tax revenues up to 11,500,000 francs by 1916, or roughly 700 million in 1952 francs. By 1952, these revenues amounted to 5,450,000,000 francs, including sums later rebated.[28] In the meantime, other sources of government revenue, especially income from the phosphate monopoly, had lessened considerably the reliance upon the *tertib*. Nevertheless, the *tertib* still remained a vital part of the tax structure of the Moroccan economy and the principal one for farmers.[29] It was riddled with exemptions, however, almost from the very beginning.

In 1916, a rebate on the *tertib* was granted to those clearing land for European-type colonization. Rebates were also given for selling grain to the army, growing soft wheat, cultivating fallow, and planting olive trees. These early exemptions from the tax led to a decree of 1923 which provided that one-half of the tax be rebated to those farmers using "European methods." (If the farmer were in soft wheat and his yield was less than 8 quintals per hectare, the entire tax was returned.) In order to qualify, the farmer's land had to be completely cleared of rocks and doum, and he had to employ a moldboard or disk plow in cultivation. The use of these methods obviously did not depend on knowledge of techniques alone; availability of credit and sufficient surfaces were also essential. It is for this reason that rebates on the *tertib* for "European methods" meant nothing to the overwhelming majority of Moroccans. During the 1952–53 season, in fact, those Moroccans receiving this type of rebate held only 153,000 hectares, which was less than 6 per cent of all Moroccan-owned land.[30]

After 1923, there were no important changes in the nature of *tertib* rebates until 1950, when the amount of the rebate for the use of "European methods" was reduced from 50 to 40 per cent. At the same time, something new was added — a 30 per cent rebate to farmers who used "improved methods" of agriculture, i.e., methods falling somewhat short of those considered "European" under the 1923 decree but at the same time more "advanced" than those of the traditional native agriculture, sufficiently so that relatively few Moroccans were able to qualify for this rebate either. However, a number of Moroccans stood to benefit from other exemptions from the *tertib* authorized in 1950. Sheep and goats less than a year old were no longer subject to tax; Moroccans were the principal herders, and around 40 per cent of their flocks qualified for this exemption. Orchards of less than twenty-five trees were also exempted, another concession to the Moroccan, who was the small farmer of the country.

TABLE 4. INCIDENCE OF THE TERTIB ON EUROPEANS
AND MOROCCANS, 1951 AND 1952

EUROPEANS	GROSS TAX (in 000 francs)	REBATE (in 000 francs)	% OF TAX REBATED
1951	842.6	329.1	39.1
1952	914.7	321.4	35.1
MOROCCANS			
1951	4,113.4	80.9	2.0
1952	4,114.1	89.4	2.2

Source: *Annuaire statistique de la zone française du Maroc, 1952*, Gouvernement Chérifien, Service Central des Statistiques (Rabat, 1952), p. 367.

Table 4 shows the European and Moroccan contributions to the *tertib* and shares in the rebates for the two years immediately after the new exemptions were authorized. As can be seen, Europeans were refunded between 35 and 40 per cent of their payments, while Moroccans received only 2 per cent of theirs. Thus Moroccans, while contributing over 80 per cent of gross tax revenues, received only around 20 per cent of the rebates.

The *tertib* had a great impact in the rural areas by forcing the fellah into a money economy. To the perils of fluctuating real yields were added the equally great perils of a fluctuating market. The farmer's anticipated gross revenue for tax purposes was based on the anticipated *average* price in the *souks*. In order to pay his taxes, however, the fellah was forced to liquidate most of his crop shortly after the harvest, a time when the market was depressed. For the fellah, therefore, the effective rate of the tax became greater than 5 per cent. There was no question of his stocking very much for a more favorable market as was possible for the European (in fact, the State stocked for the latter), since he had no savings and no credit. The activity of the markets was much increased during tax time, but the Moroccan farmer as supplier was little benefited.

LAND USE

Now that we have seen how farmland in Morocco was held and how it (or rather the produce from it) was taxed, we can turn to an examination of the various ways in which this land was exploited.

During the early years of the protectorate, relatively little was done by the Europeans to change the traditional occupations of Moroccan agriculture. The growing of cereals, particularly barley, continued to be the major activity. Within this category, however, the war years did see a beginning on the cultivation of soft wheat. In addition, a modest start was made in wine growing.

To the extent that agriculture became diversified under the protectorate, the diversification occurred largely after 1918. But even so, agriculture in Morocco still remained monoculture for the most part; around 80 per cent of the cultivated area was devoted to cereals.[31] Most of the diversification was found on European lands, where soft wheat, citrus fruits, truck crops, and vines were cultivated. The Moroccans, by and large, remained barley and, to a lesser extent, hard wheat growers.

The development of a diversified agriculture was not a spontaneous reaction to the profit possibilities of a free market, but rather was the result of direct stimulation by the government. "Statism" was very much a part of economic change in Morocco;

it was manifested in the *économie mixte* and the *économie dirigée*, the first a partnership of government and private interests and the second a detailed intervention of the government in economic life to control prices and production by means of taxation and subsidies. Thus the long French tradition of governmental interference in the workings of the economy was duplicated in Morocco.

Nowhere was the influence of the State more deeply felt than in the agricultural sector. From the beginning, if the European did not look to the State to make land available to him on favorable terms, he at least demanded that it valorize his land by valorizing his crops. The State, controlled by Frenchmen, acceded to his demands since it believed that a prosperous European agriculture was essential to its success. This does not mean that there was always complete identity of interests between the *colon* and the government; bitter controversy during the crisis of the thirties demonstrated quite the reverse. Nevertheless, the principle of state paternalism was accepted by the *colon*, and the consequences for the fellah were many. It is for this reason that the role of the State will be an essential part of the discussion of agricultural activity in Morocco.

CEREAL PRODUCTION

The extension of cultivated areas was rapid during the years of the protectorate. The area sown in cereals rose from around 2 million hectares in 1919 to almost 3 million in 1929.[32] By 1952, surfaces devoted to cereal production amounted to 4,228,000 hectares — close to 50 per cent greater than those of 1929. No clear pattern of growth emerged during this latter period, however. In 1944, there were 4,087,000 hectares in cereals; two years later, following the severe drought of 1945, there were only 2,717,000. It was not until 1952 that the 4 million mark was exceeded again.[33]

Of the 4,228,000 hectares planted in cereals in the latter year, 3,990,000 hectares were in barley, hard wheat, soft wheat, or maize. Total production of these four crops showed considerably less over-all growth in the twenty years up to 1952 than did surfaces. Yields totaled 22,300,000 quintals in 1952 — an increase of only 7 per cent. While the average annual yield within this period was 23 million quintals, production actually varied far more sharply than surfaces. A high of 38,100,000 quintals was recorded in 1941 and a low of 4,900,000 quintals in the famine year of 1945.

TABLE 5. PRODUCTION OF THE FOUR PRINCIPAL CEREAL CROPS GROWN IN THE FRENCH ZONE OF MOROCCO, 1931 AND 1952, AND THE AVERAGE, MAXIMUM, AND MINIMUM PRODUCTION DURING THESE YEARS

(in 000 qx.)

CROP	1931	1952	AVERAGE	MAXIMUM Amount	MAXIMUM Year	MINIMUM Amount	MINIMUM Year
Barley	12,852	13,212	12,988	21,824	1939	2,345	1945
Hard wheat	5,956	4,837	4,987	7,929	1941	1,188	1945
Soft wheat	2,150	2,963	2,584	5,134	1939	665	1945
Maize	1,362	2,895	2,438	4,463	1948	691	1945

Source: *Annuaire statistique de la zone française du Maroc, 1952*, Gouvernement Chérifien, Service Central des Statistiques (Rabat, 1952) p. 134.

TABLE 6. SURFACES SOWN, PRODUCTION, AND AVERAGE RETURNS FOR THE FOUR PRINCIPAL CEREAL CROPS GROWN ON MOROCCAN AND EUROPEAN FARMS IN 1951

CROP	MOROCCAN FARMS SURFACES (in 000 ha.)	PRODUCTION (in 000 qx.)	RETURNS (in qx. per ha.)	EUROPEAN FARMS SURFACES (in 000 ha.)	PRODUCTION (in 000 qx.)	RETURNS (in qx. per ha.)
Barley	1,829.9	15,573.5	8.5	54.9	597.5	10.8
Hard wheat	889.1	4,865.8	5.4	52.6	439.2	8.3
Soft wheat	260.7	1,689.4	6.5	122.9	1,383.1	11.3
Maize	485.8	2,054.8	4.2	19.5	92.2	4.7
Totals	3,465.5	24,183.5	7.0	249.9	2,512.0	10.1

Source: *Annuaire statistique de la zone française du Maroc, 1952*, Gouvernement Chérifien, Service Central des Statistiques (Rabat, 1952), pp. 140–141.

(See Table 5 for the comparable production figures for each of the four cereals included in the above totals.)

The extreme fluctuations in cereal yields show how tenuous was the lot of the Moroccan grain grower. Europeans engaging in cereal production also suffered from fluctuating yields, of course; however, the amplitude of the variations was much less in their case. The least crop of the Europeans in the years from 1940 to 1944, for example, was only 26 per cent less than the best, while the Moroccans experienced a 55 per cent variation.[34] Another important characteristic of production served to distinguish the European from the Moroccan cereal producer; average yields per hectare from the former's crops were invariably greater.[35] The 1951 season, for which European and Moroccan surfaces and yields are given in Table 6, was typical.

Table 6 also shows that, except for soft wheat, Europeans made only a minor contribution to cereal production in Morocco. Soft wheat, however, was another matter. This crop, unknown in Morocco before the protectorate, was a European specialty. Those Moroccans who took up its cultivation, while producing slightly more in total than their European counterparts in 1951, fared far less well yield-wise. They also fared far less well price-wise, as the following discussion of the evolution of soft wheat production under the protectorate will show. It also offers an excellent example of government intervention in agriculture.

Surfaces sown in soft wheat rose from nothing in 1912 to 24,000 hectares in 1920. By 1929, this crop covered 275,000 hectares. The growth in the first period can be attributed to wartime demand in France and to the development of a stable local demand as a result of the growth of the European population. The increase in surfaces to 1929 was a response to the French law of 1923, which provided that a portion of Moroccan wheat be admitted into France each year without duty. The quotas, which were to be set annually, were so liberally calculated at first that France absorbed all that Moroccan agriculture could provide through 1928. As a result, exports of soft wheat to France expanded from 493,000 quintals during the 1925 season to 1,400,000 quintals for the first eight months of 1928 alone.[36] Still, there was no surplus of wheat in France.

These were prosperous days for the *colon*. Prior to the establishment of the first quota in 1923, soft wheat brought around 22 francs a quintal more at Marseille than in Kenitra. The quota assured the soft wheat grower of being able to market his crop at this favorable price in France and also sent the Moroccan price up to within 6 or 8 francs of that in France — the difference being roughly equal to the freight charges.[37]

The honeymoon came to a close in 1929, a year in which there was general world "overproduction" and in which production in France alone was an estimated 5 million quintals over consumption. French farmers began to complain that North African wheat would spell their ruin. Arguments were advanced that Europeans in North Africa could buy or rent land more cheaply than the farmer in France, and that labor costs were also lower, so that, even with the greater distance, North African wheat could be set down more cheaply in the north of France than could wheat from the Midi. It was further argued that there was no true surplus in Morocco, but rather a shortage of storage facilities, since wheat came into the country from abroad after the exports to France. It was also alleged that foreign wheat imported into Morocco was being re-exported into France under the quota.[38]

Despite this protest in France, the exclusion of Moroccan wheat from the French market was out of the question — the Chambers of Agriculture in Morocco were much too vociferous and politically influential for that. A ban on imports of foreign wheat into the protectorate was palatable, however, to the *colon*. Since it appeared likely that future French quotas were not to be sufficient to absorb the entire Moroccan crop, then the ban would at least protect the price in the domestic market. So foreign wheat was banned by decree in 1929. (In 1933, imports of secondary cereals were also banned.) The action was a clear violation of the Act of Algeciras, but the French found justification for it in the article relating to the "necessities of public order" contained in the convention signed at the World Economic Conference in 1927. The only exception to the ban was provided by a Franco-Spanish agreement authorizing a quota of 55,000 quintals of flour to be admitted from the Spanish zone, despite the fact that the latter was a net importer of wheat and flour. This agreement was a gesture towards maintaining the customs unity of Morocco as provided in the Franco-Spanish Treaty of 1912.

France, on its side, finally agreed to admitting 1,700,000 quintals of Moroccan wheat under the quota for 1929. In 1931, when the crop was large and world prices were low, 100,000 quintals were added. The Paris Agricultural Conference of 1932 confirmed the

1931 quota of 1,800,000 quintals, broken down into 1,650,000 quintals of soft wheat and 150,000 quintals of hard wheat, as applicable annually through 1938. The importance of the quota to the *colon* during these years of economic crisis was emphasized by Amphoux when he wrote that ". . . if the high prices of the French market were to disappear, wheat growing would be ruined completely in Morocco (except perhaps in some places in the Chaouia and the Gharb where yields are quite good); and French colonization could not survive such a blow." [39]

In the meantime, the debts of the Europeans (about 150,000,000 francs), defaulted early during the crisis of the thirties, had been taken over by the protectorate government. All future indebtedness incurred by these farmers depended on the approval of the government, and all crops had to be sold to it. The sacrifice of the farmer's freedom and the burden carried to the budget by the expenses of European agriculture was the price paid for insuring the European population of the rural areas.

The protectorate government found a ready market for the grain it thus acquired. The French quotas were filled largely from the stocks of *L'Union Dock Silos* and *Le Commerce d'Exportation Marocain*, both government-sponsored European cooperatives. Although native production of soft wheat was already approaching European production,[40] the Moroccans contributed less than 10 per cent of the soft wheat sent to France each year during the thirties. Instead, Moroccan wheat either shared the domestic market with what *colon* wheat did not go to France or took its chances in the ailing world market. A look at the spread between Moroccan and French prices shows what this distinction in markets meant. Soft wheat brought an average of 94 francs a quintal in France during the 1934–35 crop year, and only 51 francs a quintal in Morocco. Comparable figures for hard wheat were 75 and 47 francs.[41]

The forties witnessed a significant change in the wheat situation in Morocco. A series of dry years during the war, culminating in the famine of 1945, brought an end to wheat "surpluses" — for a time, at least. Production, in fact, fell far short of domestic needs. Since the war rendered impossible any imports of the size needed to make up the deficit, the food supply became a critical problem.[42]

Soft wheat production after the war continued to be less than domestic requirements. Morocco therefore gave up the prewar prohibition on imports in favor of a controlled inflow. At the same time, the price of locally-grown wheat was supported at a level about one-third above the world market price. Through 1952, this program was carried in part by an export tax on barley, the principal crop of the Moroccans, which continued to be sold abroad. During the period of high world barley prices, then, the government was in effect cutting the profits of the Moroccans to increase those of the Europeans. Declining world barley prices forced the government to reduce this tax in 1953 and to drop it entirely in 1954. Under the circumstances, however, this did not improve the position of the Moroccans.

In the meantime, a bumper wheat crop was harvested in 1953. Once again, it appeared that Morocco was threatened with being swamped by surpluses, and once again the government turned to France in search of quotas. Late in 1953, after extensive negotiations and over the strenuous objections of the French Cereals Office, which argued that France itself had a surplus, the Resident-General obtained a quota of 700,000 quintals for soft wheat.[43] (In addition, France agreed to take one million quintals of barley.) Nevertheless, 2 million quintals of soft wheat from 1953 were still on hand when another bumper crop was harvested in 1954.

Again France came to the rescue, at least partially, by accepting a portion of the surplus. Another portion was sold on the world market, but only after granting an export subsidy of 2,175 francs per quintal to compensate for the difference between the price in Morocco and that in the world market, 3,960 and 1,800 francs, respectively. The total cost to the government of moving this and other cereal crops in 1954 was around 8 billion francs (over $20 million).

Despite the above measures, there was just about as much soft wheat in stock when the 1955 crop was harvested as there had been in 1954. World prices were still far below the supported domestic prices, and the French Cereals Office announced that it was prepared to accept hard wheat only. Thus the battle of the quotas was taken up once more.

In summary, the dualism in grain production had the following characteristics: European output, largely wheat, took place on lands of viable size for cash crops, particularly since the land was among the best in terms of quality and water. The European also had the skills and capital which added to the natural advantages. As a result, average yields were higher and the amplitude of yields from one year to the next lower than those of the Moroccan farmers. The tax burden also fell lightly on European shoulders. Yet, if one raises his sights to consider the world grain situation, European agriculture was marginal over-all, precisely because Morocco itself lies on the margin of the areas of the world where dry farming of grains is possible.

Farming on the margin means high costs and, in a free market, low money returns. If European agriculture was to be prosperous, then, the free market could not be allowed to do its work. Quotas from high price France and protection of the domestic market from imports of more efficient producers opened the door to prosperity. Put another way, government action assured not only good returns to European farmers, but also assured that both French and Moroccan consumers would pay the bill through higher prices in the marketplace.

The Moroccan farmer, on the other hand, took his chances on lands — given size, quality, availability of water, skills, and capital — far too small to be viable. His average yields were lower and fluctuations from year-to-year greater than the European's. At the same time, the tax burden fell more heavily on his shoulders. Although his production costs were also high, his access to high price markets was strictly limited. Concentration on drought-resistant barley, necessitated by the environment of drier lands, resulted in a crop which the government had little interest in giving real price protection since Europeans grew relatively little.

Thus, while the protectorate government concentrated its efforts on making modern farming profitable, problems of gigantic proportions were building up in the traditional sector. The two added up to economic "mis-development," a structural imbalance which has been inherited by independent Morocco and which has, as a matter of fact, extended beyond cereal production to include animal husbandry.

Animal Husbandry

Cereal growing was one pillar of traditional Moroccan agriculture; livestock production was the other. Relatively few Europeans were attracted to the latter activity; they preferred the greener fields found in cultivated crops. In the 1951 season, for example, Moroccans owned almost 22 million animals, while Europeans had less than half a million.[44]

Table 7 summarizes the growth of the three most prevalent

TABLE 7. THE NUMBER OF SHEEP, GOATS, AND CATTLE IN THE FRENCH ZONE OF MOROCCO, 1931 AND 1952, AND THE AVERAGE, MAXIMUM, AND MINIMUM NUMBERS DURING THESE YEARS

(in 000)

SPECIES	1931	1952	AVERAGE	MAXIMUM		MINIMUM	
				Number	Year	Number	Year
Sheep	6,613	*13,923	9,840	13,923	1952	6,031	1946
Goats	3,195	*9,775	6,206	9,775	1952	3,195	1931
Cattle	1,909	2,134	2,028	2,749	1943	1,326	1947

*Only those sheep and goats over a year old were counted — 9,945,000 and 7,125,000, respectively. Estimates of the younger animals were added to these counts to produce the figures shown in the table.

Source: Annuaire statistique de la zone française du Maroc, 1952, Gouvernement Chérifien, Service Central des Statistiques (Rabat, 1952), p. 135.

species of stock (sheep, goats, and cattle) from 1931 to 1952.[45] As the table shows, the cattle population actually grew very little during these years; the modest peak reached prior to the famine of the middle forties still had not been equaled by 1952. What the table does not show is the almost complete absence of any pattern of growth leading up to the 1943 high; rather the number of cattle fluctuated from year to year during this period.

While sheep, the herder's principal stock-in-trade, fared better than cattle in terms of over-all increases from 1931 to 1952, the famine years were equally disastrous for them. There were 13 million sheep in Morocco in 1942; four years later, there were not even half as many — less than there had been in 1931. The goat population, too, suffered during the dry years, dropping from 8 million in 1943 to 4.25 million in 1946.

Drops in numbers do not tell the whole story, of course; to the losses from mortality must be added the weight losses suffered by the surviving animals. Nor do total losses for the whole country describe fully the plight of all individual areas. In the region of Oujda, for example, sheep and goats had numbered 800,000 in 1942; by 1946, there were only 120,000, and these were badly emaciated.[46]

The hardy goat was the most dependable of the three major species of livestock over the years; the number of goats more than tripled from 1931 to 1952. This extension of goat raising had its drawbacks, since forest and ground cover were seriously damaged as a result. The herder had little choice, however, relegated as he was by the extension of cultivated areas to lands unfit for raising anything other than the "cow of the poor."

HORTICULTURE

Most of the fruit growers in pre-protectorate Morocco produced olives. In the south, dates were grown. Although there was some citrus production, it was not important; these fruits were seldom found in the Moroccan diet. While the years of the protectorate saw the raising of the citrus varieties develop into one of Morocco's major agricultural activities, the producers as well as the consumers were largely Europeans. Another crop which made great gains after 1912 was almonds; this, however, was almost wholly Moroccan-grown. Olives, though, still remained the trees most commonly found on Moroccan farms, where 90 per cent of them were located.

While olives are better able to withstand drought than most other fruits, yields were as precarious for the Moroccan olive grower as they were for his compatriot in barley, and fluctuations in the weather were largely responsible for a cycle which could almost be described as good year, bad year. Olive production was 530,000 quintals in 1938, the first year for which data are available, and 734,000 quintals in 1953. The average annual crop during this period, however, was 730,000 quintals — a figure barely exceeded in 1953. Production was greater than a million quintals three times during the years of 1943, 1948, and 1952; in the last year it reached 1,700,000 quintals for a record high. (Note that the following year it was well under half as much, as it also was the year before.) A low of 150,000 quintals was recorded in 1946. Olive trees covered 103,000 hectares in 1949; by 1952, the area had grown to 115,000 hectares.[47]

Surfaces planted in almond trees covered 11,500 hectares in 1929. By 1945, they had increased to 52,200 hectares, and by 1952 to 67,200. Production amounted to 300,000 quintals in 1951, as compared with 225,000 quintals in 1949 and 145,000 quintals in 1947.[48]

The growing of date palms, located in the oases south of the Atlas, was even more exclusively a Moroccan occupation than was the raising of olives or almonds. Ninety-nine per cent of the trees in the country were Moroccan-owned. The number of trees only rose from 2,962,000 in 1949 to 3,076,000 in 1952. Production, on the other hand, increased from 250,000 quintals in 1949 to 560,000 quintals in 1953. Within this period, however, there apparently was considerable variation.[49]

Citrus production occupied the great bulk of European fruit farmers in Morocco. Oranges were the major crop; they accounted for 26,500 of the 31,900 hectares planted in all varieties of citrus fruit in 1952. Tangerines, grapefruit, and lemons were also grown. The production of all these fruits gained steadily in the sixteen years from 1938 through 1953, rising from 270,000 quintals in the former year to 2,195,000 quintals in the latter.[50]

The citrus varieties were the only fruit grown in Morocco that was shipped abroad in any important quantities, with the possible exception of almonds. Over half the total crop was exported each year, the bulk of it to France. Of the 1953 crop, 1,150,000 quintals were sent to France and another 90,000 quintals went to a dozen other countries.[51]

The above figures point up the importance of the French market to citrus growers in Morocco. The extent of this market each year depended on the vagaries of French politics, for the annual quota was the subject of debate much like that which centered around the quota for soft wheat. In the case of citrus, however, the conflict arose not between the North African and the metropolitan farmer, but between the North African and the French industrialist. The size of the quota for Morocco determined how much citrus France would import from Spain, its other principal supplier. Since the Franco government dealt with France on a barter basis only, any reduction in imports of fruit from Spain brought about a decrease in Spanish purchases of French manufactured goods.

Truck farming in Morocco was similar to citrus, as well as soft wheat, production in several important respects. It expanded rapidly under the protectorate, and the major stimulus to this growth was the export trade — or more specifically, the French quota. Furthermore, it attracted a large number of *colons*. Exports amounted to 25,000 quintals in 1929. By 1950, they had reached 750,000 quintals. The total for 1952 was 524,000 quintals, of which tomatoes and potatoes, the two principal varieties, contributed 452,253 quintals. Total production of tomatoes that year was around 750,000 to 800,000 quintals, and production of potatoes was approximately three-quarters as much.[52]

All vegetables covered 51,500 hectares in 1952. A quarter of these surfaces was owned by Europeans. Almost 75 per cent of the Europeans' land, however, was irrigated, while well under half of the Moroccans' land fell into this category.[53] The area along the coast from Kenitra to Al Jadida, where the bulk of the European truck farms were located, was well-suited for this activity as regards both soil and climate. The early vegetables grown there generally matured well in advance of those grown in the countries which were Morocco's principal competitors in the French market — Algeria, Spain, and France itself.

Access to the French market dated back to 1923. The quota established that year permitted 16,000 quintals of fresh vegetables to be exported to France. By 1930, the annual allotment had grown to 42,000 quintals. To help the Europeans increase production accordingly, the protectorate government ceded them land taken over for official colonization and also granted them credit to get started.[54]

French willingness to accept vegetables from Morocco diminished sharply during the years of economic crisis and shrinking markets that characterized the thirties. It was a situation similar to that which developed in regard to wheat, except that this time the controversy over quotas was three-sided, with farmers in Algeria vitally concerned. Nevertheless, the Resident-General in Morocco obtained a French quota for 130,000 quintals of vegetables in 1932. On its side, the protectorate government assumed strict control over the quality of all vegetable exports the same year. This new government function brought about the establishment of the *Office Chérifien d'Exportation*, an organization which subsequently assumed many additional duties.

By 1935, the situation in France had reached the stage where some more effective means of regulating the quantity as well as the quality of vegetable imports was imperative. The simultaneous arrival of tomatoes from Algeria and Morocco at *Les Halles* had caused the price at one point to drop below the costs of transport — an intolerable situation from the producers' viewpoint no matter how attractive to the Parisian housewife. A conference of the North African producers was called, and a program of "harmonization" was worked out. Under this program, strict limits were set on the daily shipments of vegetables from Algeria and Morocco during May and June, when imports from the two countries overlapped and the Paris market was "glutted." Algeria was to ship all that she could during this period within the established limits, and Morocco was to make up the difference until such time as Algeria was able to fill the entire daily quota.

The "harmonization" program, in its general lines, continued in operation, with quotas for each day as well as for the whole year established annually. The division of the quotas was a constant source of irritation between the growers in Algeria and Morocco. The controversy was particularly heated when there was an early harvest in Algeria or a late one in Morocco. The French farmer was quick to join the fight whenever he felt that his interests were threatened and consequently wanted to reduce the share allotted to his North African compatriots.

VINICULTURE

Wine growing offers another example of the diversification of agriculture under the protectorate, and it exhibits much the same *raison d'être* as the production of other crops which were virtually unknown before the arrival of the French. Like soft wheat, citrus fruits, and vegetables, wine was produced by Europeans largely for European consumption. In fact, the domestic market was limited to the European population even more than in the case of other European-produced crops. For while the latter gained a certain acceptance by the Moroccans, to the extent that purchasing power made such acceptance possible, the Koranic prohibition against the use of alcoholic beverages was widely respected in Morocco. Thus it is not surprising that the availability of a market in France was as essential to the European wine grower as to his compatriots producing other crops. Both the need for this market and the resulting quotas were slower to come in the case of wine, however, as we shall see.

For the first two decades of the protectorate, viniculture in Morocco prospered greatly. If uncertain climate produced varying yields, Frenchmen found that this same climate, together with the soil, was capable of producing wines of good quality and high alcoholic content, once they had developed species of plants appropriate to the milieu. The specialized skills required were available in considerable quantity; many of the wine growers had come from Algeria and the Midi, long-time centers of wine production. A growing European population and the high prices and generally poor quality of imported wines created a ready local market for all that they could produce.

By 1929, there were 9,500 hectares planted in wine grapes in Morocco. Increasing domestic demand and a shift to wine production on the part of many farmers after 1930, when it became more difficult to market cereals in France, helped to push surfaces to slightly above 19,000 hectares in 1933 and to 24,500 hectares two years later.[55] As it turned out, the latter figure represented a prewar high, for 1935 marked the beginning of a new stage in the development of Moroccan viniculture, one characterized by numerous restrictions and regulations designed to curb the rapidly mounting output.

Over 600,000 hectoliters of wine (close to 16 million gallons) had been produced in 1934 — 180,000 more than the year before and around 150,000 more than could be consumed domestically, i.e., at a price remunerative to the growers.[56] The *colons* found no outlet for this excess in France; the French *Statut Vinicole*, which regulated all aspects of wine producing and marketing, made no provision for Moroccan wine. Furthermore, France, Algeria, and

Tunisia were also experiencing record production; and France was having ample trouble absorbing exports from the latter two countries.

It was up to the protectorate government to valorize Moroccan wine. There was every indication that the overproduction was to be chronic, rather than temporary; wine output was clearly increasing at a more rapid rate than the European population. In the apparent absence of export possibilities, limitation of production appeared to be the first step to take. As early as 1932, in fact, the government had envisaged a temporary suspension of new plantings, but had made a provisional retreat before the hostility of the Chambers of Agriculture. (In the meantime, rumors of limitation had brought a flurry of planting to beat the deadline.) The suspension finally came in January, 1935; all plantings and replantings were prohibited until September, 1936.

The next step, taken early in 1936, after another large crop the year before (520,000 hectoliters), was a program of "blockage." Under this program, domestic "needs" for the year were determined, and all stocks in excess of that amount were blocked from sale on the local market. Instead, they were to be disposed of by distillation, transformation, exportation, or destruction. The possibility of increased imports, attracted by the supported price that was the end product of the program, was anticipated by a decree submitting imports of *vin ordinaire* to the same treatment as the domestic stocks. By the middle of the year, the government was purchasing both blocked wine and alcohol which had been distilled under the "blockage" program. Furthermore, it was granting a subsidy not only on exported wine, in order to bring the grower a return approximately equal to that realized from sale on the domestic market, but on wine that had been either destroyed or transformed.

The weather granted the government a short respite from its struggle to valorize the wine crop. Contrary to expectations, 1936 production amounted to only 277,000 hectoliters, as the result of heavy mildew damage. The years that followed, however, brought more "surplus" crops, with a prewar high of 770,000 hectoliters in 1938; and the government became more and more deeply embroiled in a program of controls on both production and marketing.

The war years saw some significant changes in the situation. France finally began admitting a quota of Moroccan wine in 1941, much of which, owing to its high alcoholic content, was used to fortify domestic varieties. While the American landings in North Africa the next year brought this trade to a temporary halt, the principle was established; the wine growers now had access to the French market along with their compatriots in wheat, citrus, and truck farming. It was during the war, too, that the phylloxera finally reached Morocco.[57] As a result of this invasion and of pre-war restrictions on planting, wine production fell to 233,000 hectoliters in 1945 and surfaces declined to 15,000 hectares the next year. From 1943 – the first year of the phylloxera – to 1950, in fact, Morocco was compelled to import wine from Algeria.

The postwar period witnessed a revival of wine production in Morocco, as the phylloxera was gradually brought under control. The possibility of exporting to France and the influx of Europeans after 1945 provided an incentive not only to recover but to exceed prewar production levels. By 1951, with a record output of 1,021,000 hectoliters in the cellars, the country was on an export basis once again, with the French market, of course, as its principal outlet. France, however, was already overflowing with wine, and its ability to absorb Morocco's excess was limited. Thus by 1954, when another record crop (1,900,000 hectoliters) was pressed, production in Morocco had again exceeded domestic "needs" and export possibilities by so great a margin that viniculture was in crucial straits.

Once more the Europeans had developed a type of agriculture that apparently was unable to survive, at least in its achieved dimensions, without French quotas. European agriculture in Morocco was characterized by high costs,[58] by an insistence upon high profits, and, as a result, by high-priced products. The local market was therefore limited, not so much by custom, except in the case of wine, as by a lack of purchasing power. In the world market, price competition virtually precluded the entry of the *colon's* crops without heavy subsidization. Thus access to the French market remained his only salvation.

The fact that the quotas for all of the major crops were the subject of bitter controversy between France and Morocco gives weight to the conclusion that the agricultural varieties suited to the North African milieu were, by and large, competitive with, rather than complementary to, those of France. The illusion, held at the time of the conquest of Algeria, that here was a tropical land suited to large-scale production of rice, sugar, and cotton had long since passed. The hard fact remained that the French farmer had to share the home market with his expatriate colleague if European farming in North Africa was to endure.

RURAL LIFE

In a country as heavily rural as Morocco, the well-being of the population depends largely on the performance of the agricultural sector of the economy. Farms must produce either the basic food-stuffs required by the people or commodities capable of earning sufficient foreign exchange to secure more foodstuffs abroad. Furthermore, effective demand for these products must be created in large part through agricultural activity.

Morocco had never been sure of feeding herself, and the years of the protectorate brought little improvement in the situation. Indeed, population growth threatened to make what had been a periodic inability a chronic one. In truth, it probably cannot be said that Morocco had an abundance of food even in the most bountiful years of the protectorate. What "surpluses" there were reflected, rather, a lack of purchasing power at prices remunerative to the growers.

As we have seen, the years since 1912 were characterized in the agricultural sphere by the development of intensive-type farming in the fertile, well-watered northwestern area of Morocco. The accent was on high-value cash crops which, for the most part, either were channeled into European consumption within the country or found their way, under the quota, into the export market. In neither case was the great mass of the people benefited. The average Moroccan, without adequate credit, capital, or land, did not share in this agriculture except as he provided labor on European farms. Even when a Moroccan was able to engage in these activities, he was generally discriminated against market-wise, as our discussion of soft wheat production showed.

As far as the fellah was concerned, the principal effects of the growth of a diversified agriculture were negative ones. To promote this growth, the protectorate government took numerous steps that benefited the *colon* at the expense of the fellah. The subsidies granted to the Europeans' crops, for example, were financed largely by taxes on the Moroccans' produce or duties on their imports. Other measures designed to assure the *colon* an "adequate" return, such as limiting imports, served to raise costs for both him and the fellah. The former, however, had been compensated for his costs, while little was done to help the fellah secure a correspondingly high return.

One of the most important results of the development of diversified farming was, of course, to reduce the quality of the land available for the two major occupations of traditional Moroccan aggriculture. Grain growing was pushed into the marginal area which Despois described as one in which this activity was a gamble with the odds heavily against the player. The herder, in turn, found himself moved even farther south, onto lands offering highly uncertain pasturage at best. It is little wonder, then, that neither cereal production nor animal husbandry was able to keep pace with the population growth.

A French commission has estimated that the production of the four principal cereals declined from an annual average of 4.1 quintals per person during the years from 1934 to 1941 to less than 3.4 quintals during 1948 to 1953. The possibility of offsetting the decline in available cereals by introducing more protein into the Moroccan diet (which was traditionally one of starches) was ruled out: the number of cattle fell from 35 per 100 inhabitants in the former period to 23 per 100 inhabitants in the latter; and the corresponding figures for sheep were 156 and 134.[59]

Joly estimated that Morocco needed at least 35.5 million quintals of grain in 1945, of which human consumption would take slightly over 22 million quintals and animals and seed the rest.[60] Since these estimates were based on a total population of 7.8 million, the per capita requirements were approximately 4.6 quintals including the cereals needed for animals and seed, or 2.9 quintals excluding this amount. Of course, the "needs of consumption" is a tenuous concept; nevertheless, production not only in 1945 but in the years that followed fell so far short of Joly's estimated requirements as to suggest that undernourishment was the constant companion of Moroccans.

In not one of the years from 1945 through 1953 did cereal production equal 35.5 million quintals. It came the closest in 1953, when it amounted to approximately 33.5 million quintals. By this time, however, the population was in excess of eight million. In four of the nine years after 1945, production actually fell short of the 22 million quintals Joly estimated to be needed for human consumption alone at the beginning of the period. Nevertheless, Morocco was on a net export basis for cereals during much of this period.

THE MODES OF NATIVE AGRICULTURE

The failure of agricultural production to keep pace with population growth was sometimes attributed to the failure to adopt improved methods of farming. There are limits to the validity of this argument; the poor quality of a great deal of the fellah's land precluded any significant increase in yields regardless of the methods employed.[61] Within these limits, however, there was indeed considerable room for improvement.

The sad truth is that the modes of Moroccan agriculture did not change very much during the protectorate years. The European proved to be not a teacher but rather a farmer working for his own account. His techniques were exposed not to the landholder but to the landless, who supplied the labor for commercial agriculture and was in no position to do anything else. Even when the fellah was aware of modern methods, he did not generally adopt them. Conservatism probably played a part in this reticence, but lack of capital undoubtedly played a larger one.

On the plains, and then in the steppes, the typical Moroccan farmer was dry-farming a field of 8 hectares or less. He was still using the Roman plow, and the power to pull it was supplied by camels, donkeys, or both. He had to await the autumn rains before his weak plow and team could scratch a furrow. Thus his seed was deprived of the nourishment of the first rains. If the rains were late, his crop was further compromised. Deep plowing was impossible with his equipment, so the land could not store the water necessary for effective growth during the dry season. Neither was it possible to eliminate weeds effectively; in addition, the doum, with its deep, tough roots, could not be removed and so had to be by-passed, thus reducing the productive area.[62]

If the land was good, around 350 millimeters of rain might bring a fair crop, provided that the rain was well distributed over the year. However, the fellah was on the margin at this figure. If he was unfortunate enough to be cultivating land below the 350-millimeter line,[63] then he was lucky to recover any more than the seed. No matter how much rainfall there was, the crop was not out of danger until the harvest was in. The fellah's equipment not only failed to prepare his land quickly in the autumn; it often could not harvest the grain quickly enough to avoid the *chergui* or the locusts.

The shift of much cereal production from the plains to the drier lands of the steppes not only increased the risks associated with this activity; it seriously impinged upon animal husbandry, which was now confined largely to the high altitudes in the mountains or to the arid and rocky slopes to the south or east. As a result of this development (and the population growth which helped to bring it about), the displacements which formerly characterized animal husbandry were drastically limited. It was now seldom possible to escape extremes of climate or to find sufficient pasturage and water to maintain healthy flocks. It was for this reason that the goat supplanted the sheep in many herds; the former was better able to survive on sparsely covered land and also to withstand both the rigorous Middle Atlas winters and the extreme aridity farther south.

The tenuous balance between cultivation and animal husbandry which provided a living, if a meager one, for so many Moroccans before the protectorate was permanently destroyed. The transhumant, with his best pasture lands turned under and his migrations to the lowlands no longer possible, found himself in an intolerable situation. Consequently, transhumance declined as a way of life in Morocco under the protectorate. The semi-nomad was forced to devote himself either to cereal production on the poorest of the lands under cultivation or to animal husbandry on the even poorer lands not converted to cultivation by the press of population.

Landholdings in the fertile valleys of the High Atlas were measured in square meters rather than hectares. Maintenance of the *seguias* continued to be a time-consuming task, especially when spring rains filled the watercourses. Barley and maize continued to be grown there, but most of the production was now consumed on the spot. What was not generally went to the tax collector, and the *agadirs* fell into disrepair.

The oases were vegetating. The caravan trade practically disappeared, and with it the profit from camel raising. As in the mountains, fragmentation of landholdings was extreme. And as in the mountains, there was little excess grain for sale even in the best of years. The principal commercial crop was dates; however, lack of proper care and the prevalence of disease limited its value.

With agricultural methods little changed, many of the traditional patterns of agriculture destroyed, and agricultural production generally stagnating — all while the population was rapidly increasing — it is not surprising that migration from south to north assumed major proportions under the protectorate.[64] Many of the emigrants found employment on the European farms; more found their way to the "tin-can towns" around the urban centers. There will be occasion to discuss the life of the Moroccans in the cities in another chapter; for the moment, we will confine ourselves to a description of the farm worker's lot.

THE RURAL PROLETARIAT

One of the most important ways in which European coloniza-tion changed the face of Moroccan rural life was in its demand for wage labor. The permanent supply was provided largely by tribesmen displaced from their lands by the "needs" of coloniza-tion. Moroccans from the south were employed for the most part as seasonal laborers at the time of the harvest. Writers on the sub-ject of farm labor suggest that the more or less permanent com-plement of workers on European farms amounted to around 60,000 persons, who were earning a livelihood for about 250,000 people.[65] These people were generally landless, or at most had very small parcels which were insufficient to provide their living. Any chance that they might amass enough savings to acquire land or to extend their holdings was ruled out by the low level of farm wages.

In a rapidly growing society where the opportunities for any occupational mobility of the mass of the people are narrowly limited, the supply of unskilled labor is practically unlimited, i.e., wage rates tend toward the subsistence level. Such was the case in Morocco. There might be local shortages during the harvests which raised money wages above those prevailing throughout the year; but much of the gain was often obliterated, in real terms, by the price rises in the markets.[66]

It was only during the war, when Morocco was subject to the influence of the Vichy technocrats, that the government began to concern itself with farm labor. Workers were frozen in their jobs for the duration, work cards were issued, and salary schedules were established. After the war, the government continued to es-tablish minimum money wage rates, which were reviewed annu-ally. The European farmers were left free to fix the customary additional payments in kind, as they saw fit, which generally con-sisted of allotments of grain. (In addition, a farmer might supply the materials for a hut and a site upon which to place it.) None of the social legislation promulgated by the protectorate govern-ment after the war, e.g., family allotments and paid vacations, was applicable to agricultural workers. Furthermore, agricultural labor unions were forbidden.

Laxity in enforcement of the minimum wage and the varying dispositions of the *colons* vis-à-vis their workers led to wide variations of actual wages. The system, in the last analysis, was a paternal one; and the worker, without organization or even the right to organize, was heavily dependent on his employer for the determination of his level of life.

There is evidence that money wages did not keep pace with the general rise in prices during the years after the war. Prewar and postwar prices in the region of Fez for some of the most important commodities in the farm worker's diet were as follows:

		PRICES (IN FRANCS)	
COMMODITY	MEASURE	1938	1947
Barley	Moud	20	200
Hard wheat	"	50	600
Sugar	Kilogram	4	40
Tea	"	20	256
Olive oil	Liter	8	121
Meat	Kilogram	5	200

Among non-food items, a pair of shoes increased in price from 15 francs in 1938 to 350 francs in 1947, a *djellaba* from 50 francs to 1,000 francs. In the meantime, the daily farm wage rate rose from 6 to 65 francs a day.[67]

MEASURES FOR AGRICULTURAL IMPROVEMENT

A number of the steps that were taken to aid European agriculture in Morocco have been described. But since the bulk of the farmland in the country was held by Moroccans, it would seem that any measures to create a viable agriculture should have been directed toward helping the fellah rather than the *colon*.

Although the European occupied first place in the eyes of the authorities, it cannot be said that there was no effort to improve the lot of the fellah under the protectorate. While the European clearly failed in his role as teacher and helper, the protectorate government acted in several ways to help Moroccan agriculture. The state of the rural sector of the economy at the time of independence, however, points up the woeful inadequacy of the efforts that were made in this direction. Indeed, the outstanding success for the French was in the realm of sanitary measures, which, by promoting the growth of the population, made the problems of welfare many times more serious. Let us now see what some of their less successful measures were.

THE EXTENSION OF CREDIT

One of the most important characteristics of agriculture in pre-protectorate Morocco was the general absence of capital investment in the land. The reasons for this were many; among the most important were the lack of security and the inability of the fellah to finance such investment himself. The only source of credit was afforded by the usurer, who supplied working capital but little else. With the security brought by the protectorate one of the deterrents to capital investment was removed. It was still necessary to expand credit facilities, however, since self-financing continued to remain out of the question for the bulk of the fellahin.

Two distinct lines of agricultural credit were set up under the protectorate, one for Europeans and the other for Moroccans. For the former, the government established the *Caisse de Prêts Immobiliers,* which provided both medium- and long-term loans, the former for the purchase of livestock and equipment, the latter for investment of a more permanent nature. Short-term credit for seeds and fertilizers was also provided by the State, through the *Caisses Mutuelles de Crédit Agricole.* The funds were revolving, but initial capital and later increments were provided by the government and the National Bank. In addition, cooperatives for the Europeans were encouraged; storage facilities at Meknes, for example, were financed by an interest-free government loan.[68]

Through the *Caisse de Prêts Immobiliers,* the European could secure a loan for as much as 60 per cent of the appraised value of his property. With the establishment of the *Caisse Fédérale de la Mutualité et de la Coopération Agricole,* 100 per cent long-term financing became possible, with the latter agency supplying the remaining 40 per cent. Thus the European was in an excellent position to make capital improvements.

The same cannot be said of the fellah. The principal lending agency for Moroccan farmers was the *Sociétés Marocaines de Prévoyance (S.O.M.A.P.),* which were founded by law in 1917. Every farmer subject to the *tertib* was automatically a member of a local *S.O.M.A.P.* and had to contribute to it at the time he paid the tax. The funds thus acquired were augmented by state contributions. In 1952, there were close to a million and a half members, and they paid in 425 million francs. A few statistics relating to the operations of the *S.O.M.A.P.* during two fiscal years, taken from the *Annuaire statistique* for 1952,[69] are set out below:

	1951–52	1952–53
Number of members	1,436,000	1,449,000
Loans outstanding, end of year (in 000 francs)	2,050,580	2,393,000
Loans granted during year (in 000 francs)	1,190,853	1,499,055

The total amount of all loans made by the *S.O.M.A.P.* from the time this agency was created through 1952–53 was 7.7 billion francs. Yet, as the above figures show, loans made in just the last two years of this period accounted for about a third of the total. Even taking into consideration the greatly decreased value of the franc, it seems that little effort was directed toward making agricultural credit available to the fellah during most of the years of the protectorate.[70]

Indeed, the amounts loaned in 1951–52 and 1952–53 were negligible when contrasted with the membership of the *S.O.M.A.P.* These sums plus other loans outstanding at the time amounted to only 1,428 francs per member in 1951–52 and 1,652 francs in 1952–53. (The free exchange rate in June of the latter year was over 400 francs to the dollar.) Of course the actual average loan was considerably greater than these per capita amounts; it has been asserted that 822 farmers who qualified as "modern" received the bulk of the credit granted to Moroccans during this period.[71] This meant that the great mass of the fellahin was getting no assistance at all from the *S.O.M.A.P.*

A further characteristic of the loans granted by the *S.O.M.A.P.* should be noted. Of the total amount loaned out in 1951–52 and 1952–53, almost 80 per cent consisted of credits in kind rather than in money. The assistance thus given was generally in the form of seeds. Although seeds, if selected, could improve yields measurably, this was not enough to raise significantly the standards of agriculture.

The short-term nature of the bulk of *S.O.M.A.P.* credit is suggested not only by its composition, but also by the relationship between loans granted within a year and outstanding loans at the end of the year. In each of the two years to which our figures relate, well over half of the amount outstanding on June 30th had been lent during that year. A beginning was made in the last years of the protectorate on the extension of medium-term credit to the fellahin, but it was an extremely modest one. Long-term loans were even rarer. Since Moroccan-owned land was for the most part unregistered, it was not considered good security for this type of credit.

The activities of the *S.O.M.A.P.* in the realm of short-term agricultural credit was later supplemented by the work of rural cooperatives formed among the Moroccans. The functions of both the *Coopérative Marocaine Agricole* (formerly *Coopérative Indigène Agricole*) and the *Société Coopérative Agricole Marocaine* included the distribution of seeds to members either for cash or on credit (generally the latter). Some fertilizers were also supplied. Despite ambitious plans, however, the operations of the cooperatives were of minor importance. Both the *S.O.M.A.P.* and the cooperatives counted among their activities the giving of advice to their members. For this purpose, they employed French agricultural engineers. In 1954, there were 92 such advisers in the *S.O.M.A.P.* (or one for every 16,000 members) and 12 in the cooperatives.[72]

THE EXPANSION OF MODERN METHODS

The advice proffered to the fellah by the *S.O.M.A.P.* and the cooperatives often took the form of demonstrations of modern agricultural techniques. A somewhat more concentrated effort along these lines was made by the *Secteurs de Modernisation du Paysanat* (Rural Modernization Sectors). These *S.M.P.*, which were government-financed, dated from 1945. They operated for the most part on collective lands; a certain area was chosen to be a "model farm," and the Moroccans living there were compelled to participate in the program. The program included an attempt to deal with the social as well as the economic aspects of development. Thus, along with introducing improved agricultural methods, the directors of the program established schools and infirmaries.

The Moroccans whose lands were chosen for a sector cleared the land, built roads, erected buildings, and planted and harvested crops. All of this was carried out under the direction of Frenchmen — a supervisor of the sector and a staff of assistants. In addition, French mechanics repaired the machinery and French teachers and infirmary attendants carried out the social aspects of the program. The fellahin thus lost control of their land during the development of the modernization project. They were assured, however, that the land would be returned to them in privately-owned parcels once the project was a going concern. Just when the latter was to have been achieved is uncertain; when independence came, the first S.M.P. had been operating for ten years with no sign of the land being returned to its owners.

The establishment of the sectors did not meet with universal enthusiasm in Morocco. On the part of the fellah himself, there was worry at seeing land pass under French control. In addition, there was confusion in the transition from the camel to the tractor, confusion that was not lessened by the fact that the relationship between Frenchman and Moroccan developed as one between manager and worker rather than tutor and pupil. (The Berber institution of the governing council [jema'a] had been retained as a consultative body, but the final word rested with the French supervisor.) Indeed, the S.M.P. threatened to achieve what they were trying to avoid — the continuing "proletarization" of rural Moroccans.

The European farmer looked with disfavor on the S.M.P. for two reasons. First and perhaps foremost, he was concerned lest the projects deprive him of a cheap labor supply. Secondly, he was disturbed at the amount of the government funds devoted to rural modernization. After years of living from government largesse, he was unsympathetic with any measures that might decrease the size of the pork barrel. As a result, the size of the program was kept small by the opposition of the French section of the Council of Government.[73]

It was never intended that the S.M.P. should cover the whole country, at least directly; rather, it was the hope that each sector would form a "tache d'huile." There is, however, nothing automatic about the spreading of a new technology; it takes capital — far more than was available to the Moroccans. Furthermore, the geography of Morocco imposed fairly strict limits on the possibilities of duplicating elsewhere the programs developed in particular sectors. Even disregarding these factors, there simply were too few sectors spotted on the Moroccan landscape for the permeation to be very great. Surfaces which were in any way affected by the S.M.P. amounted to scarcely 100,000 hectares, or less than 2 per cent of the cultivated land under Moroccan ownership.[74] The bulk of this land, however, benefited only from the plowing and harvesting services which the S.M.P. offered in addition to the above-described activities. Actually, there were only 18,000 hectares in the fifty sectors of direct exploitation in 1953.[75]

Not only were the funds for the establishment of sectors limited, but there was considerable mis-allocation of what credits had been made available — at least from the short-run standpoint. The directors of one sector near Meknes, for example, invested nearly one-third of its credits in lodgings for the European and Moroccan personnel, the school, and the infirmary. Only an eighth of the funds devoted to construction was spent on farm buildings, i.e., on construction which could be expected to produce immediate returns.[76] The social measures may have been very laudable; but in view of the fact that it was imperative to increase productivity as soon as possible, it would appear that there was too much emphasis on long-term effects in the operations of the *S.M.P.* Furthermore, the level of investment was such that even the long-term benefits were necessarily confined to an infinitesimal segment of the society.

THE DEVELOPMENT OF IRRIGATION

What capital investment there was in Morocco before the protectorate was found largely in the extensive and intricate irrigation systems of the Haouz Plain, the valleys of the High Atlas, and the Saharan oases. These systems brought water to land which would otherwise have been parched throughout the year, or at least during the summer months. Even with irrigation, however, the assurance of a subsistence crop was no stronger than the run-off, which was extremely variable from one year to the next.

Irrigation was confined almost entirely to the above-mentioned areas. The great bulk of northwest Morocco was dry-farmed; the only water distribution systems here were those supplying urban needs. As a result, tribes in those areas where rainfall was marginal or submarginal devoted themselves to animal husbandry and a shaky type of extensive agriculture — regardless of the quality of their land or the possibilities of irrigation, which were in fact often excellent.

The large inland plain of the Tadla is a case in point. Through this fertile area flowed the Oum ar Rbia, the most important river in Morocco. Yet its resources remained untapped, and the people led the life of transhumants. Part of the reason lay in the fact that the population/resource ratio was such that the land could yield a living, of sorts, in its natural state. In addition, the development of irrigation would have been possible, even if the technology had been available, only with the development of a commercial agriculture; and the extensive markets required for agriculture of this type were non-existent in pre-protectorate Morocco.

With the protectorate came an unfavorable change in the population/resource ratio, and living levels began to suffer. Furthermore, the coming of the French brought a commercial agriculture into the realm of possibility. Thus two incentives for developing irrigation were provided. The second incentive proved to be the stronger, at least at first. It was the *colon* who immediately saw the possibilities of a shift from subsistence crops to those of a commercial nature, and who exerted pressure on the government to bring about this change by the development of modern irrigation. The first large project was undertaken at Al Kansera, on the Oued Beth, to serve the area around Sidi Slimane, which was one of heavy colonization.

In the execution of the irrigation works at Al Kansera, there were sins of both commission and omission from the technical standpoint. On the first score, the derivation canals were built in such fashion that the most productive lands could not be reached; rather the water was directed to less fertile land where drainage was difficult. The omissions consisted for the most part of delays in carrying out necessary measures on the land to be irrigated, such as leveling, secondary canals, and drainage facilities — all needed to bring water successfully to the land. A full eighteen years after the barrage was completed in 1935, only 10,500 hectares had been brought under irrigation, or about one-third of the potential.[77]

As for the development of irrigation elsewhere in Morocco, a dam on the Oum ar Rbia near Kasba Tadla was completed in 1939. Thus it was at last possible to begin irrigating the Tadla. Colonization had made relatively few inroads in the area up to this time, so the project presumably was more directly concerned with raising Moroccan living levels than had been the case at Al Kansera. The land irrigated by the dam near Kasba Tadla (20,000 hectares in 1953) was under the control of the Beni Amir Office. This agency was established in 1941 to direct all agricultural activity in the area, with the avowed purpose of helping the fellah comprehend the complexities of a modern irrigation system. The Office had a French overseer, or monitor, for each 1,000 hectares of land. It was his function to tell the fellah what crops were to be planted and in what amounts, to provide seeds and equipment, and to distribute the water. The cost of these services was to be paid by the farmer at the time of the harvest.[78]

The program was supposedly devised in such fashion as to maximize returns, given the nature of the soil, the possibilities of irrigation, consumption needs within the irrigated area, and the marketing possibilities both at home and abroad. Serious writers on Moroccan agriculture do not consider that the Beni Amir Office was an unqualified success, however. At the technical level, for example, the lack of proper drainage brought a problem of salting in some areas. Industrial crops, e.g., cotton, were emphasized at the expense of forage varieties; as a consequence soil fertility was threatened. (For some time, all animals were banned from the area.)

The relationship between the monitor and the fellah once again emerged as one of employer-employee. Indeed, many of the fellahin were in effect "fired"; around a quarter of the irrigated land of the Beni Amir was taken from tribal members judged incompetent by the French. This land was thereafter exploited by the Beni Amir Office for its own account or, after 1951, sold to Europeans attracted to the area by the development of irrigation. One of the major results of this development was, in fact, the growth of the European population in the Tadla.

A large new dam at Bir al Oidane, in the Middle Atlas, offered the possibility of greatly increasing the irrigable area in the Tadla; and in anticipation of this development, the territory of the Beni Moussa was added to the Beni Amir Office's orbit of control. In addition, a dam at Im Fout, on the Oum ar Rbia behind Al Jadida, made it possible to irrigate land in the Abda–Doukkala region, and one on the Oued n'Fis brought water to a portion of the Haouz Plain. Among the other, smaller projects undertaken in Morocco were works in the eastern part of the country and on the Oued Mellah, behind Casablanca — both in areas of heavy colonization.

At the time of independence, there was relatively little to show for all the time and money spent building large dams.[79] According to Dumont, the criticisms leveled against the irrigation project in the Sidi Slimane area were valid for such projects in general, not only in Morocco but in all of North Africa. The construction of dams was not preceded by sufficient technical study to avoid serious mistakes, nor was it followed by sufficient complementary construction to permit utilization of more than a fraction of the dam's capacity.

The failure to supplement work on a dam with the necessary

projects on the land intended to receive water has very serious consequences for the ultimate success of the whole undertaking. If the dam retained its potential efficiency during the time it was not fully utilized, then the "productivity" of the investment would simply be retarded. The social loss would be confined to the temporary unavailability of the productive power of the resources embodied in its construction and the permanent loss of resources devoted to maintenance. To help offset this loss, of course, there would be the dam's function as a feeder to a generating plant and the partial utilization of the water available for irrigation. However, siltage was very rapid in the dams in North Africa, and potential efficiency was not retained. Thus real capital consumption was very high at a time when the investment was under-utilized.

Dumont urged in 1949 that no new dams be begun until distribution systems for existing dams were completed, including the construction of better drainage systems in areas endangered by salting. Presumably such a program, by increasing the irrigated surfaces, would have narrowed the gap between revenues and expenses that characterized all irrigation projects in North Africa save that near Kasba Tadla.[80] In view of the amount of siltage that had already occurred, however, it may have been that measures to increase the productivity of some dams had been delayed too long.

The completion of partially constructed distribution networks does have the advantage, in ordinary circumstances, of producing fairly immediate results. So does another of Dumont's recommendations: to concentrate on the improvement of "small" irrigation techniques. For example, he recommended "spreading," a process used in Wyoming and introduced into Jordan. More could have been done to divert permanent flows, and more traditional irrigation canals could have been lined with concrete to minimize water losses through seepage. Such measures would have had the advantage of being comprehensible to the Moroccans; indeed, they often would have been only extensions of practices which the Moroccans had developed centuries before the French arrival. A further advantage, especially in view of the fact that government funds for irrigation were limited, was that they were relatively cheap. But the fact that they offered the possibility of increasing production almost immediately is the most important of all. For the real problem of the Moroccan economy concerned the race between the rate of demographic growth and the rate of increase in production. The former was ahead, and the big, expensive dams upon which the French concentrated did all too little to even the score.

SUMMARY

What was true of the development of irrigation under the protectorate was true of efforts to increase agricultural production in general; funds were not only far too limited, but were also misdirected. Morocco had some fine modern dams and some fine model farms. But the average farmer still was unable to exchange his primitive plow for a steel one, let alone a tractor to pull it.[81] In the meantime, the population was growing, and real incomes were falling. What had been, and continued to be, needed was an extensive program of relatively inexpensive measures that offered the possibility of relieving immediately the misery of the fellahin. Land had to be cleared and fertilized, selected seeds distributed widely, and irrigation canals cemented. The means to acquire simple farm equipment had to be given to the fellah. Furthermore, forage crops had to be planted on a large scale, and water points developed. The latter two measures not only would have given a much-needed boost to the livestock industry but, by reducing the overgrazing of pasture lands, would have also helped check erosion. Thus would have been achieved, at least in part, the preservation of the natural endowments with which Morocco, considering the growing population and its marginal location, was only sparsely blessed.

The protectorate government demonstrated itself as at least adverse to, if not incapable of, such a program as has been described above. In the first place, it was politically desirable to give primary attention to the most vocal group of farmers in Morocco — the Europeans. It was also relatively easy, since this was a small group with comparatively small problems. As a result, the economic change that occurred in agriculture under the protectorate took place largely in northwest Morocco, and in the most heavily colonized parts of it. The population/resource ratio for Europeans was low, and yields per man and per hectare were impressive by North African standards. For Moroccans both inside and outside this select perimeter, the reverse was true. By the time the French-controlled government was forced to turn its attention to the fellahin, the problems of the latter, long neglected, had assumed vast proportions. Perhaps the piecemeal, *ad hoc*, and long-range measures which the government was prepared to offer would have had a tangible effect if they had come earlier. As it was, however, they were a poor substitute for the bold, broad program required by the circumstances.

NEW INDUSTRY IN AN OLD SETTING

The failure of the agricultural sector of the Moroccan economy to provide a livelihood for the rapidly mounting population turns our attention to industry. While industrial activity in the Morocco of 1912 was limited to the handicraft trades, the years after the establishment of the protectorate saw the development of a modern industrial complex which, although relatively small, was a far from negligible force in the economic life of Morocco. The development was, of course, animated from the outside — mainly from France; and its direction reflected not so much the needs of Morocco as all the vicissitudes of France and all the hopes and fears of Frenchmen.

The rush of capital to Morocco after the establishment of the protectorate was in the nature of a giant bet on the future of a country where taxes were low,[1] the rate of interest was high, and the police and the army were French. Much of the early inflow went into speculation rather than productive use; nevertheless, a beginning was made on investment in industrial plant and equipment. The protectorate government did much to encourage such investment, which it viewed as a necessary supplement to populating the countryside with Europeans. To promote the formation of enterprises which were considered "indispensable" to the country, subsidies were granted, government credits were extended at low cost, and private loans were guaranteed by the State. The government also participated directly in the formation of enterprises, in the tradition of the *économie mixte*. In addition, it attempted to limit foreign competition, although its efforts in this area were restricted to a considerable extent by the open-door treaties.

The growth of French-inspired industry in Morocco up until the Second World War was impressive in percentage terms, but of course the starting position was zero. Actually, the government encountered a good deal of resistance to its program of industrialization during this period, principally from businessmen in France,

who feared low-cost competition from the colonies. With the industrial base of France so broad, it was inevitable that North
African products should compete with those of France, just as
happened in agriculture.[2] The *colons* were also a source of opposition, since they feared the loss of their cheap labor supply to
industry.

The Second World War brought about a change in French
attitudes vis-à-vis Moroccan industry. Wartime experiences and
the political uncertainties of the future in France and the colonies,
particularly Indo-China, brought a greatly increased flow of capital to Morocco in the postwar years. This time, French industrialists took an active part in the movement; and much of the
capital found its way into Moroccan branches of French industrial
firms. As French stakes in Morocco thus rose, the protectorate
government devoted an increasing share of its energies to protecting industry, although it continued to be hampered in its activities
by the inherited treaties. A measure of its success is supplied by
one observer who noted that technical management of modern
industry was wholly in French hands, and only a little over 5 per
cent of the capital in the largest firms was Moroccan.[3]

Safety of capital is a relative thing. As the years passed after the
war, and as the political uncertainties of Morocco's future grew,
the flow of private funds from abroad dwindled. Finally, during
the last years of French control, the flow was actually reversed.
Capital, especially relatively liquid capital, is the most nervous of
the factors of production. One estimate of the losses reached 35
billion francs for 1955 and 100 billion francs for 1956.[4] Another
measure of the scale of capital flight from Morocco's relatively
open economy was found in the changes in bank deposits, which
dropped from around 135 billion francs at the beginning of 1956
to 65 billion francs at the end of the same year.[5] Ironically enough,
a goodly portion of the outflow was financed by French government outlays which continued to pour in for troop maintenance
and public works, outlays designed in the first instance to keep
private investment safe and in the second to help make it pay. The
immediate effect was an almost complete cessation of the construction boom since liquid capital (bank deposits) had formed
the basis for the expansion of credit for building. Morocco was
left, however, with many evidences of the often-feverish postwar
activity, including a complex created in the image of France. To
this complex we now turn.

THE MINING INDUSTRY

Morocco fell under foreign domination during a time when the European powers were engaged in a race for controlled sources of raw materials. Actually, little was known about the mineral resources of Morocco at this time, owing to the fairly effective policy of isolation pursued by the sultans. But much was suspected; the few Europeans allowed into the interior of the country had returned with glowing reports of the potential mineral wealth to be found there. While later geological surveys showed that these reports were overoptimistic, the struggle over Morocco by the great powers centered in considerable part around control of its mineral resources.

Article 112 of the Act of Algeciras in 1906 provided that the sultan was to promulgate a mining statute based on the European forms, and also that no mining concessions were to be made until the new law had been proclaimed. The law was not immediately forthcoming; in the meantime, the ban on concessions was not completely successful.[6] As things worked out, it was the French who finally developed Morocco's mining regulations, at first in conformance with Article 112, but later in violation of it as part of a series of actions which emptied the Act of much of its content and to a considerable extent rendered it meaningless.

EVOLUTION OF THE MINING REGULATIONS

The first mining *dahir* was issued in 1914, eight years after the signatories of the Act of Algeciras had provided that one be written. The European view that mineral rights were distinct from surface rights and belonged to the State was accepted; only minerals which could be exploited by the open-pit process were designated as the property of the surface owners. The decree further provided that concessions for the mining of phosphates and nitrates be granted by open bidding; for all other minerals, prospecting permits were to be issued on a first-come, first-served basis. These permits, each of which covered 16 square kilometers, or 1,600 hectares, were valid for three years. (They were later made renewable for another three years.) At first, there was no provision that prospecting actually had to be done to retain a permit. The nominal cost made permits attractive for speculation, and a lively market developed.[7]

For those who not only prospected but wished to mine their holdings, a subsequent decree provided for the conversion of a permit for prospecting into one for exploitation, the latter valid for four years and renewable for three additional four-year periods. If the mine were of sufficient importance, it was possible to receive instead a concession for seventy-five years, with the property reverting to the State upon expiration of the concession.

A number of modifications and exceptions to the basic mining laws were made during later years of the protectorate. In cases where two or more requests to prospect a particular area were submitted within five days, for example, powers of arbitration were granted to the Bureau of Mines. In making its decision, the Bureau was to take into consideration the financial and technical capabilities of the contending parties. To prod inactive permit holders into action, a decree was also issued giving the State the right to withdraw a permit if no prospecting was carried out within a year.

In general, one of the principal aims of French policy, and thus of the laws pertaining to mining that were issued under the protectorate, seems to have been to reserve the exploitation of Morocco's minerals to the French. The development of phosphate mining is an excellent example. A few years after the establishment of the protectorate, huge deposits southeast of Casablanca were discovered by the Bureau of Mines. Under the 1914 law these deposits should have been put up for bids. But, as Hoffherr pointed out, "to abandon (them) to the hazards of tenders would have risked the consequence of their cession . . . to foreign interests." [8] To avoid this possibility, Lyautey nationalized the phosphates in 1920, putting their exploitation under the control of the Sharifian Phosphate Office. In this way, not only were foreign interests kept out, but the government gained what later proved to be a major source of revenue, and one that had the advantage of being outside the control of the French Parliament.

While phosphates were the most valuable of the minerals found in Morocco, the government did not end its direct intervention there. There was another major departure from the 1914 law in 1928, when the government established the *Bureau de Recherches et de Participations Minières*, a public corporation with the same rights and obligations as private companies. (Its initial capital was supplied by the Phosphate Office.) The activities of the *B.R.P.M.* were at first limited by law to the exploration and exploitation of coal and oil deposits, but were extended to include all other minerals, except phosphates, in 1938.[9] The organization carried out its activities in partnership with private firms, and thus was an example of the *économie mixte*. After its creation, the *B.R.P.M.* acquired participatory interests in the mining companies producing all the anthracite coal and oil, as well as those producing more than half of the manganese and one-third of the lead.

In regard to coal and oil, the State also assumed the right to grant prospecting and mining privileges to those it considered the most "qualified," regardless of the priority of application. At least one qualification seemed to be that despite the Act of Algeciras, the grantee should be French.[10]

Finally, in 1951, the 1914 definition of the ownership of minerals was changed. All solid combustibles, metals and metalloids, nitrates and salts, hydrocarbons, mica, and phosphates, regardless of the method by which they were mined, were made the property of the State. Thus there was an important departure from the former position that ores of whatever nature were the property of the surface owners if they could be mined by the open-pit process.

There was, however, one limitation on the law of 1951. It had previously been provided that Berber customary law must be respected; thus if certain minerals were considered under this law as the property of the tribe, regardless of how they were mined, their ownership did not automatically revert to the State. All that was required to accomplish the latter, however, was a special *dahir* that, in effect, authorized the disregard of the customary law. In such a case, the native owners were to be indemnified by the mining concessionnaires.[11]

Such was the development of the mining regulations under the protectorate. It was a development noteworthy for the nationalization of the principal mineral resources; for the extension of the *économie mixte;* and for a series of measures designed to give the State the right to dispose of all the important minerals in such a way as to limit their exploitation to the French. Article 112 of the Act of Algeciras, upheld in 1914, was completely cast aside.

OPERATION OF THE MINES

Twelve mines and a handful of oil wells supplied the bulk of the eight minerals that were worked in important quantities in Morocco under the French. All phosphate mining was carried on at Khouribga, southeast of Casablanca, and Youssefiah (Louis Gentil), east of Safi. All of the coal came from Djerada, south of Oujda, and virtually all of the oil from the area south of Sidi

Slimane. Four mines — Bou Beker and Touissit, south of Oujda, and Aouli and Mibladen, near Midelt — provided 85 per cent of the lead that was produced; and the first two also furnished the bulk of the zinc. Practically all the manganese was mined at Bou Arfa, near the Algerian border, and at Imini and Tiouine, in the High Atlas above Ouarzazate. Finally, all of the cobalt came from Bou Azzer, south of Ouarzazate, and almost all of the iron ore from Ait Amar, near Khouribga.[12]

The two phosphate mines were, of course, exploited by the State. The oil fields were controlled largely by the *B.R.P.M.* and the French government, with only a small share held by private interests. An alliance between the *B.R.P.M.* and the French government was again found in the coal mine at Djerada; this time, however, a half interest was held by private concerns, including a Belgian company, *Ougrée Marihaye.*

The *Banque de Paris et des Pays-Bas* had heavy mining interests in Morocco. It held a controlling share of *Pennaroya*, a company which, together with the *B.R.P.M.*, mined the lead deposits at Aouli and Mibladen and also had an interest in the manganese deposits at Bou Arfa. The *Banque de Paris* was also represented in the mines through its control of the *Compagnie Générale du Maroc*, which, along with the Epinat-Herchell Group, controlled *Omnium Nord-Africain.* Included in the many activities of the latter company was the exploitation of the manganese deposits at Tiouine. In addition, *Omnium Nord-Africain* carried on the mining of cobalt at Bou Azzer, in collaboration with the Glaoua family of Marrakech.[13]

The manganese deposits at Imini were shared by the Mokta al Hadid Company with the *B.R.P.M.* (This was the largest holding of the latter organization.) The management of this mine combined with *Omnium Nord-Africain* at nearby Tiouine to form a trucking line which carried the ore from both mines over the Atlas to the railhead at Marrakech.

The lead and zinc deposits at Bou Beker, the largest in Morocco, were mined by a firm controlled by the Walter Group, and one which remained largely aloof from the interests of the *Banque de Paris.*[14] The deposits of iron ore at Ait Amar and those of lead and zinc at Touissit were also privately worked, the latter wholly by another Belgian firm, the *Compagnie Royale Asturienne des Mines.*

The exploitation of minerals in Morocco, then, was characterized not only by limited non-French interests and almost unlimited State control, but by the concentration of private control among relatively few firms. Deconcentration of this control through the mining of heretofore unexploited deposits was unlikely without drastic changes in the laws, for prospecting permits were monopolized by the same firms that have been listed above.[15]

MINERALS AND THE MOROCCAN ECONOMY

The enumeration of the minerals found in Morocco would suggest that the country had a sound resource base for heavy industry. Closer examination reveals, however, that such was not the case. Djerada coal, for example, was anthracite and not suited to coking use; in addition, the iron ore at Ait Amar was low-grade, with many impurities. Production costs of iron and steel, making use of imported coal, would have been too high, compared with world prices; in fact, production would have been impossible without the high tariff protection which the Act of Algeciras had disallowed. (This was one area where the French had only limited success in by-passing the Act.) With protection, high production costs would have served to narrow further the already limited Moroccan market for iron and steel products.[16]

Failing the development of heavy industry, Morocco exported the bulk of its mineral products, largely in the raw state. The costs of transporting these products from the mines to the ports were both high and rigid, except possibly in the case of phosphates and perhaps also of Djerada coal.[17] As a result of this fact and of the pressures of competition on the world market, transport costs represented a very large proportion of total costs. Manganese is a case in point. Ore from the mines at Imini and Tiouine had to be carried by truck for a distance of about 175 kilometers over the High Atlas to Marrakech, whence it was transshipped by rail to Casablanca. Even the construction of an aerial conveyor system, eliminating a particularly difficult part of the truck journey, did little to reduce the share of transport costs in the total cost per ton of the manganese delivered to the Casablanca docks from an average of 75 per cent.[18]

Total costs of Moroccan mineral products were thus relatively inflexible, not an enviable situation when one considers the wide swings in world prices. Nonetheless, production under the protectorate developed to the point where, in 1951, minerals accounted for 82.7 per cent of all Morocco's exports by weight, and 36.8 per cent by value.[19]

The commercial development of Morocco's mineral resources dated largely from the period following the First World War. From the beginning, the phosphates led the way; production of this one mineral rose from a few tons in 1921 to 1,828,000 in 1930. Far behind in the latter year wère manganese (16,000 tons), lead (7,000 tons), and zinc (1,000 tons).[20] No sooner had the mining industry begun to demonstrate signs of considerable promise, however, than adversity struck, in the form of the world economic crisis. Phosphate production was cut by almost 50 per cent in 1931, and other mines either closed down completely or drastically reduced their level of operations. Not until the last years of the decade did production begin to rise again; and only a few years later, the Second World War and the resulting shortages of capital equipment and loss of contact with markets brought another halt to the development of Morocco's mining industry.

It was during the years after the Second World War that mineral production in Morocco made its greatest strides. Heavy world demand for raw materials meant that high-cost Moroccan products could enter the market. At the same time, Marshall Plan aid made it possible to reduce costs somewhat by modernizing the capital equipment of the mines and improving transportation facilities. The development continued to be paced by phosphate mining, as the 1952 production figures for the eight major minerals show:[21]

	Weight (in metric tons)	F.O.B. value at ports (in million francs)
Phosphates	3,953,098	17,868
Lead	115,269	8,795
Zinc	51,409	2,324
Manganese	426,316	6,363
Coal	460,000	2,344
Iron	650,500	1,594
Petroleum	101,027	1,010
Cobalt	9,136	914

Domestic consumption of Morocco's mineral production was confined largely to oil and coal — all of the former and about three-quarters of the latter. In addition, around 100,000 tons of phosphates were retained for domestic use. The rest was exported to European countries, principally West Germany, Spain, and the United Kingdom. West Germany and the United Kingdom also took all Morocco's iron ore production. Anthracite was exported to Italy and other countries along the north rim of the Mediterranean basin, and the zinc went to France. In addition, France's needs for lead, manganese, and cobalt were filled entirely by Moroccan output, the rest of which went to the United States; in this instance, at least, the Moroccan and French economies proved to be complementary.

Phosphates, of course, were the backbone of the export trade in minerals; and their sales, at the same time, were heavily dependent on the fortunes of agriculture in the receiving countries. The precipitous drop in output the year following the peak of 1930 showed how quickly the market could change. Over the long run, however, it would seem that demand could only increase, as more and better fertilizers are needed to maintain the productivity of long-tilled European soils. The high phosphate content of its rock, which is roughly equal to the Florida deposits and is exceeded only by those in the Soviet Union, puts Morocco in an especially favorable position over its competitors in the long-term struggle for markets. Full short-term exploitation of this position was inhibited during the protectorate years, however, by cartel arrangements with producers of lower-content rock in Algeria and Tunisia.

Unlike the Moroccan phosphate mines, those in Algeria and Tunisia were privately owned. During the twenties, there was little price competition among the North African producers; the European market was firm and Morocco's capacity had not yet been fully developed. The trouble came with the crisis of the thirties. The decline in demand appeared at a time when Moroccan output approached the combined production of the Algerian and Tunisian mines. To make matters worse, American phosphate producers began an invasion of the European market when their domestic market declined; and their position in the former was strengthened by the devaluation of the dollar in 1933. The Soviets also added to the price decline in their drive for foreign exchange. During the same period, the British market was almost completely closed by the devaluation of the pound and the consequent shift to Empire sources of phosphates.

Confronted by severely shrinking markets, the Algerian and Tunisian producers formed in 1933–34 a sales cartel, to which the *Office Chérifien des Phosphates* was associated. The organization exhibited all of the general characteristics of a cartel, e.g., quotas and delivery schedules for the members, penalties for exceeding quotas, and an equalization fund. In addition, agreements were entered into with producers in Egypt and Oceania whereby the access of these countries to the European market was limited, in return for a similar limitation on North African producers in the Japanese market. During the early years of the recovery, however, European demand for high-grade rock was met by the Soviet Union, which had refused to make any agreement limiting its shipments. The possibility of Morocco's sharing significantly in this market was ruled out by the policy adopted by the cartel which called for pushing sales of low-grade Algerian and Tunisian rock at the expense of the Moroccan products.

In 1942, during the Vichy regime, the Moroccan Phosphate Bureau became a full member of the cartel. The new yearly schedule of production instituted at this time provided that the Moroccan quota be gradually increased until it exceeded the total of those for Algeria and Tunisia. The growth of Moroccan production after 1942 and the concurrent decline of Algerian and Tunisian output suggest that the operations of the cartel were considerably more favorable for Morocco under this arrangement than they had been in the early years of the organization. However, there can be no doubt that Moroccan production would have been somewhat greater without the limitations placed upon it by the cartel.

From the financial point of view, the exploitation of minerals by the State was eminently successful as a few figures will illustrate. The government made an initial investment in the Phosphate Bureau of 36 million francs, a figure which was later increased from retained earnings. At the same time, the Bureau was able to contribute 635 million francs to the government in the following ten years, and indirectly approximately 325 million. Another indication of the profitability of phosphate production is found in the results for 1930, when exports amounted to 247 million francs and the direct contribution to the protectorate budget was over half that amount. In addition, the Bureau paid taxes, financed the B.R.P.M., and gave a large volume of business to the railroad and the port of Casablanca.[22] Finally, the Bureau spent millions on salaries, wages, and supplies from local vendors. Needless to say, the phosphate monopoly occupied a crucial place in Moroccan economic life, not only as a generator of income and public revenues internally but as a source of foreign exchange.

Revenues to the State from other mineral resources were comparatively minor. As a risk-taker in an area where discoveries, excluding the phosphates, were not impressive, the B.R.P.M. made a relatively small contribution to the treasury. Furthermore, fees for exploitation rights or for concessions were not large, and a 5 per cent tax on mineral exports, in some cases waived, did not produce a great deal of revenue.

The bulk of Moroccan mineral production was not only exported, but exported in the raw state. The 100,000 or so tons of phosphates retained in Morocco each year were processed either at a superphosphate plant in Casablanca or at three smaller hyperphosphate plants in the country. Some lead was smelted at Oued al Heimer, near Oujda, and there was an oil refinery at Sidi Kacem (Petitjean). These operations were all relatively minor, however, and additional employment opportunities afforded by giving the minerals "value added" through further processing were largely passed by.

Despite the increasing importance of minerals in Morocco's export accounts in the years after the war, the number of people engaged in mining itself did not rise significantly. Expansion of production was brought about principally through increased mechanization. As was shown in Chapter II, only slightly more than 21,000 people — or seven-tenths of one per cent of the working population — were employed in the mines in 1952.[23] A tenth of these people were Europeans; of 3,000,000 Moroccans reported in the labor force, only 19,000 were miners. Thus even the expansion of existing facilities or the exploitation of heretofore untapped deposits in response to increasing world demand would not have been likely to generate sufficient employment to benefit materially the Moroccan labor force, even with an increase in secondary activities such as the railroad and the ports.

THE DEVELOPMENT OF LIGHT INDUSTRY

While the resource complex of Morocco precluded the development of heavy industry, it permitted a limited amount of light industry. The processing of products from agriculture and fishing was the logical extension of those activities from the resource side. For example, the canning of vegetables and especially of sardines became an important Moroccan industry. Subsidiary to the latter, an olive oil industry developed, again making use of local products. Flour mills, breweries, and wineries also appeared, to complement the grainfields and vineyards. In the realm of minerals, in addition to the processing activities associated with ores mentioned in the previous section, there emerged an industry of cement manufacture. All of these activities contributed "value added" to local primary products.

A resource complex, however, cannot be discussed without reference to the character of demand, both domestic and foreign. On the domestic side, the Moroccan market was scarcely homogeneous in its demand characteristics, existing as it did within the framework of the plural society. The term "plural society" implies in itself differences in tastes among the groups, owing to cultural dissimilarities; it implies, as well, differences in economic status and therefore in real per capita incomes. In the case of Morocco, the differences arising from cultural dissimilarities were narrowed somewhat, as Moroccans, through contact, acquired European tastes. The persistence of distinctions in matters of economic status and per capita incomes, however, perpetuated the dual nature of the domestic market.

This dualism in the character of local demand served to divide the various types of light industry found in Morocco into two fairly distinct categories, including those depending wholly or partially on raw materials obtained from abroad. Sugar refineries and textile mills, both of which relied on foreign sources of supply, mainly served the Moroccan segment of the population. Wineries and breweries, on the other hand, supplied the European segment only. The same also held true, in general, for the canneries, and also for the cement industry, which supplied a burgeoning construction industry building largely for Europeans. Equipment repair shops, another activity depending on materials from abroad, primarily served the European owners of plant and rolling stock. Only in flour mills do we find an industry which depended in any substantial way on both Moroccans and Europeans for its domestic market.[24]

In general, light industry in Morocco did not look beyond Morocco itself for markets. Indeed, local production often had to be supplemented by imports from abroad to meet local demand. There were, however, two notable exceptions: wineries and canneries, both of which produced far in excess of local requirements for an almost exclusively European clientele. The struggle to obtain a foreign market for Moroccan wine has previously been described;[25] and we shall see shortly what the outlets for canned fish were.

The inventory of light industrial products manufactured in Morocco is not long. In value terms, flour, sugar, cement, textiles, and canned fish (excluding wine, which was discussed above) are by far the most important items. A brief summary of the development of production of these five products follows.

FLOUR MILLING

The rapid growth of a European population in Morocco created an increasing local demand for white flour, and the expansion of soft wheat cultivation supplied the raw material. In addition, the secular increase of Moroccans living in the urban areas added to the domestic demand. On these developments rested the growth of flour milling.

During the First World War and the first eight years of the twenties, the industry developed without serious competition. Shortages during and after the war gave Moroccan production the protection that the open-door provisions of the treaties disallowed. However, it was in this period (1923) that wheat quotas were granted by France, with the result that the domestic price of Moroccan wheat increased. The milling industry was therefore in an especially vulnerable position when the protection afforded by the circumstances came to an end. The reckoning came by the latter part of 1928, when world over-production resulted in a flow of both wheat and flour into Morocco. High domestic production costs, owing to expensive local wheat and lack of plant economies, of course precluded sales in the world market; indeed, price concessions had to be made to hold domestic customers. This happy situation for the consumer was short-lived, however; the 1929 *dahir* which banned wheat imports also excluded flour.[26]

With the new form of protection, the Moroccan milling industry continued to develop. In 1953, almost 265,000 tons of soft wheat and 79,000 tons of hard wheat were processed.[27] High-cost production of a price inelastic basic food, however, meant an increase in the cost of living in a country where purchasing power was already low.

SUGAR REFINING

The staple items in the Moroccan diet are grain products, tea, and sugar. Per capita consumption of sugar in Morocco is among the highest in the world. Domestic sugar refining was begun in the late twenties by *Cosuma*, an organization under the aegis of a large French refining combine with headquarters in Marseille. The *Banque de Paris* also held a financial interest in *Cosuma*.

Like the milling industry, sugar refining had a broad, price inelastic market. And like milling, it prospered steadily until the drop in world prices in the late twenties and early thirties, when large amounts of foreign products began to appear on the Moroccan market. Effective limitation of foreign competition was not as easily achieved in the case of sugar, however. A 1933 law established compensatory taxes on sugar imported into Morocco,[28] but protests by the signatories of the Act of Algeciras forced their withdrawal soon after. Other means of subsidization were subsequently found; long-term postponement of the payment of customs duties for raw sugar and an exemption from consumption taxes on sugar used in beer manufacture are examples.[29]

Compensatory taxes were reinstituted in 1950, and this time the protest was unsuccessful. The tax applied to imports of raw as well as refined sugar, but all sugar from countries in the franc zone was exempt. Thus protection was afforded not only to refiners in Morocco but to those in France doing business in Morocco. Furthermore, high-price raw sugar from Réunion, Martinique, and France itself was given an advantage in competition with sugar from Cuba. As a result, a kilogram of sugar cost 130 francs in Casablanca in 1950, as compared to 70 francs in then international Tangier.[30]

At the time of independence, Morocco had two sugar refineries with a combined annual capacity of around 200,000 tons. Production totaled only 158,000 tons in 1952.[31] During the year, 83,000 tons of raw sugar were imported tax-free from the franc zone and 105,000 tons, subject to tax, from Cuba. In addition, imports of refined sugar amounted to 60,000 tons, 60 per cent of which came from France.[32] Whether emanating from the franc zone or not, sugar sold in Morocco at franc zone prices. Compensatory taxes ensured that. As with milling, high-cost producers were subsidized by low-income consumers.

CEMENT MANUFACTURE

The growth of the cement industry is another story of indirect protection. During the twenties, a period of a Moroccan building boom as well as of general economic expansion, local cement manufacture grew without difficulty. Although costs of production in Morocco were higher than abroad, the local producers were able to compete satisfactorily with foreign producers in the domestic market. With the depression of the thirties, however, the precipitous drop in ocean freight rates and falling mill prices abroad combined to bring a significant increase in cement imports at the same time that demand declined. The producers in Morocco were in trouble for the first time in their short careers.

A law early in 1933 established compensatory taxes on cement imports in instances where export subsidies in the country of origin were suspected. A principal target was Belgium, a signatory of the Act of Algeciras. Belgium promptly protested the *dahir*, along with Spain and the United States; and the protectorate government rescinded the measure within a matter of weeks. In its place, however, it adopted outright subventions and rate reductions on the Moroccan railroads which kept the local cement industry going.

The cement industry prospered during the postwar construction boom in Morocco. Of the 760,000 tons of cement used in the country in 1953, local industry supplied 610,000.[33] The principal producer was the *Société des Chaux et Ciments*, a French-owned firm controlled by the *Banque de Paris*.

TEXTILE MANUFACTURING

Prior to 1939, the domestic textile industry was largely in the hands of the artisans, who struggled to compete with imports of machine-made goods from abroad throughout the period between the wars. France was the leading supplier, although its position was threatened briefly in the thirties by the Japanese. Domestic machine-made production in this period was confined to two factories carding wool for rug making; there were no factories working cotton.

During the Second World War, Morocco was thrown back on its own resources, with the result that several cotton mills were established, which were expanded when French flight capital flowed into Morocco after 1945. The cotton industry was centered in the port cities of Casablanca, Mohammedia (formerly Fedala), and Kenitra (Port Lyautey). It was not these cities' facilities for foreign transport that attracted the industry; production was intended entirely for the domestic market. Rather, the availability of power, of a cheap labor supply, and of complementary industries such as machine shops were the decisive factors. The locational advantages of the ports related only to Morocco, however; cotton textile production was still high-cost in comparison with foreign imports.

The postwar years were marked by trials and tribulations arising from this cost differential. The situation of the textile mills was thus similar to that of other French-established industry. There was, however, a point of difference. Much of the postwar foreign competition in textiles resulted from the existence in Casablanca of a group of American ex-servicemen who were engaged in importing goods from the United States. Textiles, particularly used clothing, figured prominently in their activities. The French regarded these businessmen as a threat to Moroccan textile mills, to French suppliers, and, lastly, to the position of the French franc.

In the inflation of the postwar years, France was engaged in an active program of exchange controls. The Moroccan and French francs were freely convertible, and were kept at par through the operation of a current account in the French treasury. For exchange controls to be fully effective in France, then, they also had to be enforced in Morocco. The methods by which the French sought to achieve the latter brought heated protests on the part of the American importers, and contributed to a clash between France and the United States that was finally taken before the International Court of Justice in 1950.[34]

General import regulations, including import licenses, had been instituted by Morocco as early as September, 1939. This was defined as an emergency wartime measure, and was agreed to as such by the United States.[35] Toward the end of the war, the United States agreed to the continuation of import licensing so long as it was a mere formality for American businessmen in Morocco. In the spring of 1947, however, the protectorate government began to deny some applications for licenses by the ex-servicemen, most of whom were importing *sans devises*, i.e., without securing an official allocation of exchange. Ostensibly, these businessmen were relying on their own dollar resources. However, the French authorities suspected that the dollars were coming from the conversion of franc earnings in the free market at Tangier, and claimed that the activities of these businessmen therefore constituted a leak in the dike of exchange controls.[36]

Regardless of the reasons for imposing restrictions on import licenses, the United States government saw the move as an act of discrimination against its nationals and lodged a protest with the protectorate government. The latter replied to American protests with a complete cessation of license grants to Americans importing without exchange allocations.

In September, 1947, the Resident-General backed down to the extent of declaring that products imported *sans devises* would be admitted if they were deemed "essential to the Moroccan economy." In March of the following year, the restrictions on those importing without allocations were further relaxed; the licensing requirement was removed for all but a limited number of products. By the end of the year, however, the requirement had once again been restored and licenses were being granted for only a small number of products.

Throughout this whole period of off-again, on-again import restrictions, the affected segment of Casablanca's American colony was vociferous in its protest. It even carried its complaint to the United States Congress, and it eventually produced results: the foreign aid bill, passed in 1950, contained a provision which, in effect, cut off aid to France because of the discrimination of the protectorate government against American businessmen in Morocco.[37] This time, France's response was to carry the controversy over American rights in Morocco to the International Court.

In its decision in 1952, the Court ruled that the licensing requirements imposed by the protectorate government were invalid, since they had been applied only to imports coming from outside the franc zone. This was deemed a violation of the most-favored-nation provision of the 1836 treaty between the United States and Morocco and also of Article 105 of the Act of Algeciras, which had restated the principle of "economic liberty without any inequality" expressed in the preamble of the Act.[38]

The Hague decision resulted in a greatly increased flow of foreign textiles into Morocco. Imports of American used clothing, for example, rose from 3,136 tons in 1952, the year of the decision, to 5,500 tons in 1954.[39] American importers did not confine themselves to used clothing, however. They also bought large quantities of Indian, Japanese, and Portuguese textiles — the last at one-half the domestic price in Portugal, by virtue of the fact that dollars were given an especially favorable rate. This of course gave the Americans a tremendous advantage over their French competitors in Morocco, who were not able to import without exchange allocations from outside of the franc zone; by 1954, American importers were handling four-fifths of all the textiles that came into the country.[40] It also meant more trouble for the high-cost local textile mills.

In the years following the World Court action, the demand for domestic textiles dropped precipitously. Mills either drastically curtailed their operations or closed their doors. In 1954, the government, in an effort to sustain this rapidly failing industry, suspended the import duties on raw materials used in textile manufacture. Early the next year, it provided that charges for electricity, a high-price item in Morocco, be rebated, and also that interest on equipment and reconversion loans be returned. Shortly thereafter, the protectorate government began to engage in import limitations once again.

A temporary import quota for textiles was ordered in March, 1955. It was claimed that this quota was compatible with the 1952 decision of the World Court, since the restriction was applicable to imports from the franc zone as well as from other areas.[41] Textile imports were divided by type into four categories, each of which was assigned an annual quota, by weight. The quota of each such category was then segregated according to the countries from which the imports were to come and also according to whether or not the imports were to be made with exchange allocations. Lastly, these quotas within quotas were divided among the importers doing business in Morocco in 1953 and 1954.

These regulations had the double purpose of aiding ailing local industry and of helping to restore the position of French textiles in the Moroccan market. Under the regulation, it was required that textiles imported by Americans henceforth had to come from the dollar area; thus their lucrative imports from Portugal and the Far East were barred. At the same time, the total quota for used clothing was set at only 1,500 tons, almost all of which required an official allocation of exchange. Thus the French found an effective way of once more curtailing the activities of American businessmen. Despite the regulations, it was estimated that, at the time of independence, the thirty-two local producers were supplying only 7,500 tons of the roughly 30,000 tons of annual textile consumption in Morocco.[42]

FISH CANNING

Fishing had been an occupation of Moroccans for centuries. The coastal area between Essaouira and the outlet of the Oued Noun was dotted with small Berber villages occupied by people attracted to a sea rich in sardines and tuna. Prior to the protectorate, however, poor transportation and lack of preserving facilities had kept the activity small; and fish consumption was largely confined to the smaller communities along the coast.

With the protectorate, the character of the fishing industry

changed. Improved inland transport broadened the marketing possibilities, and a growing European population increased the local
demand. On the production side, the industry became mechanized.
European owned motor-driven fishing boats, with greater range
and better equipment than the frail Berber craft, made their appearance. At first the new boats operated out of Casablanca and
Mohammedia, the former a fresh fish port, since there was a large
European population, the latter a canning port. Later, Safi, its harbor improved to permit the shipment of phosphates, and Agadir,
the best natural harbor in the country, became major fishing centers. Since local markets were not large, almost the entire catch at
both Safi and Agadir was destined for the canning industry.

The real growth of the industry, especially in Safi and Agadir,
came during the postwar years. It was sparked by the heavy world
demand for fish products as well as by the inflow of flight capital
to Morocco. As a consequence, the number of canning factories
increased from 44 to 193 in the years from 1938 to 1950, and the
tonnage handled by these factories rose from 15,000 to 57,000.[43]
Supply far outran effective domestic demand, so canned fish,
mostly sardines, became an important item in the export accounts.
In fact, it ranked second only to the phosphates in 1950, contributing 14 per cent of the total value of Moroccan exports that year
as compared to the phosphates' 21 per cent share.[44] Exports of
sardines fell from the all-time record of 2,466,000 cases (just under
50,000 tons) in 1950 to 1,678,000 cases (around 34,000 tons) in
1952. By 1953, however, they had recovered to slightly more than
2,000,000 cases, or approximately 40,000 tons.[45]

The annual French quota of 12,000 tons was one which the canners in Morocco would have liked to enlarge substantially and
which French producers hoped, at the very least, to keep constant.
In 1953, Morocco supplied one-third of the 1,800,000 cases of
canned fish consumed in France. This represented an almost
equally large proportion of all Moroccan exports of this product.[46] Here then was an industry the existence of which depended
in significant measure on a French quota, particularly since French
prices were roughly double those prevailing in world markets.

THE DECLINE OF TRADITIONAL INDUSTRY

Just as a diversified agriculture was developed at the expense of
traditional agriculture, so was European-type industry promoted
to the detriment of traditional industry. But the handicrafts hung

on, just as did the old modes of agriculture. The dual nature of the Moroccan economy as it developed under the protectorate was as evident in the industrial sector as elsewhere.

The reasons for the persistence of traditional forms of industry lie in the nature of the plural society. Disintegration of old forms is a necessary and normal part of economic change. For the process to be complete, however, the disintegration must be accompanied by a transition of people from old forms to new. At least two things are essential for such a transition: capital and mobility. Both were signally lacking to Moroccan artisans under the protectorate. The authorities deliberately planned and financed the new forms of industrial organization, but largely ignored the problems of the handicraft trades, leaving them — and the people to whom they meant a livelihood — to reap the consequences of an inability to adjust numbers and techniques to the changed situation.

Although the history of the handicraft trades since 1912 was one of a heavy decline in markets, each of the two world wars not only brought a temporary halt to the downward trend but even permitted a brief recovery. During the crisis of the thirties, on the other hand, the artisans were heavily hit by imports and by the loss of foreign markets. The same problems plagued them in the years after the Second World War.

The loss of markets at home and abroad arose not only from price competition but from product competition. The Moroccan artisan was the victim of a fundamental change in tastes. Thus not only were markets for the traditional articles usurped by other countries, but these markets were diminished sharply by a growing preference for Western-type goods, which the Moroccans were unable to supply.

The traditional overseas markets for the Moroccan handicraft products were Egypt and the Far East. These markets were taken over in the thirties by Japan, which, for example, was able to produce a cheaper *babouche* than Morocco and also an even cheaper Western-style shoe for the growing number of customers who were coming to prefer the latter. The opening of a limited market in France for native handicrafts only partially offset the loss to the artisans of their major overseas outlets. A duty-free French quota for Moroccan rugs was established in 1921 and was in force thereafter, with the amount of the quota set annually. Each rug going into the quota had to be stamped by the Sharifian Export Office as evidence that it met certain standards as to quality. In 1934, the stamping procedure was extended to other handicraft products entering France, but neither preferential tariff nor quota was given them.

The domestic market for handicraft products suffered from pressures similar to those encountered abroad. Stiff Japanese competition for the local trade during the thirties was felt not only by the artisans but by European manufacturers doing business in Morocco. As a result, the French, in violation of the Act of Algeciras, put restrictions on Japanese imports, limiting some and excluding others.[47] While the threat of Japanese competition was finally brought to an end by the Second World War, imports by American businessmen soon proved an effective substitute for goods from Japan, especially in the area of textiles.

In the meantime, the pattern of tastes in Morocco had changed to the point where it is doubtful if measures to limit American competition would have significantly improved the well-being of the native artisans, although the benefits to French manufacturers in both Morocco and France could have been considerable. In the matter of dress, for example, it has been estimated that by 1949 one-third of the Moroccan population was wearing shoes instead of the traditional *babouches*, one-fifth other Western clothing as well, and two-fifths a mixture of Western and Moroccan clothing.[48]

As a result of all of these developments, not only did the demand for Moroccan handicrafts decline, but the nature of the demand changed. An increasing proportion of the dwindling market for the traditional products was found among people who regarded them not as necessities but as luxuries. The rugs imported into France under the quota each year are a case in point. In addition to the European market, local demand arising from the tourist trade became important. This, of course, meant that the relatively inelastic demand curve of former days became a much more elastic one. Nevertheless, the development of this new type of market was indispensable in keeping the handicraft trades from suffering total destitution.

The fact still remains that traditional Moroccan industry suffered from acute unemployment or, at best, underemployment. Changes in markets called both for a significant exit from the trades and for improved technology among those remaining. An attempt to achieve the latter was instituted as early as 1918. In that year, Marshal Lyautey, always conscious of the political effects of economic difficulties, created the *Office des Industries d'Arts Indigènes* — later retitled *Service des Métiers et Arts Marocains*. As head of this new organization, Lyautey brought to Morocco an Algerian civil servant, Prosper Ricard, whose name was to be associated for some thirty years with the official efforts on behalf of the artisans. Among M. Ricard's activities was the establishment of schools of apprenticeship and pilot plants for the various handicraft trades. The aim was to spread new, cost-reducing techniques among the artisans, in order to permit them to maintain both their markets and their high standards of work. Credit was distributed through a *Caisse Centrale de Prévoyance* and *Caisses Régionales d'Epargne et de Crédit Artisanal*. However, the well-intentioned efforts of M. Ricard were not able to compensate for the lack of funds to carry out a program of the scope required by the situation.

The most pressing need was for a program of retraining and re-employment of the redundant labor in traditional industry, but in this area nothing was done. While entry into the trades was free and easy, exit was painfully slow. Left to their own resources, most of the artisans clung to their old trades and were reluctant to change them for the uncertain existence of wage labor in the new industry. Those who moved joined the unemployed or underemployed from the country in the urban "tin-can towns," their once-useful skills unwanted in a Western-type economy.

The decline of the handicraft trades was accompanied by a decline in the influence of the urban corporations. A 1917 law delivered to French authorities the municipal powers of the *mohtasseb*, including those over the artisan guilds. The function of price-making was also withdrawn from this official and assumed by the government. Other functions of the corporation were taken over by the *Service des Métiers et Arts*. In addition, the corporations suffered from the geographical redistribution of a considerable portion of the surviving handicraft activity from the inland cities to the ports, where the corporations were not well established. The artisans in Casablanca, for example, were not agglomerated by trade in particular quarters, as had traditionally been the case in the inland cities, but were scattered in small patches throughout the city.[49]

The breakdown of the corporations brought a disintegration of the social structure in the Moroccan cities that paralleled the detribalization that occurred in the countryside. As we have seen earlier, the people of Fez, the center of the handicraft industries as well as of Islamic culture, formed the stable element of the population in pre-protectorate Morocco. As the years of the protectorate passed, however, taking their toll of the artisans and their once all-powerful corporations, Fez lost this stability. Indeed, the city emerged under the protectorate as a major center of political unrest and provided Moroccan nationalism with its leadership.[50]

The merchants of Fez, by and large, proved more responsive to economic change than the artisans, and therefore fared better under the protectorate. Mobility requires not only the will to move in response to opportunity; it also requires capital. The Fassi merchants were fortunate in having both. As a consequence, Casablanca, Rabat, and Kenitra had their contingents of merchants from Fez who dealt not only in the traditional goods but also in European products. The small size of their shops was no indication of their worth. Although French control of the big commercial firms limited the participation of the Fassi to relatively small enterprises, the "leavings" proved to be highly lucrative.

THE URBAN LABOR FORCE

The development of mineral production — the first of the three major categories of industry just described — changed the Moroccan way of life very little. The rise of light industry and the decline of the handicrafts, on the other hand, were part and parcel of perhaps the most significant development in Morocco under the protectorate — the growth of a new economic and social order in the cities.

It was in the cities that the forces of the plural society were most vividly portrayed. The two minority segments of the population, the Europeans and the Jews, were heavily concentrated there, although far outnumbered by the Muslims. The Europeans were, of course, the animators of the urban economy; their influence in the cities was much more pervasive than in the rural area. They were responsible both for the shift in urban concentration from the inland areas to the coast and for the increased role of urban areas in the country's economy. It was they who opened the ports, built the factories, and established the large commercial enterprises.

The principal contribution of Muslims to this process was men. The traditional south–north migration reached a greatly increased tempo under the protectorate, with the result that there developed an urban labor pool of vast dimensions. Even the Jews, although traditionally urban-dwellers for the most part, contributed to the movement from the country to the cities. Thus industry and other urban economic activities were forced to assume an increasing share of the responsibility for providing employment for the Moroccan people.

THE MUSLIM IN THE CITIES

The Muslim and the Jew each played a role in the cities that was quite distinct in all of its major aspects. Thus the workings of the plural society dictate a basic division in discussing the life of the urban Moroccan. We shall begin with the most numerous segment of the society — the Muslims.

The bulk of the population increase in Morocco's western cities was the result of the migration from the immediate countryside of Muslims forced off their land by colonization, population pressures, or both. But population pressures, and European farmers, were present in areas of lower population density as well. In fact, the mountains, the desert, and the valley of the Sous made an even greater contribution to the urban population, in terms of their total human resources, than did the western plains. It has been estimated that as much as 80 per cent of the male population in certain areas of the south migrated to the north.[51]

The character of the migration depended to a considerable extent on the geographical origin of the migrants. The plains people, for example, were likely to move to the cities permanently, while those from the south were more often temporary residents. The latter generally moved north without their families, whom they hoped to support by remittances. In addition, it was their dream to amass enough savings for the purchase of a plot of ground "back home" — an incentive for migration among land-hungry peasants anywhere. Whatever their intentions, however, a fairly substantial portion of the "transients" remained in the cities definitively, thus joining the ranks of the *déracinés*.

A notable exception was found among the Chleuh, particularly the members of the Ammeln tribe from Tafraout, in the Anti-Atlas. A number of families from this area owned grocery stores in the cities along the coast as far north as Tangier. The management of a store was rotated among the male members of the family.[52] In this way, no individual was away from home too long, and family relationships as well as the tribal structure were maintained. The large, well-constructed homes at Tafraout, which were far more elaborate than would be possible on an income derived solely from local resources, testified to the success of some Ammeln grocers.

The movement to the cities had a profound influence in the rural areas. When migration was of a permanent nature, as was most often the case, the whole social structure of the affected area — based on the tribe — was broken down. In the case of temporary migration, there was actually a reduction of cultivated land in some areas, in the absence of a large proportion of the able-bodied males. On the other hand, animal husbandry was often expanded, since this was an occupation suitable for the very young or very old. In any event, remittances from migrant relatives became indispensable to the maintenance of a subsistence level of living in southern Morocco. The most far-reaching effect of temporary migration, however, resulted from the return of tribal members, exposed to European living levels, to their homes. In this way, the pattern of "citified" wants was transmitted to even the remotest country areas.

In the meantime, what happened to the migrants, whether temporary or permanent, whether from the mountains, desert, or plains, when they reached the cities? They arrived totally unskilled in the context of a modern industrial society. They were, in addition, largely illiterate. But they were eager to find work, and to better themselves and their families, both economically and socially. Unfortunately, the opportunities awaiting them in the cities were very limited. They became part of a huge, unskilled urban labor pool from which relatively few, e.g., the Chleuh grocers, were able to emerge.

The rules of the plural society severely restricted the occupational mobility of the Muslim in the city. The existence of a European *petite bourgeoisie* meant that even the semi-skilled jobs were in demand by the dominant minority. Under these circumstances, it is perhaps not surprising that little was done to encourage the urban Muslim to acquire modern skills or to put to use such skills as he might have developed.

Even at the lowest level of employment, however, the lot of the Muslim was highly uncertain. His principal opportunities lay in unskilled jobs in industry or transportation, or in performing any of a wide variety of menial services required in an urban area. But while an urban complex of not insignificant proportions was developed in Morocco under the protectorate, the population had grown even more rapidly. Thus there were simply too many men in the urban labor pool for the jobs available. As a result, members of the urban proletariat were plagued by unemployment and underemployment, just as the artisans (a number of whom, as we have seen, traded their plight for that of the proletariat). A further result was that wage rates for unskilled labor were without exception low. The minimum wage for industrial workers in the Casablanca area, for example, was brought by an increase in 1956 to 67 francs an hour, or 536 francs (around $1.35 at the then-current free market value of the franc) for an eight-hour day.[53] In other areas, the official minimum was even lower.

Any attempts on the part of the members of the urban proletariat to improve their lot through the formation of labor unions were largely ruled out under the protectorate. Unions were flatly prohibited until 1936, at which time the right to organize was given to Europeans alone. Not until 1950 were Moroccans officially permitted to join the European unions, although a considerable number had in fact been admitted before this time. However, the unions, many of which were affiliated with the Communist-dominated French unions continued to be controlled by the Europeans, so that the Moroccans stood to benefit from their membership only in those few instances where their interests coincided with those of the controlling minority. The real significance of Moroccan union membership during the protectorate lay not in the economic sphere but the political. Organizing experience gained by the Moroccan trade unionists served them in good stead during the fight for independence. After the Casablanca riots of 1952, the leadership went underground where it played a crucial role in the struggle. Emerging in 1955, the leaders formed the *Union Marocaine de Travail* which claimed 600,000 members by the following year. In any event, this union became a major force in both Moroccan economic and political life.

The plight of the Muslim in the cities was nowhere better exemplified than in his housing. Under the rules laid down by Marshal Lyautey, who decreed that the European quarters of each town be separate from the *medina*, or Moroccan quarter, the development of housing to accommodate the influx of Muslims to the cities was limited by the proximity of the two quarters. In addition, the newcomers did not have the necessary capital to build permanent housing, and adequate government assistance was not forthcoming. There were two consequences: overcrowding of the *medinas;* and the growth of "tin-can towns," or *bidonvilles,* on the outskirts of each urban area.

Contrary to the information contained in official publications, the problem of housing for Moroccans was not born during the Second World War, when construction came to a standstill; rather it antedates the war by many years. A *bidonville* was to be found in Rabat, for example, as early as 1927.[54] It would be more correct to say that there was little official cognizance of the housing problem prior to the war, and that the wartime suspension of building merely aggravated an already serious situation.

The population of the "tin-can towns" in Casablanca was estimated at around 75,000 (roughly a fifth of the Muslim population of the city) in 1950.[55] Public housing, including the model development of Ain Chok, was developed on a small scale and was able to accommodate only a small minority of the Muslim population. Thus the great mass of the people outside of Casablanca's *bidonvilles* were found either in the old *medina* near the port or in the new *medina,* which dated from the twenties and lay east of the European town.

The "houses" in the *bidonvilles* were made of old packing cases, bits of cloth, and discarded gasoline cans. Any construction in concrete was forbidden by the authorities, because this would have suggested permanence. Even the construction of a new shack required official permission, which was not readily given. As a consequence, spatial expansion of the towns was limited somewhat. Nevertheless, as the population continued to increase, more living quarters were surreptitiously created in the courtyards of what appeared to be single dwelling units. Furthermore, rooms in the shacks were sublet to new arrivals to the point where it was a rare family that had more than one room. The hazards to health that resulted from overcrowding were further heightened by the absence of sewage disposal facilities and the rarity of water points.

When one considers the quality of the "housing" in the *bidonvilles,* rents were high. According to Adam, the rentals paid by 180 families, each living in one room at Ben Msik at Casablanca, averaged 473 francs per month at the end of 1949. At the same time, the cost of building a one-room shack of frame construction and walled with tin cans was 3,500 francs; a "deluxe" model, made entirely of old boxes, cost from 10,000 to 15,000 francs. Thus the annual return on a 15,000-franc shack which rented for 500 francs a month was 40 per cent.[56] High returns on such investments were not a new phenomenon; in the Douar Debbagh *bidonville* at Rabat, returns to owners ran as high as 80 per cent a year in the thirties.[57] The tenant, however, had no choice. He had no capital with which to purchase a shack and no alternative to living in one.

The pattern of one room per family also permeated the *medinas*. Houses that previously were dwellings for single families now sheltered at least as many families as there were rooms, with people often living in jerry-built structures in the courtyards. Running water was scarce; and where it existed, there was only one faucet for the entire house. With the continued crowding of families into the limited space of the *medinas*, syphilis, trachoma, and tuberculosis were even more prevalent here than in the "tin-can towns." [58]

The effects of the housing shortage also extended to what public housing had been constructed for Moroccans. High construction costs meant high rents, with the consequence that the occupants tended to sublet rooms. Thus, even here, a pattern of one room per family was rapidly developed.[59] All in all, living conditions for the Muslims in the cities worsened considerably, as their numbers increased. The average member of the urban proletariat was underemployed, poorly paid, and poorly housed.

Although reliable figures are always difficult to come by in Morocco, there is some quantitative evidence concerning the economic situation of the average Moroccan family. In 1956 — and it should be emphasized that there had been considerable inflation since 1949 when Adam compiled his figures — the average family income in a "tin-can town" was estimated at 14,000 francs ($35) per month or, assuming an average family of five, $7 per capita; this works out to $84 per year. It was further estimated that 20 per cent of the urban population lived in *bidonvilles*. That the Muslim living in the *medina* was little better off is suggested by the same author when he calculated that 80 per cent of urban families had an income of less than 15,000 francs per month.[60] An indication of the distribution of income between the segments of the plural society is offered by Page when he notes that the "Muslim sector, which constitutes 95 per cent of the population, certainly does not receive 50 per cent of the income." [61] Another indicator is Waterston's estimate of $190 as annual per capita income for the whole population in 1958 which, when juxtaposed to the $84 figure cited above, suggests that the gap between European and Moroccan incomes is wide indeed.[62]

The Position of the Jews

The role of the Jews in the plural society has been outlined in Chapter II, so we need do little more here than summarize their place in the economic and social structure of Morocco's cities.[63]

Like the Muslims, Jews streamed to Morocco's western cities, particularly Casablanca, during the years of the protectorate. Some came from the *mellahs* of the south; others abandoned the inland cities as commerce shifted to the coast. Unlike the Muslims, a high proportion of the Jewish migrants came to Casablanca and neighboring cities skilled in the ways of commerce or in the handicraft trades.

To this basic advantage of the Jewish migrant over the Muslim must be added the benefits resulting from the spirit of mutual aid found among Jews both in Morocco and elsewhere. The newcomers to the cities were aided immeasurably in establishing themselves in their new surroundings by those who had preceded them. Furthermore, the work of the *Alliance Israélite Universelle* in the areas of education and medical care was indispensable. American Jewry also took an active interest in the welfare of Moroccan Jews in the later years; the establishment of a trade school in Casablanca was one manifestation of its concern.[64] Undoubtedly the most important advantage of all was the favoritism shown the Jews by those in control of the country during the years of the protectorate. With the exception of the period during the Vichy regime, the Jews in Morocco's cities enjoyed a freedom of movement and of opportunity, virtually unknown among the Muslims, which gave them wide scope for their considerable talents.

As a result of all these factors, the urban Jews were far better off than the Muslims on almost all counts; in fact, many Jewish merchants and bankers amassed sizable fortunes under the French regime. Many, too, made a successful transition from rural areas to white collar jobs in European-controlled business or government offices. Even the average Jewish artisan probably fared better than his Muslim competitor. Relatively few Jews were to be found in the ranks of the urban proletariat, and those who did were assured by French policy of a higher wage than Muslims for equal work.

There is, however, one area in which the Jews fared even more poorly than the urban Muslims — in the matter of housing. No *bidonvilles* sprang up to shelter Jewish migrants to the cities. Thus the only escape valve for the *mellahs* was the European quarters of cities. This avenue was indeed utilized by many of the more

successful members of the Jewish community, resulting in a movement almost unknown among the Muslims in the *medinas*. Even
so, the influx of immigrants to the traditional Jewish quarter far
more than offset the exodus; as a consequence, there was overcrowding in Jewish quarters that was also without parallel among
the Muslims. Halpérin, writing in 1952 of Casablanca, noted that
the population density of the city as a whole was approximately
6,000 per square kilometer, while in the principal Muslim quarters
there were 92,000 people per square kilometer. The comparable
figure for Casablanca's *mellah*, however, was no less than 215,000.[65]

MOROCCANS IN FRANCE

Not all of the movement from the south of Morocco to urban
areas had its terminus within the country. To the contrary, many
Moroccans found their way, at least temporarily, to the cities of
France — Paris in particular. Estimated at 12,000 in 1947, these men
formed, together with migrants from Algeria and Tunisia, an
urban proletariat which was significant to French industrial activity.[66] They also played an important role in their country of
origin, both in their absence and after their return.

Moroccan emigration to France dated from World War I. Although most of the migrants came from a rural milieu, relatively
few went into agricultural employment in France. They were attracted, rather, to the cities and to the unskilled industrial jobs
which France, with a low population/resource ratio, was generally
not able to fill with its own nationals. France incurred relatively
little social cost by the presence of the Moroccans; as aliens, they
were not eligible for the benefits to which French workers, or
even Algerians, were entitled. In addition, the migrants were all in
the most productive years of their lives, so that there were neither
young nor old to become public charges.

Another advantage to France was that the Moroccans were
available or dispensable as the needs of the economy dictated. The
size of the inward flow was fairly closely regulated, and the return
flow was largely self-regulating. When the necessity to cut back
the labor force arose, the Moroccans, as marginal labor, were
among the first to be laid off; and in the absence of employment
opportunities, they returned to their homes. When times were
good, on the other hand, the outward flow was small.

Thus Moroccan migration to France was one of ebb and flow,
depending, with one exception, on business conditions in France.
The exception resulted from a situation that developed in Mo-

rocco in the late twenties. Capital expansion during this period
brought a sharp rise in wage rates. Since the expansion was predicated on low wages, the situation was viewed as an acute labor
shortage in Morocco, and emigration to France was banned. By
the time the ban had been lifted, the depression in France had
eliminated employment opportunities there.[67]

In addition to the possibility of finding a fairly steady job in
Paris, rather than perhaps only intermittent work or even no work
at all in Casablanca, wage differentials between France and Morocco were an incentive to emigrate. Depending on the type of
job, wages in France were often two or three times as high as in
Morocco. Of course living costs in France were also higher, but
not enough to negate the difference in wages. Nevertheless, the
North African workers in France underwent severe privations in
order to send remittances home. Eight or ten workers living in a
small, unheated room was not uncommon, and expenditures on
food and clothing were kept at the barest of minimums. As a result, the North African quarters in and around Paris became dis-
ease-ridden slums.[68]

The social repercussions of this migration of Moroccan workers
was much greater in their own country than in France. Remittances from workers in Paris, like those from workers in Casablanca, were an essential complement to real yields for families in
the south of Morocco. The perpetuation of life there came to
depend on both forms of income; and the coincidence of depression and drought meant famine. In the longer run, the Moroccans
who lived and worked in France were a major source of political
discontent at home. They joined with the migrants to Casablanca
and other coastal cities to give the Moroccan nationalist movement
its mass support. And like those who migrated to Casablanca, they
spread discontent to those areas of the country not directly exposed to European influences.

Thus the development under the protectorate of a large urban
proletariat — part of it in France — served to hasten the demise of
this latter-day form of colonization. French control of Morocco
brought benefits to Frenchmen and, to a lesser extent, to the Jews.
The flow of Muslims between the country and the cities brought
to the great mass of the people a rising awareness of these benefits,
benefits in which it could have a chance to share only by changing
the form and spirit of government.

V

THE DEVELOPMENT OF TRANSPORT, TRADE, AND PUBLIC FINANCE

We have now examined the major economic changes wrought by the French in Morocco since 1912; and we have also noted many of the consequences for the Moroccan people. Reduced to its simplest terms, the economic change in Morocco under the protectorate amounted to an opening up of the country. Prior to 1912, as we have seen, Morocco's was a relatively closed economy, and a real one. The French contribution to economic "progress" was to bring the country a money economy, one predicated on a volume of domestic and foreign commerce unheard of in pre-protectorate days.

The development of a commercial agriculture and mineral production in the countryside and of a modern industrial and commercial complex in the urban areas necessitated a revolution in the means of transport. The new economy was the end product of the opening up of the country; the development of a modern transportation system was the means.

DIRT TRACKS TO STEEL RAILS

Improvements in inland transport were the first order of business for the French when they came to Morocco. The existing system was totally inadequate for the task of pacifying the country; artillery pieces, for example, were not readily divisible into camel-sized loads. It was military even more than economic considerations, therefore, that dictated the course taken in developing transport facilities in the early days of the protectorate. Military and economic needs were to some extent coextensive, however, since it was the economically interesting part of Morocco which was the first target of the pacification.

The French were immediately faced with two obstacles to the rapid development of effective transport. The first was provided by the Germans, the second by the First World War. The Franco-German Treaty of 1911 had stipulated that no railroads for commercial use be built before the completion of the Tangier–Fez line; in this way, the Germans hoped to keep an outlet for their trade in central Morocco. The treaty did, however, allow the construction of narrow gauge military railroads; but under no circumstances were commercial products to be carried over these lines.[1]

The outbreak of the war relieved France of this diplomatic restraint on railroad development, and the Treaty of Versailles later absolved her permanently from all agreements with the Germans concerning Morocco. However, the war also brought shortages of capital goods, so that construction of railroads continued to be confined to narrow gauge roads for several years. Limited though it was, this construction was an integral part of the Lyautey-type pacification. Keeping subdued tribes busy on public works projects considerably reduced the possibility of their slipping back into revolt.

Much greater effort was devoted to the development of a highway network in the early days of the protectorate. The Franco-German Treaty of 1911 had made no mention of highways, and the limited need for capital equipment in their construction meant that the war was not a particularly inhibiting factor. At the same time, the great need for manpower in road building dovetailed well with the Lyautey policy. It should be remembered also that the motorcar was already well developed by 1912; and the war years brought considerable reductions in its real costs, and consequently great increases in its acceptance. From the beginning, the automobile offered serious competition to the Moroccan railroads for freight and passenger traffic; and the competition stiffened with the rapid development of both forms of transportation after the war.

RAILROADS

The first segment of the Moroccan rail network, connecting Casablanca with Rabat, was a product of pre-protectorate French activity. Begun in September, 1911, this narrow gauge road was opened to traffic in December. Traveling time between the two cities was cut from more than two days to a few hours. At the same time, the line demonstrated the possibilities of reduction in the cost of distance. Savings realized from moving military goods by rail instead of by camel were estimated to equal the entire cost of this line after only eight months of its operation.[2] In 1915, when France was no longer encumbered by agreements with the Germans, the Casablanca–Rabat line and other narrow gauge roads subsequently constructed for military use were opened to commercial traffic, thus making substantial savings in freight charges possible for civilians as well.

Operating costs on the narrow gauge roads were relatively high, however. Thus new construction in the postwar period, when capital equipment was once again readily available, was almost all standard gauge. Furthermore, the old routes which continued to carry commercial traffic were converted to standard gauge. Bousser estimated that a locomotive operating with a three-man crew on a narrow gauge line consumed 7 kilograms of coal per kilometer (around 25 pounds per mile) hauling 30 to 40 tons of freight. With the same crew on a standard gauge line, a locomotive could haul 175 tons while consuming only twice as much fuel.[3]

Morocco's rail network spread rapidly after 1920, during the period when colonization was developing apace. In 1923, a line was completed from Sidi Kacem to Rabat via Kenitra, and the Sidi Kacem–Fez section of the Tangier–Fez railroad was also finished. By 1927, the whole Tangier–Fez line was open to traffic. In the meantime, the Casablanca–Rabat line had been converted to standard gauge. Casablanca was connected by rail with Marrakech in 1928, and a branch of this line was run to the phosphate center of Khouribga and the nearby farming center of Oued Zem. Thus, by the end of the decade the plains of northwest Morocco were linked by standard gauge rail to Casablanca, Rabat, Kenitra, and Tangier. A connection with another western port was made in 1936, when a line was constructed from Benguerir, on the Casablanca–Marrakech road, to Safi. This line provided transport for the phosphates mined at Youssefiah.

To the east, the imperial link with Algeria was finished in 1934, with the completion of the Taza–Fez portion of the line. (The section from Taza to Oujda had been completed earlier.) Later on, a branch line south from Oujda was extended until it reached the anthracite coal of Djerada, the manganese of Bou Arfa, and the soft coal of the Kenadsa basin near Colomb Bechar in Algeria.[4]

In its completed form, the Moroccan rail network had around 1,600 kilometers of track.[5] It was a comprehensive system — perhaps too comprehensive. On the surface, the rail service in northwest Morocco would seem justified, in terms of reaching both domestic markets and the western ports. However, distances in this area were relatively short, and road transport was able to compete successfully with the railroads on almost all scores. Indeed, it took concerted government action to prevent the railroads here from being forced out of business by truck and bus competition in the thirties. Only in the transport of minerals did railroads maintain a superiority over highway transport. Due to the heavy emphasis on export trade in Morocco's mining industry, only the Khouribga–Casablanca and Benguerir–Safi lines in the plains area appeared to have economic justification.

It is more difficult to defend the line from Fez to Tangier on economic grounds; as events worked themselves out under the protectorate, the line was a failure. Here it was more a question of the total amount of traffic than of the superiority of transport by road. Tangier was largely by-passed as an entrepôt for the French zone under the protectorate. While France participated in the international administration of Tangier, its control was far from complete; furthermore, the Spanish zone lay between the city and the French zone. The authorities, in their efforts to keep the development of their area in French hands, were unwilling to depend on trade routes outside of their political control. Thus the ports of Casablanca and Kenitra were developed at the expense of Tangier; and the Tangier–Fez line proved to be largely a carrier of passengers, rather than freight.

The economic justification of the railroad east from Fez to Algeria is the most obscure of all. Trade to the east was never very important in Morocco, and the coming of the French did little to increase it. The Moroccan and Algerian economies were competitive rather than complementary. Prior to 1923, however, some foreign products, notably British cottons, came to Morocco through the "back door." The duty on these goods was only 7.5 per cent, as compared with 12.5 per cent on goods entering through the ports; but the costs of moving them were high. Thus when improvements in transport facilities promised a reduction in freight costs, the importers on the Atlantic coast protested the tariff differential. As a result, the protectorate government authorized the collection of an additional 5 per cent on goods moving west of Taza in 1923. In 1936, the customs barrier was moved to the border town of Oujda.

The railroad from Fez to Oujda — like that from Fez to Tangier — was primarily a carrier of passengers. Similar to the roads of the western plains, it was only the spurs carrying minerals, i.e., coal from Djerada and Kenadsa and manganese from Bou Arfa to the Algerian port of Nemours, which supplied an economic need.[6] The main road did have a military function, however; the completion of the link from Fez to Taza meant that it was possible to move troops by rail all the way from Marrakech to Tunis. Unfortunately, troop transport brings no direct economic return. Deficits still had to be met, which was a task that put a heavy burden on the Moroccan economy.

The largest revenues of the Moroccan railroads were earned from the transport of minerals, particularly phosphates. The rail net as a whole operated at a loss. It was maintained primarily by government subsidies, which were eventually transformed into dividends for the holders of railroad stocks. To the extent that the minerals did not pay their way, the mine owners were also being subsidized. In effect, however, part of the subsidy was no more than government bookkeeping, since the protectorate government shared in the ownership not only of the mines but of the railroads themselves.

Highways

As already noted, restrictions imposed by the Germans and by wartime shortages of capital equipment served to limit railroad construction in the early years of the protectorate. There was urgent need, however, for the development of a transport system permitting the expeditious movement of men and matériel for the pacification campaign. With the rapid development of the automobile, highways were the obvious answer; and they offered in addition an excellent way in which to keep pacified tribes busy.

Thus highway construction had a head start on railroad building in Morocco. Despite the rapid development of a rail system after the war, the highways were able to maintain their advantage. The reduction in freight costs resulting from the substitution of rail for camel transport — impressive as it was — ran a poor second to the savings possible through the use of motor transport. Part of the reason lay in the fact that fuel for motor transport was relatively inexpensive in comparison with the costs of electricity, and especially coal, for the railroads. Electricity, in fact, was more than twice as expensive as in France and was consequently a large factor in the high production costs in the modern sector. The railroads and also the mines, however, were particularly heavy users of power, most of it thermal, produced by *Energie Electrique du Maroc*, a firm owned jointly by the government and private interests.

The roads also had the advantage of reaching sections of the country inaccessible to the rail system. Road building was at first concentrated in much the same area that received railroads, that is, western Morocco and the region to the northeast. As the pacification spread southward, however, so did the roads. Thus the Moroccan road network, as it evolved, was an extensive one, ranging from fine, modern highways that blanketed the north all the way to *pistes*, or dirt tracks, leading to remote desert regions.

By 1919, when the railroads were just getting under way, Morocco already had 1,639 kilometers of primary roads and 374 kilometers of secondary roads, as compared with only 822 and 66 kilometers, respectively, just three years before. By 1953, there were almost 49,000 kilometers in the highway network, 15,000 of which were in all-weather roads.[7] Morocco indeed had an impressive network of highways and roads, from macadam to *piste*. But it was an expensive one, in a poor country. The important question is whether it was utilized fully. A look at the French attempts to "rationalize" transport under the protectorate may suggest an answer.

THE "RATIONALIZATION" OF TRANSPORT

Through the period of rapidly expanding economic activity that characterized the twenties, Moroccan railroad and highway networks were developed simultaneously, and competition between them posed no serious problems. The Moroccan economy, with a heavy emphasis on primary products, was a "fair weather" one, however. The calamitous drop in the world prices of these products during the crisis of the thirties meant severe reductions not only in the revenues of the producers, but also in receipts of the transporters. Both groups laid their troubles in the lap of the protectorate administration.

Among the transporters, complaints emanated chiefly from the management of the railroads. Now that times were bad, it felt the full force of motor transport's competitive superiority and demanded immediate help from the government. In response, the government initiated a program designed to maintain the railroads, whatever the cost. The crisis of the thirties, then, was the short-term reason for the "rationalization" of transport in Morocco. The secular reason lay in the continuing pressure of competition on the railroads resulting from improvements in the road network and the motorcar.

The railroads, as was pointed out above, were largely dependent on the carriage of minerals, especially phosphates. By 1932, revenues for the hauling of phosphates had dropped by almost half from the 1930 high of 35 million francs. A revival of phosphate tonnage in 1933 could not compensate for the losses of traffic incurred elsewhere by the railroads; their share of the transport of the export cereal crop declined, for example, from 93 per cent in 1930 to only 36 per cent in 1933.[8] Thus the freight activity on the railroads suffered not only from a heavy absolute decline, but from a shift to highway transport. To make matters even worse, passenger traffic demonstrated similar characteristics.

It was at this point that the government stepped in. A sudden concern for the public safety arose in official circles: M. Lucien Saint, the Resident-General from 1929 to 1933, noted that there was "great urgency to make road traffic less dangerous and to make insurance against accidents obligatory." [9] Laws early in 1933 required that all public vehicles be licensed, the licenses to be granted only after a safety check. Operators, too, had to be granted official approval. In addition, the insurance of all vehicles was made mandatory. Other restrictions levied on highway transport at the same time made it clear that the government's concern extended beyond safety considerations. For example, no new public carriers were to be allowed, and existing ones were required to obtain route franchises. Furthermore, minimum rate schedules for both merchandise and passengers were established.

To deal especially with truck transport, the particular thorn in the side of the rail operators, the *Office Général de Transport Marocain* was set up. Controlled by the railroads but financed by treasury advances, the *Office* bought up trucks, many of which it then proceeded to retire permanently from service. This step was taken when it became clear that the depression made it relatively easy to get rid of an operator, but not to eliminate his equipment — which was written down in value and then sold to someone else.

A primary effect of all of these measures was to improve the railroads' competitive position. However, the "rationalization" of transport did not end with the attempt to valorize the rail network. The *Compagnie des Transports Marocains*, the largest bus company in Morocco, had for some years been subsidized by the government both through outright subventions and through price reductions on gasoline and equipment. In the depression years, however, the *C.T.M.* initiated, with government financial aid, a concerted drive to buy up competition. Despite considerable success in this area, the *C.T.M.* was unable to achieve one of its major objectives: to eliminate Valenciana, a Spanish bus line and its most serious competitor.[10] As Valenciana could not be bought out, it was restricted. Central locations in the towns were denied to it, and the choice routes, e.g., Casablanca to Marrakech, were reserved to the *C.T.M.*

While the *C.T.M.* was swallowing competition with the aid of the government, it in turn was being swallowed by the largest railroad company in the country, the *C.F.M.*, or *Compagnie des Chemins de Fer du Maroc*. Again the influence of the authorities was apparent, since ownership of the *C.F.M.* was vested in the protectorate government and a consortium headed by the *Banque de Paris et des Pays-Bas*. Thus this was another example of the way in which transport was "rationalized" under the protectorate. Through consolidation of companies, regulation of rates, barring of entry, and the forcing out of small operators — especially Moroccan ones — the government maintained a system of rail and road transportation that was profitable for the European owners but unnecessarily expensive for the users.

TRANSPORT AND THE MOROCCANS

Despite the elevation of rates which resulted from government intervention in the development of the new transport, the benefits to the Moroccan people were great. The casual traveler in Morocco was likely to have the impression that the transport system was designed primarily to serve the modern portion of the dual economy, and he would have been correct. But he might have deduced from this that the traditional segment benefited from the system very little, and here he would have been wrong. It was true that passengers in his first or second class railroad car would all be dressed *à l'européenne* and would be speaking French, but it was also true that almost five million Moroccans rode fourth class coaches during 1952.[11]

The traveler may have been similarly deceived when he drove along one of Morocco's fine paved roads and saw it disintegrate into a dirt track the moment the last European farm was reached. In reaching this European landholding, however, the road was likely to pass by, or at least near, fields owned by Moroccans, thus bringing them some partial benefits. At the same time, the traveler may have noticed the dirt paths alongside the highways, where Moroccans and their slow-moving donkeys were safe from the hazards of European cars on the road. It is true that the narrow strip between road and path marked a separation of centuries, but it is also true that many Moroccans spanned the gap during the four decades of the protectorate. While they might continue to use the traditional means of transport for short trips, they boarded the many busses found on the new highways to cover longer distances.

The reduction in the cost of distance profoundly affected Moroccan society. The Sous and the Tafilalet, once remote, were now within hours of Casablanca. Indeed, improved transport was an important means by which the Moroccans were able to substitute a national consciousness for tribal loyalties. This contribution of the French-built transportation net to Moroccan life, while unintentional, was probably its greatest.

Aside from its role in the rising nationalist movement, the modern transportation system had a deep influence on economic life in the countryside. As costs of transport were reduced, the radius served by a market was increased; consequently, the number declined. (The same held true for the *fondouks,* or wholesale houses.) As part of the process, permanent *souks* appeared; big centers such as Khemisset and Tiflet, on the Rabat–Meknes road, and Souk al Arba du Gharb, on the road from Kenitra to Tangier, were unknown before the protectorate.[12] In many instances, both farmers and traveling merchants exchanged their donkeys and camels for a seat on a bus for themselves and space on its roof for their goods. In the case of the merchants, some were able to purchase small cars or trucks to carry them on their rounds.[13]

As Moroccan travelers and Moroccan freight shifted to the new forms of transport, the traditional forms underwent a secular decline. The demand for the talents of the desert nomads for raising camels and running caravans, already declining before the protectorate, largely disappeared. The change was reflected in camel prices at Goulimine, south of Agadir, the largest market in Morocco; despite the depreciation of the franc since the twenties, camels brought little more in 1956 than they did earlier. While these animals still had a place in agricultural activity, the only caravans to be found in Morocco were infrequent ones moving a party of transhumants and their belongings from one area to another. The nomads were left stranded by twentieth-century transport technology.

Few Moroccans were able to enter the transport business as it developed under the protectorate; the "rationalization" of the thirties saw to that. Among the few were some *caids*, especially from the Sous, who managed to make the transition from the caravan to the truck or bus. However, they lived on the sufferance of the authorities, and had to make their way on the fringes of the transportation network. More Moroccans acquired cars and became clandestine transporters of passengers. This group lived despite the authorities and operated on some of the best routes reserved to the *C.T.M.* Information on the latter transporters, naturally, is lacking; but continuous French efforts to suppress their activities suggest that they were doing well under the umbrella of high official rates in a country where purchasing power was low.

PORTS AT THE THRESHOLD OF THE "OPEN DOOR"

Much of the domestic transport net described above was developed as a means not of tapping interior markets but rather of tapping interior resources for foreign markets, in France and elsewhere. To get Moroccan products abroad, however, more was needed than rails and highways. As was noted in Chapter I, Morocco's port facilities were poor indeed when the French assumed control over the country. Thus improvements to the ports received high priority among the plans for development. In fact, the French had begun work of a minor sort on the port of Casablanca five years before they formally received their protectorate.

DEVELOPMENT OF THE PORTS

The geographic and political configuration of the French zone of Morocco dictated that foreign commerce should pass through the Atlantic ports. The zone had only a very small opening on the Mediterranean, and attempts to develop the tiny port of Saidia-Port Say there had to be abandoned in the face of a serious siltage problem. The nearby port of Melilla, in the Spanish zone of control, was also ruled out. Although the Franco-Spanish agreement of 1912 provided for the customs unity of all Morocco, the French were unwilling to rely on Spanish goodwill for an outlet to their zone. As a result, the outlet for eastern Morocco was the Algerian port of Nemours, which was supported by Moroccan public revenues. However, the traffic through this port was largely confined to minerals from Morocco's eastern mines. The economically interesting part of the country from the French viewpoint was much farther west.

There were two ports on the Strait of Gibraltar — Ceuta and Tangier. The former had never been an outlet for the area which was to fall under French control; the Riff Mountains were an effective barrier. Tangier, on the other hand, had played an important role in Morocco's foreign trade, limited though it was, in the years before the protectorate. But being only partially under the control of France, it was to lose out in the years after 1912. During the protectorate, it was a relatively unimportant entrepôt for the hinterland, and instead led a precarious existence as a haven for flight capital from Europe.

The political facts of life were even more evident in the decline of the Atlantic port of Larache, which, prior to 1912, had been the international outlet for heavy articles from Fez. Included in the Spanish zone by the Franco-Spanish agreement of 1912, the town languished in a backwash, its port rapidly silting up.

The very considerable expenditures for port development after 1912, therefore, were concentrated in the area along the coast from Kenitra to Agadir — all under complete French control. In this area, the great bulk of the effort was directed toward developing Casablanca; as a result, the volume of merchandise moving through this port was several times greater than that of all the other ports taken together.

The development of the port of Casablanca was a result largely of historical accident. Many of the European traders in pre-protectorate Morocco were located here; and their numbers were swelled by the arrival of other merchants and speculators after the landing of French troops in 1907. Thus by the time the protectorate came into being, Europeans were firmly established in Casablanca. And by the time a French *Commission des Ports* had determined that Al Jadida should become Morocco's principal port, it was too late. Marshal Lyautey could scarcely ignore the demands of his countrymen already in Morocco; and he chose Casablanca, one of the poorest natural harbors, to become the first port of the country.[14] Consequently, heavy capital investments had to be made to compensate for the deficiency in natural endowments, and this meant high port charges from the very beginning.

Under the guidance of the protectorate government, what was

little more than an inhospitable roadstead in 1912 was transformed into a great modern port. Long jetties were constructed into the open sea to create an artificial shelter for ships. Loading facilities were constantly improved, especially for phosphates; elevators for the storage of grains were constructed; and a fishing port was also added. All of these projects were financed in the tradition of the *économie mixte*. Contracts for the construction and operation of the ports were let by the government, in return for a share of the revenues, to a private French consortium in which the *Compagnie Marocaine*, a large holding company, was the principal participant. Bond issues were floated in the name of the consortium but were guaranteed by the State. This formula was also used in the construction of port facilities at Kenitra and Rabat-Salé; but other ports in the country were improved on the initiative of the government alone, since the expected returns did not attract private capital.

One of the most important of the secondary ports was Safi, which was developed to receive phosphates from Youssefiah. Another was Kenitra, which was constructed to substitute for Larache and Tangier as an outlet for the Gharb. Down the list was Fedala, an appendage of Casablanca which received Morocco's petroleum imports. Agadir, the outlet of the Sous, was modestly developed, largely as a fishing and fish canning port. Essaouira, on the other hand, continued a decline begun when the caravan routes lost their importance; and Al Jadida, for which the French commission held such promise at the beginning of the protectorate, vegetated in the shadow of Casablanca. Rabat, which saw some development in the early days of the protectorate, later silted up.

The early favor accorded Casablanca by the government assured its primacy not only over all other ports but over all other cities in the country. All highways and railroads led to Casablanca; its businessmen were in the enviable position of standing athwart the sole channels of both domestic and international trade. They had little worry of serious competition from elsewhere.

PORT ACTIVITY AND BALANCE OF PAYMENTS

Figures relating to the flow of goods through Morocco's ports offer convincing evidence of the dominant position of Casablanca. In 1953, products leaving Morocco from the ports totaled 6,343,000 tons, and were valued at roughly 83 billion francs. Imports, on the other hand, amounted to 2,150,000 tons, with a value of around 162 billion francs. Casablanca's share of the imports was 80 per cent by weight, 92 per cent by value. Altogether, the activity of this one port accounted for 75 per cent of the tonnage and no less than 84 per cent of the value of all products leaving or coming into Morocco by sea in 1953.[15]

The above figures suggest more than Casablanca's supremacy, however. As can be seen, little more than half of the imports entering through the ports were covered, in value, by exports. This was not a situation peculiar to 1953; on the contrary, a large passive balance of payments had been a chronic problem under the protectorate. The total foreign commerce of Morocco, including a relatively small amount passing over land routes, rose from one billion francs in 1923 to over 265 billion francs in 1953. Save for 1941, when exports totaled 2.5 billion francs, while the war restricted imports to only 2 billion, the country had a deficit in its international accounts every year during the period. It was the greatest in 1930, when less than a third of the imports were covered by exports. In the last years of the protectorate, 50 to 60 per cent was generally the rule.[16]

In view of the depreciation of the franc, tonnage figures offer a more accurate measure than valuations of the increased activity under the protectorate. Imports and exports taken together totaled 888,000 tons in 1923. By 1953, they had risen to 9,259,000 tons, and thus were over ten times greater.[17] Since Morocco's exports to a large extent were composed of primary products, phosphates in particular, it is not surprising that exports consistently outweighed imports. Of the total tonnage in 1953, for example, exports accounted for 6,830,000, of which phosphate exports alone came to 4,143,000.[18]

It is also not surprising to find France involved in a large portion of Morocco's foreign commerce. In 1953, France took 47 per cent of Morocco's exports, by value, and supplied 56 per cent of the imports, for a 53 per cent share of the total trade.[19] Put another way, two-thirds of Morocco's deficit on trade account was with France. Of the other currency blocs, Morocco ran a consistent deficit with the United States and a constant but small surplus with the sterling area. Generally speaking, the country also had a small deficit with its remaining trade partners. Since the French treasury was committed to maintaining the Moroccan and French francs at par, deficits with non-franc areas meant a draft on French foreign exchange reserves.

In the last analysis, the yearly deficits were filled by capital inflows mostly French, public and private. In the ten years after 1946, public and private funds invested in Morocco totaled nearly 700 million francs ($2 billion). Before 1949, the capital for public and semi-public investment came from loans made in the French capital market and guaranteed by the French government. After the inaugural of the Moroccan modernization and investment plans in 1949, the capital came directly from French investment funds in the form of long-term low interest loans. The two plans (1949–53 and 1954–57) entailed expenditures of $1.1 billion, largely concentrated in transport, communications, irrigation, and electric power.[20]

Throughout much of the period of the struggle for independence, then, the French government continued to pour funds into Morocco to develop an "infrastructure" which, together with troops, would make the country attractive to foreign investment. Evidence that the private investor was not confident of its success is suggested by one observer who noted that the share of public and semi-public funds in the capital inflow during the period 1951–56 rose from a low of 63 per cent in 1952 to 88 per cent in 1956.[21] Thus, the French taxpayer was still paying, as he had ever since 1912, even after the private investor had decided that the game was no longer worth the candle.

PUBLIC FINANCE

The Moroccans were also making their contribution to European enterprise, not only as consumers, but as taxpayers. An examination of figures published by the United Nations relating to sources of public revenues in 1952 shows how heavily the tax structure in Morocco was biased toward the European segment of the population under the protectorate.[22]

Of the 42½ billion francs raised by taxation in Morocco in 1952, less than 14 billion came from direct taxes. The *tertib* was the principal such tax, contributing 13 per cent of the total tax revenues. The burden of the *tertib* fell more heavily on the Moroccans than on the European farmers.[23] Other direct taxes were license taxes on businesses and levies on various forms of personal income; all together, they contributed 19 per cent of the revenues from taxation in 1952. The license tax was levied on net revenues; for any business making over 700,000 francs per year (around $2,000), the rate was a flat 15 per cent. The tax on salaries, fees, wages, pensions, and annuities was a flat 10 per cent, with deductions for family allowances and professional expenses. Thus these two taxes not only contributed a relatively small portion of the total revenues, but, by being proportional, tapped high income brackets only lightly.

Indirect taxes brought almost 29 billion francs in 1952. Customs duties alone contributed over two-fifths of all revenues raised by taxation. Consumption taxes on tea, sugar, beer, and alcohol represented around 14 per cent of the revenues, and registration and stamp taxes around 10 per cent. Thus a heavy proportion of tax revenues was raised from levies which were regressive, i.e., levied on consumption; and the greatest burden fell on the Moroccans whose marginal propensity to consume was close to unity.

The prosperity of Frenchmen in Morocco, then, was at the expense of both the Moroccans and Frenchmen in France. Even if the latter had been willing to continue the arrangement indefinitely, such was not the case with the Moroccans. On March 2, 1956, in the ultimate manifestation of their mounting discontent, the Moroccans won their independence. Their legacy was a high cost, ill-structured, and vulnerable economy heavily dependent on France for money, markets, and skilled manpower.

VI

EPILOGUE AND PROLOGUE

Just as the judgment of Lyautey's work and that of his successors had to be based on the character of the "raw materials" — natural, capital, human and institutional — available to them from 1912 to 1956, so too must the judgment of their Moroccan successors rest on the materials they were bequeathed. These materials are the assets and liabilities accumulated over forty-four years, items to be increased, varied, and refined in the first case and to be eliminated, or at least minimized, in the second. Some, of course, vanish immediately in the new logic that is automatically created by the shift in political control. Others, fortunately or unfortunately, depending on which side of the "balance sheet" they appear, persist and are therefore the stuff of which Moroccan economic history is made.

The epilogue of this book, then, is concerned with the relatively long-term assets and liabilities inherited from the French; in addition, it is concerned with what the Moroccans have done with, and about, them during the few short years since independence. The prologue, on the other hand, is concerned with the problems and prospects of Morocco; as such, it is an attempt to isolate those factors which, when the future has become history, may prove to have been both durable and vital.

Neither epilogue nor prologue can be meaningfully written without reference to an ultimate goal. It is the goal which makes the assets and liabilities, as well as the problems and prospects, identifiable and classifiable. In any underdeveloped country, the ultimate goal must be economic independence. Economic independence is of course a meaningless concept without political independence, but the latter will prove to be ephemeral without the former.

There are a few things that should be said immediately about what economic independence means. First and foremost, it is a condition in which, over the long term, a nation is able to pay its own way in the world. Secondly, it is not, or should not be, synonymous with a state of autarky, where the real advantages of international specialization are eschewed for the sake of self-sufficiency. Thirdly, and this follows from the previous point, it implies a state where the alternatives — sources of supply and places to sell — are many. Unlike autarky, where, in theory, outside markets are not entered at all, economic independence means that market ties with the outside world are ideally so numerous and so diffused that no single tie can inhibit freedom and flexibility of economic and political action. Obviously, the goal is only a theoretical one, an ideal which cannot be attained completely; but the goal nevertheless remains as a reference.

To achieve as well as to maintain any significant degree of economic independence requires the conscious, purposeful, and continuous shaping of an appropriate domestic economic organization. The process through which this organization is created entails undoing as well as doing. (Although the acts are performed simultaneously, they are analytically distinct.) In the case of Morocco, the undoing is perhaps best described by the word "de-colonization," and involves the elimination of those factors which were deliberately designed during the protectorate to make the country an appendage to the French economy and which are incompatible with economic independence.[1] The doing requires the development of other factors which will prevent Morocco in the future from becoming an appendage to somebody else. The total process might be termed national economic integration.[2]

The basic need is to create those institutions, kinds of economic activity, and, indeed, frames of mind *on a nation-wide basis* which will allow *all* Moroccans to contribute a full measure to the goal of economic independence and to receive a just reward for their labors. While these words may be appropriate ones for the Minister of Labor and Social Affairs to use in the flush of a May Day parade of workers in Casablanca, they also seem appropriate to the reality of the present-day world of growing aspirations at home and power politics on the international scene.

It is obvious that integration is not solely an economic process; it is also political and even more basically social. In this age of specialization, however, there are fairly rigid limitations on what one is willing to try. Here it is proposed to leave the problems of political and social integration largely in more competent hands.[3]

Where trespass is unavoidable, it will be brief and proximate to the central problem of economic integration. We begin by a short indulgence of this self-granted prerogative.

THE SETTING FOR ECONOMIC INTEGRATION

Economic integration, even under the most propitious circumstances, is a difficult never-ending process which cannot wait, and Moroccans have been far from blessed with a favorable complex of circumstances during the years of independence. As a result, precious time and timing have been lost in a country where the grim race between population and production makes the losses critical to say the least.

Because ties with France have been so close and so many faceted, a redefinition of those ties in the light of Moroccan independence is obviously a first order of business. The Algerian war, however, has prevented consideration of first things first. Events in Algeria inevitably reverberate in Morocco. They have impeded the orderly change of institutional arrangements with France, so necessary to keep the delicate economic process working. Instead of comprehensive agreement concerning the course of future relations with France, there have been substituted a few partial measures. An example is a Technical Aid–Cultural Exchange Treaty signed early in 1957.[4] Mostly, however, relations continue on an *ad hoc* basis with all the uncertainties, disappointments, and mutual recriminations associated with one party's guessing badly what the other will do next.

Morocco is also Irredentist. Franco-Moroccan and Spanish-Moroccan relations are strained by conflicting claims concerning the historic Moroccan Sahara, parts of what is now southwestern Algeria, Ifni, Rio de Oro, and, more recently, the Mediterranean presidios.[5] Proved minerals, e.g., the iron ore of Tindouf, significant mineral possibilities, ports, and, above all, principles are at stake. In the atmosphere of the Cold War too, bilateral disputes quickly become issues for a larger forum. Soviet policy has won friends in Morocco. The United States, at the same time, has become an uncertain quantity for Moroccans as it walks a taut rope between its European commitments and a plunge into ex-colonial Africa.

Morocco, in the interest of national integration, must not only decide where it will stand in the Cold War; it must also decide the character of its pan-Maghreb, pan-Arab, and pan-African relations, which, on balance, are probably more competitive than complementary. Finally, the nature of economic relations with Europe presses for decision as the Common Market takes clearer shape. Morocco, in short, must find its identity among nations by developing international political and economic links which are compatible with economic independence. Obviously, Moroccans can expect many decisions to be thrust on them from the outside, or, perhaps more accurately, the range of choice to be narrowed considerably by the decisions of others. Nevertheless the Moroccans are a long way from the Algeciras of 1906 when the powers negotiated *over* Morocco. Negotiation *with* Morocco is much more the order of today.

On the domestic side, no windfalls have come to hasten the integration process since 1956. On the contrary, the influence of non-economic factors has been pretty much negative. For example, the year 1957 was marked not only by a massive capital flight with a consequent stagnation in the industrial sector, but also by a serious drought which resulted in far-below-average crop yields. Both led to a critical balance of payments problem, and the year was virtually lost as far as economic progress was concerned. Both also demonstrated two critical legacies of the protectorate: a modern sector which turned out to be unstable once the assumption of continued French control turned out to be false, and a traditional sector still largely submitted to a capricious nature.

The year 1960 saw the earthquake which destroyed Agadir, the port for the Sous and much of southern Morocco. The drought returned again in 1961, but its consequences were far overshadowed by the greatest blow of the post-independence period, the sudden death of King Mohammed V. The King, the symbol of the hard struggle for freedom, was endowed with a charismatic personality together with great wisdom and political acumen. It would not be too strong to say that he single-handedly held in check those centrifugal forces which appeared in Moroccan political life after 1956.

The natural catastrophes can be absorbed in time, but time is the scarcest factor in Moroccan economics. Agadir can be rebuilt; the fellahin can be helped over the deficit years; but the fact remains that, since resources must be diverted for these current purposes, the process of investment for integration is delayed. Whether the loss of the King, who was the catalyst for integration, can be overcome remains to be seen.

Enough has been said in previous chapters to show that, in accordance with the *système*, Europeans, mostly French, controlled and operated not only the government but also the modern part of the economy.[6] In other words, Muslim Moroccans were effectively blocked from entry into positions occupied by Europeans even if qualified, although many Jews were allowed to filter through.

After independence, some Europeans, especially those in the lower echelon government jobs requiring little skill, could be replaced immediately. In the interests of good public relations, European industrialists also tended to replace their compatriots in this category. At the other end of the spectrum, the logic of independence demanded that Moroccans be placed in top-level policy positions, also immediately. Owing to the thinness of cadres, many technically trained persons and private businessmen whose skills were badly needed have found themselves engaged in administration and policy making. As one observer put it, "Morocco's able young men are all in senior posts, and broadly speaking, there is no middle layer; below the elite comes the proletariat."[7]

The really serious consequence of the *système* lies then in the large void in the middle of the hierarchy. Ideally, to minimize the shock to the economic process of a changeover in personnel, the rate of withdrawal of Europeans should, in terms of numbers and kinds of skills, be equal to the rate of development of Moroccans qualified to take over. Achievement of the ideal, however, presupposes a willingness on both sides to wait.[8]

The willingness has not been present. Many French administrators proved unable psychologically to make the transition to a subordinate status; they have long since returned to France. Others have left in the wake of civil disturbances, e.g., the Meknes riots in the fall of 1956.[9] Still others, while living on what appears to be borrowed time in Morocco, are being attracted by seemingly permanent well-paying jobs opened up by the boom in France. Official anxiety over the exodus is reflected in offers of generous work contracts *(contrats de travail)* and liberal exemptions from exchange controls on transmission of earnings to France.

The process has had a multiplying effect. As the government officials return to France, so do those who serve them — merchants, restaurateurs, skilled mechanics, etc. While many of the latter cannot be considered a serious loss, in many cases the officials and some of the skilled civilians cannot be replaced adequately in the short run.

Certain elements in Morocco, principally the anti-regime Union of Popular Forces, consider the exodus too slow or, to put it another way, the rate of "Moroccanization" too slow. Since the government cannot remain indifferent to the pressures for "Moroccanization," it has been forced into the ambivalent position of hastening the process for political reasons and delaying it for reasons of efficiency. The interplay of motives on both the French and Moroccan sides has not led to even an approximation of an ideal rate of replacement. There is no doubt that the lack of cadres will be overcome in time but, in the interim, management resources must be used intensively to say the least. Thus, the development of efficient administration and administrators takes its place as a part of the process of economic integration. By that much, their contribution to the process itself is reduced.

Accurate figures on the extent of net European emigration are hard to come by since procedures for recording entry and exit are inadequate. According to one source, however, almost 19,000 of the 28,000 French officials left the country in the four years following independence.[10] At the same time, of the total European population in the ex-French zone estimated at 400,000 in 1955, only one-half remained five years later.[11] While the rate of emigration had begun to level off by 1960, it has been forecast that by 1965 the European population would be reduced to 100,000, with almost all the minor officials gone.[12] The reduction through emigration has been somewhat mitigated by the entry of new government employees — especially teachers, magistrates, agricultural technicians, and civil and mining engineers — who serve on an individual contract basis. The substitution of these employees, whose actions are not colored by memories of a bygone colonial era, for those whose actions are so affected, is not all gain since the former are handicapped by an unfamiliarity with the country and by the hard fact that organizational effectiveness suffers from large-scale substitution of personnel over a relatively short period of time.

The Jewish population has also been affected by emigration, much of it clandestine in the direction of Israel. Since 1956, when Morocco joined the Arab League, postal service with Israel has not only been cut but organized emigration has also been disallowed. This has been partly in deference to other league members. Another factor has been the unwillingness of the government to lose the business and professional skills of the urban Jews at a time when the country seeks to reduce its dependence on the French in the conduct of the modern economy. The Jews, in the official view, are full citizens of Morocco and are a precious asset in its economic life.[13]

Since the emigration of the Jews has been largely illegal, accurate data are even harder to obtain than in the case of the Europeans. It is only possible to say that the figure is greater than 50,000, the number that the Zionist organization working in Morocco is reported to have sent to Israel before this activity was closed down shortly after independence.[14]

The reduction in numbers of the two minority groups has had a significant impact on the Muslims. As a result of the liquidation of enterprises owned by the minorities, many Moroccan employees have been discharged. Other jobs have not been easy to find in a situation where an estimated 20 per cent of the urban labor force is chronically unemployed.[15] On the social side, the loss of professional people has been very serious. For example, while the doctor-population ratio was never good, by 1960 it had been reduced to one doctor per ten thousand inhabitants. (The comparable figure for France was one per thousand.) Of the slightly more than one thousand doctors, only one-tenth were Moroccans. At the same time, expected but nonetheless revealing was the fact that 40 per cent of the physicians were in Casablanca although only 8 per cent of the population lived there. Vast areas of the countryside were thus without medical service. Mitigating this gloomy development was the report that around 150 Moroccan students were studying medicine in France and Spain.[16]

Most encouraging of all have been the strides made in general education since independence. According to one source, the percentage of school-age children in attendance rose from 15 per cent in 1955, the last year of French control, to 40 per cent in 1961. Despite this most creditable performance, the magnitude of the task confronting Morocco is revealed by the number of illiterates under fourteen years of age. These were estimated for 1955 at 77 per cent in the cities and 93 per cent in the rural areas.[17]

These statistics tell only part of the story. The 1960 census figures suggest the rest by showing all too graphically that Moroccans must run hard even to stay where they are, not only in education but on all fronts. The census showed a population total of 11,600,000 people, a 25 per cent increase over 1951–52. The figures broke down at roughly 11,000,000 Muslims, 160,000 Jews, and an undifferentiated 400,000 foreigners including French, Algerians, and Spanish in both ex-zones and in Tangier. Most significant, however, are the figures for the Muslim Moroccans who comprised 95 per cent of the population in 1960 and are likely to represent an even larger share in the future owing to emigration of Jews and Europeans. In the ten years between censuses, while the European and Jewish populations were reduced one-quarter by emigration, the Muslims increased by 30 per cent, with an annual average growth rate of about 2.5 per cent.[18] Even if one allows for considerable error in the previous and present censuses, any approximation of a 25 per cent growth startles. Although the magnitude is history, it presents the contemporary challenge. The 2.5 per cent growth *rate* is alarming because it is the source of a Herculean task — one that is increasing in geometric proportions. In a real sense, this figure, more than any other, emphasizes the Moroccans' problem and is the principal legacy of the protectorate.

TERRITORIAL UNITY

Adding to the complications produced by the unfavorable windfalls and the rough-cut readjustment of the numbers and relationships of the elements in the plural society have been the efforts designed to bring unity within present Moroccan borders. (These efforts are aside from, although they are related to, those made in attempting to recover territories still controlled by others.) The melding of the ex-French and -Spanish zones with formerly international Tangier, even formally, has been a time-consuming task of decolonization.

Although the central government took formal control of the old Spanish zone in 1956, effective control was not obtained until early in 1958 with the withdrawal of the peseta as the fiduciary currency there. The delay can be attributed to the slow negotiations with Spain concerning the conditions — the exchange rate and the terms of settlement — of the changeover. Political events, e.g., the dispute over Ifni, also played a part. As it turned out, the Moroccan government used the roughly one billion pesetas withdrawn to satisfy part of past debts owing the Spanish government.[19]

The adverse effects on business of the uncertainties connected with the currency exchange were compounded by the great disparities in basic conditions between the two zones. By comparison, the inhabitants of the old Spanish zone, largely Riffian, are poor relations when contrasted with their compatriots to the south. Extremely limited agricultural possibilities and poor communications in rugged terrain combine to produce this situation. But when the level of living was lower before the currency exchange, so was the price level.[20] The monetary unification of the two zones has meant that the prices of the south have come to prevail in the north to the dismay of its inhabitants. For the south, Riffian migration has complicated the already critical problem of chronic unemployment. Add to these difficulties differences in administrative procedures, educational systems, and even languages crystallized over forty-four years, and the magnitude of the integration problem comes into sharper focus. On balance, the ex-Spanish zone brings little other than problems to the Moroccan administration and economy.[21]

Moroccan freedom of action concerning Tangier was more readily accomplished than was the case with the ex-Spanish zone; the powers associated with the international administration of the city turned control over to the government in the fall of 1956. The delay in full integration with the rest of the country until 1960 was unilateral and related to official uncertainty over exactly what role the city was to play in the country's economic life. The uncertainty had its basis in history. Over long stretches of time the city has been effectively cut off from the rest of Morocco. These have been periods when overseas contacts, not the hinterland, gave Tangier its *raison d'être*.[22] The thirty-three years of international control were largely one of these periods.

At the time of independence, Tangier was a city of banks where a free money market prevailed, import duties were a flat 10 per cent, and internal taxes were practically non-existent. Its role as entrepôt for Moroccan foreign trade was minimal, since the French had done much to favor Casablanca and the Spanish had done the same with Ceuta. Port facilities did little more than serve local needs and act as a transit point for tourists and European residents of the other zones en route to and from Europe. Without a readily accessible hinterland, local industrial activity was also minor. Tangier was largely a provider of services, a vault for large gold deposits, and a base for legitimate international business activities and some not so legitimate.

The Royal Charter for Tangier, which took effect in the summer of 1957, appeared designed to assure, for the most part, the continuity of the city's traditional functions; in retrospect, it proved to be a first step toward a complete integration precluding those functions. Under the Charter, provisions were made for continuing freedom of the exchanges and for free import and export, subject, however, to the new Moroccan tariff schedule but not to the quota restrictions applicable in the rest of the country. Offsetting the latter, however, was a 4 per cent supplementary tax on all imports and exports transiting Tangier. Alarming to the freewheeling Tangier businessmen was the Charter's Article V which provided for six months notice by the government of any change in the provisions. That any change at all might be contemplated, notice or not, was enough to scare many of them to more hospitable Zurich, Monaco, and Beirut.

As business fell off in Tangier, prices went up as the tariff schedule took effect. High port charges also had their leavening influence. Finally, since Tangier was not included in the clearing accord with the French Treasury, importers were compelled to purchase foreign currencies on a weakening parallel market, which meant another fillip to the price spiral.[23]

In the meantime, there was agitation among some Moroccan political groups in opposition to the government to do away with the "special status" of Tangier. As with the question of "Moroccanization," the government could not safely ignore this ferment, and it chose the occasion of the establishment of the national currency in the fall of 1959 to announce the abrogation of the Charter of Tangier effective, in accordance with the delay provided by Article V, in the spring of 1960.

With a relatively minor exception, the abrogation meant that Tangier was completely integrated into Morocco and that its usual functions were a thing of the past.[24] Freedom of exchange, import and export, were eliminated. As a result, business activity sank to new lows, and prices rose to new highs. Some representative price changes are listed below:[25]

	BEFORE	AFTER
	(IN FRANCS)	
Gasoline (liter)	40	70
Olive oil (liter)	190–200	220–230
Sugar (kilogram)	55	110
Flour (kilogram)	33	50

The wrench of integration leaves Tangier in the doldrums, because it deprives the city of its accustomed occupations. As the powers gave it a special status in 1923, so too must Moroccans recognize its special character, even though the principle of integration stands. Thus, the then-Crown Prince, Moulay Hassan, made several remedial proposals in a speech at Tangier in the fall of 1960. These included further development of the port so that it might serve to clear trade from the northern Gharb and the central Riff, assurance that Tangier merchants would get their share of import licenses and allocations of foreign exchange, subsidies and low interest loans to industry not granted elsewhere, and, specifically, a new textile plant with part of the shares held by the government.[26] There has also been talk of making Tangier a free port, or at least endowing it with a free zone.

The problem of territorial unity then has been largely one of how the relatively well-endowed south can absorb the poverty-stricken ex-Spanish zone and maverick Tangier. The weight of the past, largely determined by bargaining in Europe among European powers, makes the process difficult indeed. The withdrawal of the peseta and the abrogation of the Charter are in reality only first steps, and are certainly far from the last, in restoring the territorial unity of Morocco.

PLANNING AND INSTITUTIONS

Earlier it was stated that the ideal goal for Morocco must be economic independence, and that this may be approximated through the creation of multiple and diffuse relationships between the outside and of an appropriate domestic organization — appropriate in the sense that it allows Morocco to pay its way. In turn, this domestic organization must be created and re-created through the continuous process of national integration. The goal then sets the task, which is a continuing one because conditions, both external and internal, are constantly changing. Finally, the task is urgent because it is made increasingly difficult by population growth.

It is extremely doubtful if the process of national integration will go far enough or fast enough if dependent upon laissez-faire any more than a political "laissez-faire" would have produced independence in 1956. Also, just as the "unseen hand" is most unlikely to bring about a state of autarky, neither is it likely to result in multiple outside liaisons appropriate to economic independence. The realities say otherwise. If the apple is to drop in this case, someone must shake the tree.

Moroccans have no choice but to adopt bold national planning and to mobilize people and resources in the struggle for national economic integration. They must develop clear consistent plans together with the skills and determination necessary to its execution.[27] They must also be prepared for surprises. The execution of plans not only leads to discovery of parameters not known *a priori* (or if known not given sufficient weight) but also to new parameters which appear over time. From this it follows that the planners must forsake rigidity in execution as well as devotion to fixed time spans, e.g., two-year or five-year plans, for the pragmatic and even the *ad hoc*. Mobilized resources are certain to need directing to new paths, no doubt with annoying frequency to both the planners and the public. In fact, the biggest task of all is probably that of keeping resources effectively mobilized during reorientation periods.

Planners must have tools (institutions) with which to work and a framework (supplied by legislation and treaties) for carrying out their tasks. In Morocco, both appear to have been developed with the following in mind. First, in an economy where roughly a fifth of the national income arises in foreign trade, possible actions are weighed in terms of their eventual effects on the balance of payments. Will a given action promote exports or reduce imports? Second and no less important, will a given action lessen dependence on France, both as a market and as a source of aid? Third, will a given action promote national integration?

In the matter of institutions, Morocco became a member of the International Bank for Reconstruction and Development and the International Monetary Fund in 1958; it made a drawing from the latter in the fall of the next year when the national currency (the dirham) was established. During the same period, the Bank of Morocco was established and took over from the old French-controlled *Banque d'Etat* the note issue and depository function for the government. The Bank was also charged with the responsibility of negotiating payments agreements and of dealings with the International Monetary Fund.

Other banks were established, among them the National Bank for Economic Development, Bank for Foreign Trade, National Savings Bank, and National Agricultural Bank. The first mentioned was designed to promote the development of relatively large-scale enterprise, while the financial needs of small business were recognized in 1960 with the establishment of the so-called *Banque Centrale Populaire*. Finally, the government instituted the

Bureau d'Etudes et de Participations Industrielles (B.E.P.I.), an agency which, much like the *Bureau de Recherches et de Participations Minières (B.R.P.M.)* established in 1928 in the mining sector, shares the ownership of industrial firms with private interests in the tradition of the *économie mixte*.

The biggest step toward providing a framework for planning was that taken in the matter of the national currency. National economic policy could have neither meaning nor effect if prices, wages, and other costs were beyond government control; such was the case when Morocco was in the franc zone and subject to the regulations of the French Treasury, regulations taken largely in the interests of the French economy.

After a series of monetary actions carried out in France after the return of General de Gaulle, most of which were distinctly unfavorable to Morocco, the Moroccan government established the dirham in the fall of 1959 and backed it with gold (at least one-ninth of the note issue) instead of the franc. At the same time the currency was devalued by slightly more than 20 per cent; the drawing was made from the International Monetary Fund as a stabilization measure; the Royal Charter for Tangier, which included freedom of exchange, was withdrawn; and exchange controls were extended to the franc zone. The last were confined largely to capital transfers, however, and the movement of goods remained practically free. Although certain ties to the franc zone remained, for most intents and purposes, Morocco severed its connections with the franc. Inflation in France during the years the currencies were tied, however, had left its mark in Morocco. Although the franc was gone, high costs remained.

Control over the currency and the exchanges were the main features on the monetary side, but behind money lie real goods and services. The flow and composition of trade has been regulated by a comprehensive tariff schedule first established in 1957 and revised in 1961, a quota system, and export subsidies; the direction of trade has in part been determined by a series of bilateral trade and payments agreements with countries in both the Eastern and Western blocs.[28]

Policies concerning foreign aid and investment give further guidance to planners. Foreign aid has been received from several countries, including the United States, West Germany, and the Soviet Union. Private foreign investment has also come from many countries, among them West Germany, Italy, and the United

States, as well as France. The net flow of funds has, nevertheless, been outward as capital repatriation by Europeans continues.

At the same time that Moroccans have sought to establish multiple trade, aid, and investment ties with the outside, they have also tried to spread the benefits from those ties widely over the country. For example, achievement of national economic integration through dispersion of new industrial investment appears to be a basic policy. More specifically, the policy is to reduce the importance of Casablanca and its environs as *the* industrial and commercial nucleus of the modern economy. Thus, the Moroccans are attempting to reverse the long-time French policy of concentration begun in early protectorate days when Lyautey first chose to make Casablanca the principal port of the country.[29]

With the setting for national economic integration established, it remains to assess the progress made since 1956 in the several sectors of the economy. Following the format of the middle chapters of the book, we shall discuss in turn agriculture, industry and mines, and transport and trade. In a sense, the comments and observations will serve as addenda to those chapters. Finally, there will be a concluding but inconclusive note, necessarily inconclusive because students of fast-moving events cannot really overtake them.

DEVELOPMENTS IN AGRICULTURE

The broad lines of Moroccan agriculture are somber, and the keynote over-all is stagnation. Farm output, heavily weighted by cereals, continues to swing as nature decrees around an average dating from the thirties. The cereals category accounts for about one-third of the gross national product and usually somewhat less than 20 per cent by value of Moroccan exports.[30] The dual character of agriculture — traditional vs. modern — persists as does continued reliance on privileged access through quotas to the high price French market.[31] Despite migration to the cities, roughly three-quarters of the population still live in the rural areas but unemployment reduces by half the number who work there. Underemployment is also chronic.

The broad objective for planning in agriculture is easily stated: greater production at lower unit cost. With growing population, yields must be raised immediately, and this calls for measures with a quick payout even if an early asymptote. Over the longer term, progress must be sustained by longer term measures.

The question remains of where the measures are likely to be the most productive. The configuration of current land use and additional possibilities suggest that efforts should be concentrated on presently cultivated surfaces rather than on extension of the margin. (In fact, higher yields per hectare now under the plow would reduce the pressure on marginal lands.) At the same time, the existing pattern of land ownership and agricultural methods requires that efforts be directed toward the preponderant and traditional Moroccan sector rather than toward the small and modern European one. Stated differently, the protectorate policy of dealing with the relatively little problems of Europeans while neglecting the big problems of Moroccans should be reversed, and the battle for production fought in present Moroccan fields with the goal of relegating the word "dual" to history.

Higher farm yields are a very large key to Moroccan development but, if they are to be really meaningful, they should be accompanied by lower unit costs. The resulting wider spread between input and output should in turn be shared by lower product prices and increased farm incomes. Lower prices for food and fiber to consumers would help to stimulate development in other sectors of the economy; they would also give Moroccans a better chance to compete in world markets, thus reducing dependence on France.

Increased farm incomes should be divided among a higher level of living for the fellah, more mechanized equipment, and the maintenance through crop rotation of Morocco's most precious patrimony, the fertility of the soil. The introduction of forage varieties into the rotation would have the further advantage of raising the efficiency of animal husbandry. All would combine to reduce the tendency, well established during the protectorate years, of agriculture and animal husbandry to move farther and farther out on the margins where neither could develop.

Although the period since independence has been relatively short, the government has taken several steps to increase farm production, both in the short and long run. Some of these steps are discussed below.

LAND TENURE

One of the fruits of independence has been a more detailed and therefore clearer picture of the land tenure situation in Morocco. During the protectorate years, one had to be satisfied with an average figure of 17 hectares per Moroccan farm, 8 of which were cultivable.[32] Data on the distribution by size were not published. By 1959, an indication of size distribution began to appear, even though statistically it still left much to be desired. The weakness of the average as a measure was amply demonstrated, however, when the Ministry of Agriculture estimated that 50 per cent of the rural families had less than 3 hectares; 25 per cent had no land at all; and only the remaining 25 per cent had "viable" farms. Further evidence was found in a sample of 40,000 hectares which came under the Operation Plowing program in 1959, of which more below, where it was shown that 92 per cent of the parcels comprised less than 3 hectares. In the region of Tetouan, located in the ex-Spanish zone, another sample revealed that 99.6 per cent of the parcels were less than 10 hectares, 84 per cent less than 4 hectares, and 67 per cent less than 3 hectares.[33]

These figures certainly indicate not only smallness as typical of Moroccan agriculture but also fragmentation of individual holdings, both inimical to the "industrialization" of agriculture. These disadvantages can be reduced through cooperative organization and consolidation of parcels. Both cooperation and consolidation have become keystones of government agricultural policy, particularly in the areas under large-scale irrigation. Cooperation has also been promoted as an adjunct to grants of credit, the services of Operation Plowing, and the cession of domanial lands and those collective lands, formerly rented to Europeans, which have been recovered by the State.

In general, it is safe to say that the land tenure situation has changed relatively little in the few years since independence, but that the little change may portend greater changes in the future. Some *melk* land acquired by Europeans during the protectorate has been sold to Moroccans,[34] and a start has been made in the distribution of the limited amount of domanial land. As an example of the latter, there is the case of 750 hectares in the Triffas, located in eastern Morocco, which were broken down into 287 parcels and distributed in 1958. Another distribution took place in the Gharb during the same year where 2,350 hectares in 156 parcels passed into the hands of the fellahin.[35]

Title to domanial lands remains with the State. The right of usage can be inherited, however, but the parcel cannot be broken up among heirs. Fragmentation of what are already small holdings is thereby avoided. The farmer pays no rent for the land in any crop year if his yield is less than 5 quintals of hard wheat equivalent per hectare. Succeeding increments of yield above 5 quintals are assessed rentals on a regressive basis ranging from 15 down to 8 per cent of crop value for yields in excess of 15 quintals. It is hoped that the regressive schedule of rents will be an inducement to increase yields. Also in the interest of stimulating larger output is the requirement that cooperatives be established.

Another noteworthy development has concerned those collective lands which were rented to 114 Europeans during the protectorate. A *dahir* published in the summer of 1959 called for government recovery of the roughly 45,000 hectares of such land, three-quarters of which had been leased in perpetuity. Most was located in the fertile regions of Casablanca, Rabat, and the Tadla.[36]

Under the decree, the lands were divided into three categories: (1) properties under perpetual lease which reverted to the government immediately; (2) properties under perpetual or long-term lease which were converted to rentals for three years or, in exceptional cases where large investments had not yet been amortized, for five years; and (3) properties whose leases would continue but with the rent payments revised.[37] Control of the recovered lands was to remain in government hands, and recipients were required to form cooperatives.

Since the total area affected by the decree represents less than 4 per cent of the *colons'* land, it does relatively little to alter the distribution of holdings between Europeans and Moroccans, but the action raises certain speculation concerning the future. For example, a case might be made for taking back the collective lands which had been acquired "in the public interest" and sold to Europeans, since these lands comprise a significant proportion of the approximately 300,000 hectares transferred under the protectorate program of official colonization. It might not be difficult to argue that the public interest had changed. Domanial, *guich*, and *habous* lands now in European hands might also be included in the same argument.

Along with its distribution of domanial and the rented land, the government has adopted the policies of continuing official control and "compulsory cooperation" by the fellahin. Their efficacy may be doubted, however, in the light of experience during the protectorate, particularly in the *Secteurs de Modernisation du Paysanat* and in the cooperatives required in the areas under large-scale irrigation. In both cases the overseer-worker relationship quickly prevailed over any spirit of cooperation, and considerable hostility was generated among the Moroccans involved. But at the same time, it should be remembered that the monitor who had been French is now Moroccan. The significant difference is that the same action taken to the same end by a colonial power and an independent government is often greeted by the people concerned with hostility in the first case and approbation in the second.

TAXATION

The principal agricultural tax, the *tertib*, came under considerable fire with the advent of independence. It will be remembered that the *tertib* was a proportional tax of 5 per cent levied on estimated *gross* farm income, but that there was a schedule of rebates to be made in cases where either "European" or "improved" methods were used. The rebate system did much to modify the incidence of the levy by shifting the relative *net* tax burden from the qualified modern European farmer to the traditional and therefore ineligible Moroccan farmer.[38] The abolition of the rebate system in 1957, while greeted with much enthusiasm in Moroccan agricultural circles, also served to switch the focus to other aspects of the tax.

In the vanguard of the campaign against the *tertib* was the *Union Marocaine de l'Agriculture*, an organization of Moroccan farmers formed shortly after independence. In a study published by the group in 1959, it was argued that, since the tax was based on gross income, it took into account neither cost of production nor, more specifically, the break-even point *(seuil de rentabilité)*. In addition, the tax was based on *estimated* gross income, and bad estimates by the authorities often led to capital levies. Further, the exemption from tax of 3 quintals per hectare, then in force, was alleged to be a capital levy since the money returns from 3 quintals did not cover production costs. As a minimum, the *Union* wanted an over-all exemption of 8 quintals, and even an exemption of yields above that figure if the fellah were working a very small plot.[39]

The response of the government in 1959 was not so generous, but it did represent a significant break with the past. In the first place, the basic exemption was raised from 3 quintals to 4 which meant that an estimated 1,300,000 hectares undoubtedly worked by small farmers, or about 50 per cent of the crop land, would be relieved of tax.[40] At the same time, the proportional tax of 5 per cent was abandoned in favor of a progressive schedule ranging from 2 to 10 per cent depending on estimated per hectare yields. The importance of this change is shown by some comparative rates in the higher brackets of yield for 1958 and 1959. On land yielding above 20 quintals per hectare, the 1958 tax for hard wheat was 4,680 francs per hectare, while the comparable figure for 1959 was 7,130 francs for yields between 20–25 quintals, and 11,310 francs for returns above 25 quintals, a new category. For soft wheat, the corresponding figures were 3,900 francs, 6,030 francs, and 9,570 francs, while the tax on barley was raised from 1,920 francs to 3,020 francs, with 4,790 francs collected when yields exceeded 25 quintals.[41] While the tax did something for "fiscal justice," its performance in raising revenue was still dependent on two characteristics which have made Moroccan agriculture uncertain — wide swings in yields from year-to-year and, in the upper ranges of yields, dependence on annual French quotas.

The final break with the *tertib* was made in the summer of 1961 when King Hassan II announced its abolition, giving as his reason the incompatibility of the tax with his long-run program of agrarian and fiscal reform. The announcement was also timely since drought had reduced the 1961 crop to an estimated 14 million quintals, a little less than half the average of the six years between 1950 and 1956.

At the present writing, the substitute that will be adopted for the *tertib* is not clear. A real property tax would be difficult to assess with thousands of hectares of still unsurveyed land in the country; a tax on marketed crops would require control of hundreds of *souks;* and an income tax would present a host of administrative problems. In any event, it would seem that the substitute should do at least two things: to provide exemptions for that overwhelming majority of the farmers who live on or close to the subsistence margin, and to promote greater efficiency in agriculture. It is evident that the government must take steps — and one of them could be in the area of taxation — to raise farm production significantly before it can hope to raise significant revenues from the agricultural sector.

Land Use

Although land use has changed relatively little since independence, its history after 1956 is interesting primarily because it points up the increasing acuity of Moroccan agricultural problems. These problems are a mixture of both deficit and a particular kind of surplus. They are perhaps best shown by a brief review of the evolution of the major product categories: cereals, animal husbandry, horticulture, and viniculture.

Cereals dominate Moroccan agriculture by any significant measure or combination of measures, such as area utilized, weight, or value of output. Table 8 shows its outline for the past thirty years. Closer examination of the figures will only confirm the first impression that cereal production is in "dynamic equilibrium" and,

TABLE 8. AVERAGES OF AREA SOWN, PRODUCTION, AND RETURNS FOR FOUR MAJOR CEREALS, 1931–1960

YEARS	AREA (ooo ha.)	PRODUCTION (ooo qx.)	RETURNS (per ha.)
		Hard wheat	
1931–1935	916	5,455	6.0
1936–1940	918	4,376	4.8
1941–1945	951	5,384	5.5
1946–1950	773	4,697	6.0
1951–1955	960	5,965	6.2
1956–1960	1,090	6,823	6.3
		Soft Wheat	
1931–1935	305	2,511	8.2
1936–1940	426	2,929	6.9
1941–1945	372	2,515	6.8
1946–1950	325	2,206	6.8
1951–1955	535	3,951	7.4
1956–1960	460	2,960	6.4
		Barley	
1931–1935	1,491	11,418	7.7
1936–1940	1,879	14,648	7.8
1941–1945	1,967	13,323	6.7
1946–1950	1,576	11,882	7.5
1951–1955	1,994	16,281	8.2
1956–1960	1,676	11,640	6.9
		Maize	
1931–1935	369	1,562	4.2
1936–1940	469	2,531	5.4
1941–1945	508	2,657	5.2
1946–1950	509	2,970	5.8
1951–1955	497	2,699	5.4
1956–1960	468	2,818	6.0

Source: *Annuaire statistique du Maroc, 1957*, Royaume du Maroc, Service Central des Statistiques (Rabat, 1957), p. 108; *La situation économique du Maroc en 1959*, Royaume du Maroc, Ministère de l'Economie Nationale et des Finances (Rabat, June, 1900), p. 7; *La Vie Economique*, January 13, 1961, pp. 1, 4.

with population more than doubled during the period, a very low level one at that. Fluctuations from year to year result from the forces of nature, and man has failed even in his minimum task of dampening them significantly. Thus, he falls a long step short of overcoming the forces sufficiently to produce a growth trend.

Morocco pays a stiff price when production is on the downside. Admittedly, the year 1961 is an extreme example since the harvest of 14 million quintals, exception made for the famine year of 1945, was the worst in thirty years; but the example is a recent one and that alone makes the costs worth consideration. One source estimates that in a normal year, the harvest would total 28 million quintals with a value of around 100 billion francs ($200 million). Although the estimate is probably a little too high, the 1961 harvest of 14 million quintals then meant a *trou* on the order of 50 billion francs.[42] But this was just the beginning. The Minister of Agriculture reported that the government had set aside the equivalent of $14 million to provide employment on public works for the fellahin in the worst-stricken areas and an additional $2 million for barley seeds, enough to sow 500,000 hectares for the next year. The burden on the budget and foreign exchange reserves was lessened, but it was far from removed, by the receipt under the United States Public Law 480 of 200,000 tons of soft wheat and 100,000 tons of barley which helped to relieve the suffering of men and animals in the countryside. Exchange-using imports of additional cereals were still needed to supply urban areas.[43]

Yet another aspect of Moroccan cereal production was illustrated during the 1960 growing season when 22 million quintals were harvested. Although 1960 was a year of shortage for all grains, soft wheat was especially in short supply, a typical situation even in good years. To alleviate the situation, Morocco entered into an arrangement with France whereby 85,000 tons of Moroccan hard wheat were exchanged for 125,000 tons of the soft variety. Since the value of each lot was roughly equal, the transaction was in effect a barter.

The case is interesting for the manner in which equal value was achieved. The Moroccan grain was purchased by France at NF 490 per ton at the same time that Canadian hard wheat was entering the French market at a world price ranging from NF 350–380 per ton. France in turn sold the soft wheat to Morocco at the world price of NF 323 per ton, while the prevailing quotation in France was NF 490 per ton.[44] The element of French subsidy in the transaction is obvious. The two examples show that grain growing is hardly a solid backbone of Moroccan agriculture. On the contrary, "Achilles heel" would be a better description since its present state is a very large obstacle in the path of economic independence. Without a viable agriculture, there can be no viable economy.

Animal husbandry exhibits the same fundamental characteristic as cereals, stagnation if not regression. Certainly Table 9 shows no growth pattern, so the number of domestic animals per capita declines as population grows.[45] As a consequence, urban consumption of meat and dairy products continues to be maintained only by imports which make demands on precious foreign exchange.

Nature is responsible for the static and sad situation in animal husbandry. The seasons and years continue to be read in the physical condition of the animals. The spring is the period of relative abundance, and the animals fatten rapidly from nature's bounty. But nature demands a price for her generosity, and the bill comes due in the rainless summer when the natural forage disappears and the stubble from the harvests substitutes only temporarily. Weight so rapidly gained in spring is quickly lost in summer. The late fall rains mark a partial revival of the pastures and enough forage to assure a shaky existence until spring. All this describes a good year. In a bad year when the rains fail, lack of nourishment combines with heat and cold to decimate herds and flocks. Rebuilding is both slow and precarious.

Perhaps even more than the cereal grower has the herder submitted to the will of a capricious nature. Shelters, accumulation of forage for the dry season, selective breeding, and veterinary care are exceptions rather than the rule. Overgrazing, however, is the rule, and marginal lands become more so as the herder borrows heavily today on future land productivity to build the flocks and herds which have been called his only savings bank. ("Le troupeau est la banque du fellah.") In the short-term logic of survival, it is easy to see why the expectation that his capital will be lost through drought and disease does not deter him from trying to accumulate some.

Vision, at least in earthly matters, is not ordinarily associated with subsistence life in cold mountains or on rocky plateaus. For this reason alone, the Moroccan herder cannot be expected to win that measure of victory over nature which would be his real salvation. As with cereals, the government must step in to help

TABLE 9. THE NUMBER OF SHEEP, GOATS, AND CATTLE IN MOROCCO, 1955–60, AND THE AVERAGE OF THE YEARS, 1931–52
(in 000)

SPECIES	1955	1956	1957	1958	1959	1960	AVERAGE 1931–52
Sheep	12,181	9,768	10,158	10,423	10,262	9,260	9,840
Goats	7,302	5,591	5,429	5,404	5,349	5,056	6,206
Cattle	2,466	2,350	2,542	2,883	2,560	2,591	2,028

Source: *Annuaire statistique de la zone française du Maroc, 1952*, Gouvernement Chérifien, Service Central des Statistiques (Rabat, 1952), p. 135; *Annuaire statistique du Maroc, 1957*, Royaume du Maroc, Service Central des Statistiques (Rabat, 1957), p. 127; *La Vie Economique*, September 1, 1961, p. 1.

convert animal husbandry from a present liability in the struggle for economic independence to a future asset. In fact, the two should be related. Mixed farming (crops and animals on the same property) has not been characteristic of Moroccan rural economy, although it is sound both in terms of cash returns and continued real productivity of the land.

On the surface, two bright spots in the agricultural sector appear to be citrus growing and truck farming. Unlike cereals, each has increased markedly in both area and production since independence. Also unlike cereals, part of which are consumed on the farm, fruits and vegetables are predominantly cash crops for export where prices, costs, and markets are critical variables. It is the marketing aspects which remove much of the glitter from the production records.

The story of Moroccan citrus is primarily that of the orange since this variety is by far the most important by weight and value. In the eight years after 1952, the area in orange groves almost doubled from 26,500 hectares to over 50,000 hectares, with 60 per cent occupied by producing trees. During the same period, output increased from 219,500 to 415,000 metric tons. A constant domestic consumption of 100,000 tons and an expansion of the French quota to 177,000 tons (from 115,000 tons in 1952) meant that the amount to be sold in other markets rose from 4,000 in 1952 to 138,000 tons in 1960.[46] In effect, production rose far faster than the French quota, thus forcing high-cost Moroccan producers to turn to other markets already flooded by oranges of Mediterranean competitors who themselves were engaged in expanding production.

Apparently Moroccan growers are headed for even more difficult times because the area now in orange groves has not yet reached full producing capacity. Even bigger tonnages will therefore have to be sold in the less lucrative markets when full capacity is reached. The importance to the country as a whole of a very possible market glut is pointed up by the fact that in 1958, citrus exports brought 14 billion francs in foreign exchange, or 10 per cent of total export earnings.[47]

The history of truck crops parallels that of citrus in many ways. Total area planted in vegetables expanded from 52,000 hectares in 1952 to 82,000 hectares in 1960. (By 1957, tomatoes alone covered 67,000 hectares.)[48] Exports rose from 52,000 for all vegetables in 1952 to 150,000 tons for only tomatoes in 1961. The French quota for tomatoes, the major variety, lagged behind the production increase — 90,000 tons in 1961 — which meant that Moroccan producers were forced to seek less attractive markets for larger amounts. In fact, the Moroccans at times had difficulties even in France, particularly in 1959 when, despite quotas, prices fell precipitously at *Les Halles*.[49] Throughout the period too, the size of the annual quota was in annual jeopardy as Algerian producers sought to reduce competition in the French market by reducing the Moroccan share.[50] As in the case of oranges, the problem of markets for tomatoes has no easy solution. Hopefully, the situation will be different with respect to wine.

Wine growing has also registered sizable gains in recent years; but production has increased more than area planted in vines. In 1954, there were 54,000 hectares of modern vineyards; six years later there were an additional 5,000 hectares. During the same period, the 1954 output of 1.9 million hectoliters, a record to that date, was surpassed by 850,000 hectoliters in 1959, and the average for the six years was close to the 1954 figure.

Local consumption has moved in the opposite direction. Moroccans provide little or no market, owing to religious prohibition, and emigration of Europeans has meant a drop from a long time constant domestic consumption of around 600,000 hectoliters per year to an estimated 225,000 hectoliters for 1961. Thus the pressure to export increases as an alternative to the unprofitable distillation or "blockage," roughly the Moroccan equivalent for wine of the American grain storage program.

The willingness of France to take Moroccan wine exports depends on the state of its domestic supply. The Moroccan quota went to an all-time high of one million hectoliters in 1958–59. The year 1958 had been a deficit one in France to the profit of Moroccan growers, but 1959 saw a decided improvement in French production with prices plummeting well below Moroccan production costs. For the following year, the quota for Moroccan wine was cut back to 700,000 hectoliters where it has since remained.

If the present French quota and current domestic consumption are subtracted from an average production of around two million hectoliters, then roughly half the output must be sold in other markets if distillation and blockage are to be avoided. The problem of these other markets was put succinctly by M. Kebbaj, the Minister of Agriculture, when he noted that "the great consuming countries are also the great producing and great exporting countries." [51] Although Moroccan wines face tough competition in world markets, their high quality merits serious promotional efforts and, as the Minister pointed out,[52] wine accounts for 6 per cent by value of all exports, and 10 per cent of all agricultural exports — a not-inconsiderable contribution to exchange earnings. At the same time, the dimensions of this particular agricultural problem are likely to stabilize fairly well on the production side, as the government has limited vineyards to the area currently planted.

Measures for Agricultural Improvement

A rising production curve in agriculture is the product of many factors, among them better soil preparation and conservation, selected seeds, fertilizers, insecticides, and often irrigation. In certain cases, consolidation of parcels and the formation of cooperatives can also play a part. Some of the factors, e.g., selected seeds and fertilizers, are relatively inexpensive and bring quick payouts if properly used; others (irrigation projects) are very costly and, even if properly developed, offer only delayed returns. Either in the short or long run, however, it is technology and the credit mechanism which give these factors shape, mutual consistency, and scope. With neither technology nor credit is Morocco well endowed.

Moroccans also have very limited land, living as they do on the margin of the grain-growing area of the world. Rising output then must result from increased productivity per hectare presently cultivated and ideally, where there is chronic underemployment and unemployment in the countryside and few alternatives in the cities, increased productivity per person now in agriculture.[53] Within the limits of land, technology, and finances, the Moroccans have tried to move forward in the years since independence.

One of the programs designed to raise farm output has been Operation Plowing *(Opération Labour)*. This program is the successor to the old *Secteurs de Modernisation du Paysanat* which were established by the French, the first one in 1945. Unlike the sixty-two Sectors, however, where the administration in effect assumed direct control of the land and concerned itself with social as well as economic measures, the one hundred Works Centers *(Centres des Travaux)* of Operation Plowing do not control the land directly and are interested only in increasing farm output.[54]

The program combines the short-run objective of raising output immediately with the long-run goal of creating a viable agriculture. In essence, it attempts to do for the fellah what he cannot do for himself, owing to lack of know-how, capital, and land of sufficient size to allow the efficient use of modern machinery. Basically, as the name implies, the program provides mechanized plowing services; it also supplies on request other services connected with preparing the land for planting. But the program goes even further by requiring that the fellah do certain things, including using selected seeds and fertilizers. He must also combine with neighbors to create parcels of at least 100 hectares; this together with the requirement that they elect a *Comité de Gestion* to deal with the personnel of the Work Center provides the first elements of a cooperative which, the government hopes, will eventually be self-sustaining.

The potential advantages of Operation Plowing are several: no longer must the farmer, with only animal power at his disposal, wait for the fall rains (which may be delayed) to turn over his soil; the tractor does it for him in advance. At the same time, the farmer does not become an idle bystander. He sows the selected seeds, spreads the fertilizer, weeds and harvests the crop. The results of at least one season have been significant. A sampling of land worked by Operation Plowing in 1958 showed a 95 per cent probability that the increased yield lay between 5.13 and 6.85 quintals of hard wheat equivalent per hectare, up from 8.92 to 10.06 quintals per hectare, also with a 95 per cent probability. The sampling was admittedly taken on above-average land, but it was also taken in a year when the yields were generally below average.[55] On a money basis, increased quality and yield brought a return, after deduction of additional expenses, of about 24,500 francs per hectare, up from 17,000 francs before Operation Plowing.[56]

On the debit side, there have been technical mistakes: some of the cultivation undertaken by the Works Centers has been poorly executed; in addition, the kind and amount of fertilizer have not always been suited to the soil or, if appropriate, not distributed to farmers at the proper time. Hand-spreading of the fertilizer by the farmer has also left much to be desired.

The financial aspects of the program are also subject to debate. From the beginning, the government has tried to put the program on an almost self-sustaining basis, the principal element of subsidy being the administrative overhead which was to be borne by the government budget. (At first, the fertilizer was distributed free, but later a charge was made.) Since no amount of "scientific" farming can completely compensate for drought, the farmer has been saddled with heavy charges in years when there was little or no yield.

In 1960, a new schedule of charges, based on hard wheat equivalents, was announced for the 1961 season. If the land yielded less than 3 quintals per hectare, the only charge was for the seed. In fact, the 3-quintal deduction applied to land in all categories of yield. From 3 to 8 quintals, the incremental charge was 50 per cent of the yield; above 8 quintals, 80 per cent. The schedule was considerably modified in practice, however, by the proviso that those in the higher categories of yield would pay more than the actual expenses to a maximum of 150 per cent — this to help compensate the government for those who paid less. Even with a schedule of charges thus devised, there is no assurance that the program will be self-sustaining, especially in a drought year such as 1961 when yields fell precipitously. At the same time, there *is* the possibility that the farmer charged a sum in excess of actual costs may seek to reduce his payment by having the Centers work, not his best, but only his marginal land.

A real question is whether the government, in keeping its subsidy to a minimum, can expect Moroccan agriculture as a whole to pull itself up largely by its own bootstraps or whether Operation Plowing may founder owing to the means of financing adopted. Technical mistakes present an additional hazard since they take a toll of meager finances. In sum, when both technology and money are in very limited supply, their leverage is correspondingly very limited. This hard fact, it should be added, does not obfuscate the principle of large-scale modernization, but it does reduce its efficacy in practice. As a result of the divergence between principle and practice, there has been no secular growth in the area under Operation Plowing; on the contrary, total area has decreased from a high of 288,000 hectares in 1959 to 173,000 hectares in 1961.[57]

The development of modern irrigation has continued slowly and expensively since independence. Of 500,000 hectares of irrigable land in the five major areas of large-scale projects, roughly 116,000 were equipped by 1960, but only 59,000 hectares, or a little more than 10 per cent, were actually irrigated during that year.[58] In the Five-Year Plan, begun in 1960, approximately 500 million dirhams (about $100 million) was budgeted to equip an additional 78,000 hectares in these areas.

The major change thus far has been the establishment in 1960 of a National Irrigation Office to manage the five major projects along with several smaller ones. As was stated earlier, administration at the project level during the protectorate left much to be desired. It will be a long step forward if the Office can correct some of the deficiencies which were apparent in that period. The question still to be answered, however, is whether bringing the full 500,000 hectares under irrigation represents the best allocation of resources, given the relatively short "life expectancy" of the dams and alternative uses of scarce funds budgeted for agriculture.[59]

The most important experiment with new crops is that being carried out in the irrigated area of the Gharb at Sidi Slimane, where the growing of sugar beets was inaugurated in 1959. The experiment has been under the auspices of the government's *Bureau d'Etudes et des Participations Industrielles, Cosuma*, a French-owned sugar refining company located in Casablanca, and a Belgian group. Apparently the experiment has been a success. According to one source, average beet production per hectare in the experimental plots was 43 tons, well above the European average, while sugar yield per hectare was an average 10 tons, as compared with 3 less for Europe.[60] On the basis of this experience, a refinery will be built in the area and is scheduled to begin operation in 1963. Annual capacity is calculated at 30,000 tons of refined sugar, or approximately 10 per cent of current domestic consumption which incidentally is among the highest per capita in the world.

If the results of the Gharb experiment have any general application, it would represent a major breakthrough in Moroccan agriculture. Assuming production costs competitive with those prevailing elsewhere, domestic sugar production could mean a major saving of foreign exchange,[61] a large boost to animal husbandry through the production of by-product fodder, and increased agricultural income and employment. As with all assumptions, however, those of broad application of the experiment and competitive costs remain to be verified. The test comes largely with practice.

The efficacy of credit in getting resources efficiently allocated depends on many things. Good organization and management of credit institutions, potentially at least, assure rapid appraisal of applications and grants of loans; they also assure that the turnover rate of funds approaches the planned maximum through repayments made on time and that write-offs are minimal. Good organization and management, however, can only be as effective as the condition of the borrower allows. In the case of agricultural credit, the farmer must have land of sufficient size and productivity so that use of the loan proceeds will generate the funds for repayment over the agreed term.[62] In case of default, the land must also be good security, i.e., it should be registered. Equally important, fluctuations in income, owing to fluctuations in yields and/or market prices, must not impede the capacity to repay on time and in full.

All of these conditions lead to efficient use and therefore to minimum cost of agricultural credit. In fact, until these conditions are met, it is largely meaningless to say that credit is in short supply. In other words, the volume of credit is a concept without real meaning if efficiency in use is not considered.[63] Credit for Moroccan agriculture during the protectorate was largely short term, a means of tiding the farmer over until the next harvest. Seed loans predominated. Slowness in processing applications and the requirement that real property be pledged as security helped to keep medium-term loans for equipment small. There were virtually no long-term facilities for Moroccans. Credit, then, did little to raise productivity, but served only to maintain it at a low level.[64]

While the credit worthiness of the fellah left much to be desired, so did the organization of the credit institutions. For example, the medium-term credit agency — Les Caisses Régionales d'Épargne et de Crédit (C.R.E.C.) — made loans to the artisan trade and for urban construction as well as to agriculture; thus the attention of the loaning authorities and available funds were divided among disparate activities. The loan officers in the Sociétés de Crédit Agricole et de Prévoyance (S.O.C.A.P.), the source of short-term credits, was the local Moroccan governor, "assisted" by the French Contrôleur Civil. These officials had a host of other duties, and making loans did not rank high on the list.[65]

The reform of the agricultural credit system in 1961 was designed to correct some of the deficiencies. Briefly, the new system provides for a National Agricultural Bank, several regional banks, and many local banks.[66] Provision is made for assessment of credit needs of Moroccan agriculture as a whole and for the require-ments of the localities. Funds will come from the "stockholders" of local banks (only stockholders will be eligible for loans), loans from the National Bank, subventions from the State, and deposits by the government. Loans of all maturities are provided for, and control of the banks is shared by the stockholders and government representatives, the latter heavily weighted toward those con-cerned with agriculture.

The organizational part of the reform holds much promise that credit can now play an effective role in raising agricultural pro-ductivity. Whether the management will measure up technically is another matter. Then, too, there are those conditions of the borrower, cited above, which credit extension can only partly ameliorate. Credit, new crops, irrigation, "Operation Plowing," land and tax reform, cooperatives – all are points of leverage in Moroccan agriculture. In the last analysis, however, their effec-tiveness will depend on the knowledge, skills, understanding, and cooperation of the men involved, from the Minister of Agriculture to the fellah in the remotest corner of the country.

MINING AND INDUSTRY

The post-independence developments in mining and industry in general make pleasant reading. Mineral production curves, led by phosphates, have largely been rising and promising explorations have been carried out. At the same time, the list of new industrial firms lengthens, and old ones revive behind trade barriers. Indus-trial activity is also becoming somewhat more dispersed geograph-ically, as is ownership where foreign investments are involved. (While French ownership still predominates, others are coming in.) Thus, the industrial sector makes its contribution to economic independence as areal dispersion furthers national economic in-tegration, and as the changing character of ownership contributes to multiple ties with the outside.

Enthusiasm should probably be tempered, however, by at least one fact and two serious prospects. The fact is that the increase in national product contributed by mining and industry and the impact of the increase on the balance of payments have remained relatively small.[67] Admittedly, the time period has been very short, but market limitations, both domestic and foreign, un-doubtedly also make only small gains possible. Given limited market potential, one prospect is that the obvious opportunities, especially in the industrial sector and specifically in light industry, will be rapidly used up. In other words, there is a clear chance that industrial growth will level off at an early date, thus duplicating the experience of cereals production during the protectorate years.

Wide cyclical swings are not to be ruled out either. Producers for the domestic market must contend with fluctuating purchasing power which basically reflects the varying fortunes of a shaky agriculture, while mineral producers must face world markets characterized by large price movements over the cycle. Even the anticipated processing of certain minerals in Morocco cannot be expected to alleviate the situation very much, since any realistic development along this line would still leave the products in the price-sensitive category of industrial raw materials. Thus price instability may have a dampening effect on sustained growth by its adverse effects on profits available for reinvestment by already-established firms and on the anticipations of those considering new investment.

The government is doing much on many fronts to forestall the possibility of stagnation. Tariff protection, of course, is a classic device, and the Moroccans are using it to assure local producers a measure of monopoly in the local market. By the same token, the government assures itself also that import substitution will in fact result from the establishment of new industry, thereby saving foreign exchange. On the domestic side, an additional measure of monopoly is added by government control of new entry, and permission is refused where "unnecessary" duplication of facilities would result. Thus, in contemplating investment in Morocco, an eligible manufacturer need largely concern himself only with identification of the total market potential for his product; he has less need to undertake the more difficult task of estimating market share as in the case where more competitive conditions prevail.[68] Of course, that in itself is a large inducement to invest.

There are others. For example, the *Bureau d'Etudes et Participations Industrielles (B.E.P.I.)* will often purchase shares in enterprises; in fact, it may insist on it, much as the *Bureau de Recherches et de Participations Minières (B.R.P.M.)* has done for many years in the mining sector. The government also offers a subsidy *(prime d'équipement)* of up to 20 per cent of investment to firms willing to locate in places other than Casablanca and Mohammedia, now the major centers of industrial activity; and it will give partial and often full relief from import duties on imports of necessary capital goods. Safety of capital is increased by provisions of an investment law covering such matters as nationalization and guarantees of earnings and capital repatriation. Along this line, a treaty has also been negotiated with the United States which will make American investments eligible for the U.S. Investment Guaranty Program.

The impact on investment of the tax reforms, which went into effect at the beginning of 1962, remains to be seen. The substitution of a flat 30 per cent income tax rate on corporations for the former moderately progressive structure is a case in point. Perhaps more interesting is the additional requirement that amounts ranging from 3 to 15 per cent, varying according to earnings, be paid into a so-called National Investment Fund which pays no interest on monies received. Rebates are made, however, in cases where the taxpayer makes an additional investment, which is approved by the government, in an amount at least equal to tax paid. To qualify for a full rebate, the taxpayer must invest a sum twice the amount of the tax.[69] The wisdom of tying so closely the rate of net investment to tax paid in any given year remains to be demonstrated.

MINING

The nationalized phosphates account for more than half of mineral output by value and continue to lead other minerals in relative tonnage increases. Production in 1960 totaled 7.5 million tons, up from approximately 4 million tons in 1952, while the others, notably lead, zinc, manganese, iron, and cobalt, registered smaller gains. For example, manganese rose only from 426,000 to 483,000 tons in the same period, and the other minerals exhibited a similar tendency.[70] While the boom in Europe was a major factor in the expanded phosphate sales, undoubtedly part of the increase can be attributed to the fact that Morocco left the *comptoir*, a marketing cartel which for many years had held down the rate of increase in production of high grade Moroccan rock in order to provide a market for the lower grades of the Algerian and Tunisian members.[71]

The slow production increase of other minerals can be explained partly in the trend of world prices, one which has been largely downward in the period covered. As has been the case before, the drop in mine net returns has exceeded the price declines, since transport charges, in the case of Morocco high ones, have remained relatively fixed.

Coal and oil production actually dropped during the period, coal owing to a lagging demand and oil because of a reduction in productivity of the Gharb fields. Both developments emphasize Morocco's critical need for cheap energy resources: the coal is anthracite with limited industrial uses while the oil is pumped from small wells which means high cost of production. Further, domestic crude production covers less than one-sixth of domestic needs, so the difference must be financed by precious foreign exchange. Thermal and hydroelectric power remain expensive, the latter partly because output is as uncertain as the Moroccan rainfall.

Mineral exploration has shown promise. Natural gas has been discovered near Essaouira, and large pyrite deposits have been found which will form, along with the phosphates of Youssefiah, the basis for a chemical complex planned for nearby Safi. Oil and mineral explorations are also being made south of the Atlas, most notably by the *B.R.P.M.* in association with *Petrofina* (Italian) and *Teknoexport* (Czech), respectively. Thus, while the list of minerals has not lengthened significantly since independence, the considerable activity in exploration should tell the Moroccans at a fairly early date what their prospects are.

INDUSTRY

While industry established during the protectorate, most notably textiles, began to revive behind the trade barriers which were first set up in 1957, the years since independence have also witnessed the appearance of many new industrial firms on the Moroccan scene.[72] For the most part, the industries are thus far of the light variety, using a large percentage of imported components, although in several cases the percentage is being decreased through the development of local suppliers. For the most part, too, these firms are producing for the local market.

The development with the greatest potential impact on the balance of payments was the construction of an oil refinery at Mohammedia which went on stream at the end of 1961. Less costly imports of crude oil can thereby be substituted for refined products. The refinery has a capacity of 1,250,000 tons per year. The throughput forecast for 1962 was 600,000 tons which together with the much smaller production of the oil refinery at Sidi Kacem, would supply Morocco's estimated petroleum needs for the year. The figures also show that the installed capacity will continue to meet the country's requirements for some time to come. The refinery is jointly owned and operated by *E.N.I.* (Italian) and the *B.E.P.I.*

Vehicle assembly has seen an outstanding success, an apparently outstanding failure, and one yet to prove itself. The success is Berliet (French), a manufacturer of heavy trucks whose Moroccan plant has an annual capacity of 2,000 units, more than adequate to meet both civilian and military needs. As a consequence, Berliet is on an export basis and has been making a considerable contribution to balancing the trade account with Mainland China by selling trucks there.[73] The failure was the "national" farm tractor, the *Tarik*, a wheeled type whose manufacture was undertaken by the *B.E.P.I.* and two French concerns. Exactly what happened has not been clear but, among other things, it was said that the vehicle was "ill suited" to Moroccan agricultural conditions. In the meantime, the farmers were suffering, since imports of competing types continued to be banned even though local production had been suspended.

Facing the test is a new auto assembly plant in which Simca, Fiat, and the National Bank for Economic Development are involved. Their chances of success are greatly enhanced, however, by trade barriers which will assure a lion's share of the market. Complementary activities to be developed include the manufacture of batteries, seats, and radiators. Already on the scene is a tire company, owned by an American firm and the *B.E.P.I.*, with a capacity of 125,000 tires and 75,000 tubes per year. Output falls short of domestic consumption, roughly 200,000 tires in 1960, so imports continue.[74]

A final development of note is a modern textile plant which was constructed at Fez. Wholly owned by Moroccans consisting of the *B.E.P.I.* and individual investors, the plant is noteworthy because it indicates that Moroccans are willing to invest in equities which, in many countries, has proved to be a long and difficult step from the typical small family-owned and -operated enterprises.[75] Until Moroccans can be trained to take over, the plant will be operated by Italian technicians.

Heavy industry is on the horizon. Underway is the construction of several chemical plants at Safi. Making use basically of phosphates from Youssefiah, the plants will first produce super triple phosphate (a high grade fertilizer) and phosphoric and sulphuric acids. Later an ammonium sulphate plant is anticipated. The estimated cost of the plants themselves is over $20 million, with almost twice that sum to be spent on highways, railroads, port facilities at Safi, and other complementary works. Thus, the government hopes to add value in Morocco to phosphates, the backbone of the mining sector, and thereby to increase employment and export revenues.

Along with the restoration of the Spanish zone to government control came the Riff iron mines, located near Nador. The ore, now wholly exported through the presidio of Melilla, is much higher grade than that at Ait Amar in the south. The principal stumbling block to the development of a steel industry is that Djerada coal, which is anthracite, is not suited to coking use with present technology. One is tempted to predict that, barring any technological breakthrough, Morocco will have no steel industry, since the economics, including imports of coking coal, would preclude it. It has been proved elsewhere, however, that the arguments of economics cannot defeat a determined government where a steel industry is concerned, and official spokesmen continue to refer to the possibility whenever they discuss economic prospects.

TRANSPORT AND TRADE

Moroccan transportation history is largely a story of costs sunk in steel and concrete, both noted for their durability and immobility. Since transport facilities represent very large and very long-term investments and since the French were "roadbuilders," the new government finds itself heir to a comprehensive rail and highway network whose density, configuration, and probably costs will be present for a long time to come.

From the economic welfare point of view, whether the story is a happy or sad one depends on how "wise" the investment seems to have been in the light of subsequent developments — economic, political, technological, and random. These developments essentially determine whether there will be profits or losses over the long life of the investment.[76] In the case of losses, to paraphrase an old saying, there is little use in crying over sunk costs. The only question is who is to pay, the public or the investor, for what subsequently has turned out to be a mistake.

During the protectorate the public paid. Given distances, types, and volume of products to be moved, highway transport would have been the more efficient technology in most cases. (Shipment of phosphates would be a notable exception.) "Rationalization" of the network, however, involved adjustment by the government of competitive relationships between the railroads and highway transport by subsidy of the former and, in general, taxing the latter. On balance, transport costs were raised all around in order to assure returns to railroad investors. Thus, it is doubtful if the transportation system efficiently served even the colonial purposes for which it was built.[77]

As noted earlier in the chapter, the Moroccans have elected to be economic planners and, in the transport sector, their agency is the National Transport Office *(Office National des Transports)*, successor to the *Bureau Central des Transports* which had been established to control the media in 1937. The *Office* has its work cut out because it stands to reason that if the system turned out to be ill-suited to French purposes, it is probably even less likely to serve Moroccan aims. At the same time, given the long-term nature of transport facilities in both construction and use, it is not surprising that there has been relatively little change since 1956.

At the time of independence, all major transportation links in the former French zone fanned out from Casablanca. The Spanish road system, meager as it was, consisted largely of a poor east–west connection, while north–south routes from the presidios petered out in the Riff. The major exceptions on the north–south axis were limited to a road from Tangier across the Spanish zone to Casablanca and the railroad from Tangier to Fez. Both were largely used for passenger transport, since the French and Spanish preferred not to depend on each other for transit of freight and thus kept such traffic within their respective zones.

Improvements of north–south communications must be high on any agenda of national economic integration, and even higher on those for political and social integration. An early manifestation of Moroccan concern on this score is found in the construction of the *Route de l'Unité*, a road begun by nationalist volunteers and finished by the Ministry of Public Works, which runs from Fez north across the Riff to Ketama. Widening and resurfacing of the road south from Tangier is also underway.

But the main work of developing a system suited to Moroccan purposes lies in the future, and planning a coherent network is hampered by political uncertainty. For example, barring any early return of the Spanish presidios of Ceuta and Melilla on the Mediterranean coast, the Moroccans feel it necessary to improve the port facilities of Alhucemas rather than rely on Spanish goodwill in the matter of transit. Far to the southeast there is another problem originally created by French boundary makers who, early in the century, put part of the road to the Moroccan oasis of Figuig in Algerian territory. Costly re-routing of the road may be necessary no matter what the future holds for Algerian-Moroccan relations.

In the ex-French zone, particularly in the western plains where the system is the most comprehensive, the policy of national economic integration through dispersion requires obliteration of the fan from Casablanca by the development of communications to other ports and through the improvement of lateral roads.[78] In the meantime, the old system remains, and it does not come free. Maintenance costs of highways continue, and losses of the railroads *(Les Chemins de Fer du Maroc)* and the transportation company *(La Compagnie des Transports Marocains)* must be made good, in considerable part to French owners who received the concessions during the protectorate.[79] Although the concessions are not now a really active political issue, it seems safe to predict that their public utility nature will make them so in the future.

Economic growth over time can partly correct the mistakes of the past by gradually taking up some unused transport capacity. In the interim, however, resources are diverted to debt service and maintenance charges, thus reducing the amount available for investment in growth itself. The Moroccans, in sum, inherited a costly imbalance in the transport sector which will require considerable ingenuity and perspicacity to correct.

The same ingenuity and perspicacity will be required in the trade sector. Here the legacies have been basically two: an "open" economy to the degree that a substantial portion of the national income arises in international trade, and a chronic balance of payments deficit. It is not surprising, therefore, that on both scores, the government seeks, as one way to assure economic growth, close control over the international accounts. Given the importance of trade to national income, it is not surprising either that previous sections of this chapter have repeatedly included references to foreign trade.

Since much of the ground has already been covered, a recapitulation here should suffice to bring out the salient characteristics of the foreign trade problem. From these characteristics, it will be possible to identify some of the important questions the Moroccans must face in the future.

The recapitulation can perhaps best be made through a brief examination of the 1961 balance of payments. The year was admittedly a particularly bad one in the agricultural sector, but the results in the international accounts serve only to bring into sharper focus a deficit situation which has been almost consistently the rule ever since 1912 when the protectorate was established.[80]

In 1961, Moroccan imports by value rose to roughly DH 2.5 billion, an increase of 8 per cent over 1960, while exports declined to DH 1.7 billion, a drop of 3.4 per cent. The deficit on trade account was thus DH 800 million, or approximately $160 million, as compared with a deficit of DH 300 million in 1960. Owing to the crop failure, imports of foodstuffs went up 26 per cent over 1960 while exports in the same category were falling by 9 per cent. Hard wheat, barley, and corn were virtually eliminated as export items, but the fall was checked somewhat by an increase in shipments of citrus fruits and canned fish. At the same time, phosphates, the largest single export of any product, declined in value owing to a price reduction, this despite an increase in tonnage. Imports of steel and capital equipment increased almost 15 per cent as industrialization went forward, and imports of consumption goods rose 5 per cent. The capital account registered a net outflow of DH 7 million since private transfer payments and capital movements of DH 252 million were not completely offset by U.S. grants and loans of DH 245 million.

An over-all measure of Moroccan performance in international trade and payments for 1961 is found in the changed gold and foreign exchange position of the commercial banks and the Bank of Morocco from the previous year. The decline in gold and foreign exchange holdings of these institutions was approximately 23 per cent, or $53 million. Reserves at the end of 1961 totaled $178 million.[81] Global figures such as these are really only quantitative measures of the results of actions taken by both private enterprise and government. For a clearer understanding of what happened, it is necessary to look behind the figures.

The continuing weakness of cereal production is certainly demonstrated in the 1961 results, and enthusiasm for the continued increase in citrus exports must be moderated by the continued heavy dependence of growers on the French quota for successful operations, a quota which continues only on a year-to-year basis.

At the same time, the government profoundly influenced not only the volume of trade but its composition and direction as well.

In the fall of 1961, the serious situation in the balance of payments led the government to take several emergency measures, some of which are likely to become permanent. A case in point was the increase in duties on a considerable number of consumption goods, avowedly raised not only to reduce imports of "luxury" items but to protect local industry as well. Thus duties on jewelry were raised from 50 per cent to 100 per cent; electrical appliances from 35 per cent to 70 per cent; tires from 25 per cent to 40 per cent; beef from 30 per cent to 80 per cent; and beer from 40 per cent to 80 per cent. Duties on shoes and clothing reached new highs of 80 per cent and 40–60 per cent, respectively.[82]

In addition, the government required from businessmen an advance deposit of 25 per cent of import value for many products; however, it also made many exemptions. The requirement together with the exemptions were designed to influence the volume, composition, and direction of the import trade. Imports made under the U.S. aid program were not subject to advance deposits, nor were shipments from the ten countries which had bilateral trade and payments agreements with Morocco. Certain products were also excluded from the requirement, among them cereals, sugar, tea, pharmaceuticals, chemicals, rubber, copper, tin, and machinery. In effect, by its actions the government was assuring essential foodstuffs for the people and the necessary raw materials and equipment for the expanding industrial sector.

Any set of rigid import controls can ameliorate a balance of payments deficit, since it limits and rations the use of scarce foreign exchange; but it cannot correct a deficit in any meaningful way unless it contains the seeds of its own destruction, i.e., unless it eventually renders itself moot by contributing to an increased capacity to provide import substitutes and to a greater capacity to export. But even if a set of import controls were designed to optimize these capacities, success would not be a certainty in the light of at least two possibilities. The first is that trade is a two-way street, and Moroccan plans could be foiled by the reluctance of trading partners to take an increased volume of exports. The second possibility is that perhaps Morocco could neither generate domestically nor borrow abroad capital resources in amounts sufficient to develop the capacities.

Since the prospects are uncertain concerning both the intentions of trading partners and the matter of capital mobilization, one is led, however reluctantly, into the realm of speculation. Given the geographical location of Morocco, the present trade pattern, and future production possibilities as suggested by domestic resources, the answer to the export problem would appear to lie in Europe, and not with the distant countries of the Eastern Bloc or with the United States. The countries of the Common Market provide 62 per cent of Moroccan imports and take 58 per cent of the country's exports. If the United Kingdom joins the Community, the shares will be raised to 66 and 65 per cent, respectively.[83] A breakdown by product is even more revealing. In 1959, the Common Market countries took 80 per cent of Moroccan agricultural exports, 45 per cent of the canned fish, more than 50 per cent of phosphates, and 100 per cent of the lead, zinc, cobalt, and copper.[84] Europe then holds a big key to the future of Moroccan exports, and there is reason to believe that it might be willing to unlock the door.

Associate status of Morocco with the Common Market would assure commercial access to all member countries, particularly important since there is the possibility that Morocco's principal competitors — Spain (citrus fruits), Portugal (canned fish), and Algeria (wine and truck crops) — will seek such favored relations. At the same time, since Morocco accounts for only 5 per cent of Common Market exports, including those from France, it would seem doubtful that the Community would object to protection of local industrial enterprises, at least during the near future.[85] Further advantages of association would include eligibility for capital from the Investment Fund set up by the Common Market countries for overseas territories and access to the European labor pool, a possibly important palliative to the chronic unemployment problems in Morocco. While association does not suggest economic independence in the fullest sense of the term, it does suggest a step in that direction, especially when contrasted with the *pacte colonial* of protectorate days when the Moroccan role was to remain on the periphery of the twentieth century as the satellite of a single power. The realities indicate that although Morocco should move with deliberate caution vis-à-vis Europe, they also indicate that it should move with deliberate speed.

Apparently the country will have a powerful sponsor in France. One of the by-products of the French agreement with Algeria (which was concluded while this work was being written and which stands as graphic proof that events do not wait for their students) has been a rapprochement of France with Morocco. Not only is France prepared to maintain quotas for Moroccan exports, but it is also requesting that similar favored treatment be extended by its Common Market partners. Nor is this all. For the last six months of 1962 France extended a credit of NF 300 million ($60 million) to be divided equally among the purchase of goods and equipment, the government development budget, and the balance of payments deficit. In addition, French private investment will be encouraged through the development of a credit insurance scheme. A new credit line has thus been opened, one which will help to ease the strain on the balance of payments and to alleviate the critical shortage of domestic capital. Finally, France will provide salaries for 1,000 teachers in addition to the 8,000 already in Morocco.[86]

American aid has been a factor ever since independence and will presumably continue in the future. Running between $40–50 million per year, the grants and loans have been devoted to technical assistance and the development budget. In addition, surplus agricultural commodities have been furnished to relieve the distress caused by drought. The Soviet Union has also extended aid, to date mostly military.

Like most underdeveloped countries, Morocco's capital needs far exceed domestic supply together with that which other countries have thus far been willing to provide. Making up for lost time is expensive, and Moroccans are a long way from closing the gap. All this is to say that Morocco does not have economic independence now and that such independence can only come, if at all, through the joint efforts of Moroccans and the more affluent elsewhere who realize that their own best interests are identical with those of the underprivileged in a shrunken world.[87]

CONCLUDING NOTE

Especially for the student of history is the course of future change likely to look capricious. Only with the long backward view of the historian can one discern what was after the fact inevitable and, for the more venturesome, the what might have been. The historian has a chance, risky to be sure but nevertheless a chance, to bring order and logic to happenings more or less past.

To look ahead, one abandons the hazards involved in identifying crucial events, in developing a thesis concerning the events, and in an analysis of the events for the far greater risks of prediction. The best counsel then is caution, for the facts of the past and present suggest many different outcomes. The long odds against success of a specific forecast, which therefore would undoubtedly serve no useful purpose, militate in favor of a few relatively general observations concerning the future. The comments below fall into the latter category.

One thing is manifestly clear. The Moroccans seek economic independence while living geographically on the margin of that part of the world which has fertile land, ample water, temperate climate, and a vigorous population. Relatively then, but only relatively, they have a better chance of achieving viability than others who find themselves outside this select perimeter. More specifically, the country has a plural society and a dual economy, inherited from the protectorate, both of which are likely to disappear through continued emigration of Europeans and by the increasing absorption of "traditional" Moroccans into the modern economy. Only those Europeans psychologically capable of assimilation to Moroccan culture will remain; the task of adjustment will be easier to the extent that French culture has left an indelible and no doubt durable imprint on the minds of the Moroccan elite. Negotiations with France concerning mutually desirable relationships will be successful, because the points at issue are so numerous as to create a wide bargaining range conducive to compromise. In a sense, the Moroccans will themselves be reaching the stated, but unachieved, objective of the protectorate, which was to bring about reforms and assure the integrity of the government.

The government will continue to plan, despite false starts, lags, and failures, primarily because it has no choice.[88] Eventual success in planning will be dependent on rapid improvement in strategy, techniques, and execution to say nothing of finance, because the time available undoubtedly leaves little margin for the luxury of error. To make matters even more critical, the margin narrows as the time is reduced by fast-increasing population with wants to match.

A catalog of Morocco's problems, among them population growth, widely-fluctuating agricultural yields, and illiteracy, makes a somber and sobering document with a long history, part of which has been examined in the preceding pages. The items on the extensive list, however, are generalizations as they stand, and generalizations often hide much more than they reveal. Indeed, hope for the Moroccans lies in the complexities hidden by these generalizations, in the interstices where meaningful leverage can be applied — and in time. The belief that such interstices exist may be an expression of faith without substance and if so there can be no hope, but it can also be a philosophy which can lead, if there is substance, to many effective courses of action.

All mankind has a stake in the outcome of the fight for a better life, not only in Morocco but in all countries similarly engaged. It may well be that the future belongs not to the most vocal claimants in the East and West, but to the hungry two-thirds of the world. For this reason, people of goodwill everywhere and even those with simply common sense will wish Moroccans, and others like them, every success in an endeavor worthy of the dignity of man.

REFERENCES

NOTES

REFERENCES

Adam, André, "Le 'bidonville' de Ben Msik à Casablanca," *Annales de l'Institut d'Etudes Orientales*, VIII (1949–50).

Amphoux, Marcel, "L'évolution de l'agriculture européenne au Maroc," *Annales de Géographie*, 42nd year (March, 1933).

Ashford, Douglas E., *Political Change in Morocco*. Princeton, 1961.

Aubin, Eugène, *Le Maroc d'aujourd'hui*. Paris, 1908.

Barbari, Mouslim, *Tempête sur le Maroc, ou les erreurs d'une politique berbère*. Paris, 1931.

Barbour, Nevill, ed., *A Survey of North West Africa*. New York, 1959.

Barennes, Yves, *La modernisation rurale au Maroc*. Collection des Centres d'Etudes Juridiques, XXVI. Paris, 1948.

Baron, R., *et al.*, "Conditions d'habitation des émigrants indigènes à Rabat," *Revue Africaine*, LXXIX (3rd and 4th quarters, 1936).

Baumont, Guy, "L'avenir des corporations artisanales au Maroc; l'exemple de Meknès." Thesis, Ecole Nationale d'Administration, Section Economique et Financière, 1949.

Benoist, Michel, "La mise en valeur des hauts-plateaux du Maroc Oriental." Thesis, Ecole Nationale d'Administration, Section Economique et Financière, 1950.

Bernard, Augustin, *L'Afrique du Nord pendant la guerre*. Paris, 1926.

————, *La main-d'oeuvre dans l'Afrique du Nord*. Paris, 1930.

Blardone, Gilbert, *et al.*, *Initiation aux problèmes d'outre-mer: colonisation, décolonisation, sous-développement*. Lyon, 1959.

Bondis, A., *La colonisation au Maroc: l'action des autorités de contrôle*. Rabat, 1928.

Bourdet, Claude, "Les maîtres de l'Afrique du Nord," *Les Temps Modernes*, 7th year (June, 1952).

Bousquet, G.-H., "L'Islam et la limitation des naissances," *Population*, 5th year (January–March, 1950).

Bousser, Marcel, "Note sur le coût des transports au Maroc," *Bulletin Economique du Maroc*, I (January, 1934).

————, *Le problème des transports au Maroc*. Paris, 1934.

Boutin, François, *L'expansion commerciale du Maroc*. Paris, 1928.

Bovill, Edward W., *The Golden Trade of the Moors*. London, 1958.

Breil, Jacques, "Quelques aspects de la situation démographique au Maroc," *Bulletin Economique et Social du Maroc*, IX (October, 1947).

Broderick, Alan H., *North Africa*. London, 1943.

Brunot, Louis, *La mer dans les traditions et les industries indigènes à Rabat et à Salé*. Paris, 1920.

Campon, Ludovic de, *Un empire qui croule: le Maroc contemporain*. Paris, 1886.

Célérier, Jean, "Chez les Berbères du Maroc: de la collectivité patriarcale à la coopérative," *Annales d'Histoire Economique et Sociale*, 8th year (May, 1936).

——————, "Les conditions géographiques du développement de Casablanca," *Revue de Géographie Marocaine*, XVIII (May, 1939).

——————, "Les conditions géographiques du développement de Fès," *Hespéris*, XIX (1st quarter, 1934).

——————, "L'économie montagnarde dans le Moyen-Atlas," *Revue de Géographie Marocaine* (January, 1939).

——————, "La modernisation du paysanat marocain," *Revue de Géographie Marocaine* (January, 1939).

——————, "La transhumance dans le Moyen-Atlas," *Hespéris*, VII (1st quarter, 1927).

Celier, Charles, *et al.*, *L'industrialisation de l'Afrique du Nord*. Paris, 1952.

Chardonnet, Jean, "L'expansion industrielle du Maroc," *Bulletin de la Société Royale de Géographie d'Egypte*, XXIV (November, 1951).

Chevalier, Louis, *Le problème démographique nord-africain*, Institut National d'Etudes Démographiques, Travaux et Documents, no. 6. Paris, 1947.

Chouraqui, André, *Les Juifs d'Afrique du Nord*. Paris, 1952.

Clerc, M. F., *Bulletin Economique et Social du Maroc*, No. 82 (October, 1959).

Coon, Carleton S., *Caravan: The Story of the Middle East*. New York, 1951.

Cowan, L. Gray, *The Economic Development of Morocco*. Santa Monica, 1958.

Cruickshank, Earl Fee, *Morocco at the Parting of the Ways: The Story of Native Protection to 1885*. Philadelphia, 1935.

Damade, Pierre, *La vigne et le vin au Maroc*. Paris, 1936.

Darré, M., "L'économie montagnarde chez les Ait Youssi de l'Amekla," *Revue de Géographie Marocaine*, XVIII (January, 1939).

Demonrosty, R., "Le Maroc économique," *Le Bulletin Colonial* (November, 1932).

Despois, Jean, *L'Afrique du Nord;* vol. I in *L'Afrique blanche française*. Paris, 1949.

Donon, Jean, *Le régime douanier du Maroc et le développement du commerce marocain jusqu'à nos jours*. Paris, 1920.

Dresch, Jean, "La prolétarisation des masses indigènes en Afrique du Nord," *Chemins du Monde* (October, 1948).

Dumont, René, *Etude des modalités d'action du paysanat*, Cahiers de la Modernisation Rurale, no. 3. Rabat, 1948.

——————, "Evolution récente et perspectives de l'agriculture nord-africaine," *L'Observation Economique*, Special Study, no. 3 (May, 1949).

——————, "Projet de rapport à M. le Commissaire Général Jean Monnet sur l'accroissement de la production agricole en Afrique du Nord." Mimeographed, 1949.

Esquer, Gabriel, *Histoire de l'Algérie*. Paris, 1950.

Essafi, Tahar, *Au secours du fellah*. Marrakech, 1934.

Fazy, Henri, *Agriculture marocaine et protectorat*. Paris, 1948.

Flournoy, F. R., "Political Relations of Great Britain with Morocco from 1830 to 1841," *Political Science Quarterly*, XLVII (March, 1932).

Gaignebet, Jean, "Marrakech, grand carrefour des routes marocaines," *Revue de Géographie Marocaine*, VII (4th quarter, 1928).

Gallagher, Charles F., "The Royal City of Tangier," *American Universities Field Staff Reports* (July, 1957).

Garcin, P., *La politique des contingents dans les relations franco-marocaines*, Collection des Centres d'Etudes Juridiques. Paris, 1937.

Gondal, Jean, *Destin de l'Afrique*. Paris, 1933.

Guillaume, Albert, *L'évolution économique de la société rurale marocaine*, Collection des Centres d'Etudes Juridiques, XLVIII. Paris, 1955.

Guillon, Jean, "Du collectif à l'individuel dans une terre marocaine." Thesis, Ecole Nationale d'Administration, Section Economique et Financière, 1951.

Halpérin, V., "Structure et perspectives de la population juive en Afrique du Nord," *Politique Etrangère*, 17th year (March, 1952).

Hardy, Georges and Jean Célérier, *Les grandes lignes de la géographie du Maroc*. Paris, 1933.

Harris, Norman D., *Europe and Africa*. New York, 1927.

Harris, Walter B., *Morocco That Was*. Boston, 1921.

Hicks, Ursula K., *Development from Below: Local Government and Finance in Developing Countries of the Commonwealth*. New York, 1961.

Hoffherr, René, *L'économie marocaine*, Collections des Centres d'Etudes Juridiques, III. Paris, 1932.

—————, "Le marché économique du Maroc et son investigation rationelle," *L'Afrique Française*, XLII (May, 1932).

Joly, Fernand, "L'agriculture céréalière au Maroc," *Bulletin Economique et Social du Maroc*, VIII (January, 1946).

—————, "Casablanca, éléments pour une étude de géographie urbaine," *Les Cahiers d'Outre-Mer*, I (April–June, 1948).

Joly, Fernand, *et al.*, *Géographie du Maroc*. Paris, 1949.

Jouannet, Jacques, *L'évolution de la fiscalité marocaine depuis l'instauration du Protectorat*, Collection des Centres d'Etudes Juridiques, XXXVIII. Paris, 1953.

Kerr, Clark, *et al.*, *Industrialism and Industrial Man*. Cambridge (Mass.), 1960.

Knight, M. M., "Economic Space for Europeans in French North Africa," *Economic Development and Cultural Change* (February, 1953).

—————, *Introduction to Modern Economic History*. Berkeley, 1940.

—————, *Morocco as a French Economic Venture: A Study of Open Door Imperialism*. New York, 1937.

—————, "Water and the Course of Empire in French North Africa," *Quarterly Journal of Economics*, XLIII (November, 1928).

La Batut, Géraud de la Borie de, "L'industrie de la sardine à Safi." Thesis, Ecole Nationale d'Administration, Section Economique et Financière, 1951.

Labonne, Eirik (pseud. E. Jussiaume), *Réflexions sur l'économie africaine.* Paris, 1932.

La Chapelle, F. de, "Une cité de l'Oued Dra sous le protectorat des nomades," *Hespéris,* IX (1st quarter, 1929).

Lacouture, Jean and Simonne, *Le Maroc à l'épreuve.* Paris, 1958.

Langer, William L., "The European Powers and the French Occupation of Tunis," *American Historical Review,* XXXI (October, 1925 and January, 1926).

Laoust, E., "Pêcheurs berbères du Sous," *Hespéris,* III (2nd quarter, 1923).

Latron, A., "Problème foncier et bled marocain," *L'Afrique Française,* XLVIII (February, 1938).

LeNeveu, C. A., "France and Italy in North Africa," *Foreign Affairs,* VI (October, 1928).

Le Tourneau, Roger, *Fès avant le Protectorat.* Casablanca, 1949.

Lucas, Georges, *Fès dans le Maroc moderne.* Paris, 1937.

Lyautey, Louis H. G., *Paroles d'action.* 5th ed. Paris, 1948.

Marquez, G., "Les épiciers Chleuhs et leur diffusion dans les villes du Maroc," *Bulletin Economique du Maroc,* II (July, 1935).

Massignon, Louis, "Enquête sur les corporations musulmanes d'artisans et de commerçants au Maroc," *Revue du Monde Musulman,* LVIII (1924).

Mikesell, Marvin W., "The Role of Tribal Markets in Morocco," *The Geographical Review* (October, 1958).

Montagne, Robert, *Les Berbères et le Makhzen dans le sud du Maroc.* Paris, 1930.

————, *Un magasin collectif de l'Anti-Atlas.* Paris, 1931.

————, *Naissance du prolétariat marocain.* Cahiers d'Afrique et d'Asie, III (1952).

————, *Révolution au Maroc.* Paris, 1953.

————, *La vie sociale et la vie politique des Berbères.* Paris, 1930.

Moon, Parker T., *Imperialism and World Politics.* New York, 1929.

Mothes, Jean, "Considérations sur les divers aspects du problème de l'artisanat marocain," *Bulletin Economique et Social du Maroc,* VII (July, 1945).

Myrdal, Gunnar, *An International Economy: Problems and Prospects.* New York, 1956.

Nesry, Carlos de, *Les Israélites marocains à l'heure du choix.* Tangier, 1959.

Olivier, F., "Répartition des tribus et de la propriété dans la banlieue de Meknès," *Bulletin Economique du Maroc,* IV (July, 1937).

Page, André, "Regards sur l'économie marocaine," *Revue d'Economie Politique* (March–April, 1954).

Passeron, René-Eugène, *Les grandes sociétés et la colonisation dans l'Afrique du Nord.* Algiers, 1925.

Peyronnet, F. R., *Le vignoble nord-africain*. Paris, 1950.

Pic, Edouard, "Les problèmes de la coopération chérifienne." Thesis, Ecole Nationale d'Administration, Section Economique et Financière, 1949.

Rézette, Robert, *Les partis politiques marocains*. Paris, 1955.

Ricard, Prosper, "Les corporations d'artisans au Maroc," *Bulletin du Travail (Maroc)*, (1929).

————, "Pour une première étape dans la modernisation de l'artisanat marocain," *Bulletin Economique et Social du Maroc*, VIII (October, 1946).

Roberts, Stephen H., *History of French Colonial Policy, 1870–1925*. London, 1929.

Rosier, René, *Les sociétés indigènes agricoles de prévoyance au Maroc*. Paris, 1925.

Roussillon, Jean, "Problèmes de la main-d'oeuvre de colonisation au Maroc." Thesis, Ecole Nationale d'Administration, Section Economique et Financière, 1948.

Sayous, André, "L'agriculture française et la concurrence de l'Afrique du Nord," *Revue Economique Internationale*, I (July, 1929).

————, "La réglementation du transport en commun des voyageurs par route au Maroc Français," *Revue Economique Internationale*, V (September, 1933).

Schaefer, René, *Drame et chances de l'Afrique du Nord*. Paris, 1953.

Spencer, Daniel L., *India — Mixed Enterprise and Western Business: Experiments in Controlled Change for Growth and Profit*. The Hague, 1959.

Spillmann, Georges, *L'Afrique du Nord et la France*. Paris, 1947.

Staley, Eugene, "The Mannesmann Mining Interests and the Franco-German Conflict over Morocco," *Journal of Political Economy*, XL (February, 1932).

Stuart, Graham, *The International City of Tangier*. 2nd ed. Stanford, 1955.

Surugué, P., "Quelques aspects de la question du paysanat marocain," *La France Méditerranéenne et Africaine* (2nd quarter, 1938).

Trotter, Philip D., *Our Mission to the Court of Morocco in 1880*. Edinburgh, 1881.

Waterston, Albert, *Planning in Morocco*. Baltimore, 1962.

Wendel, Hugh C. M., "The Protégé System in Morocco," *Journal of Modern History*, II (March, 1930).

NOTES

1. Since the physical geography is, of course, the same today as it was when the protectorate came into being, the present tense will be employed when it is being discussed. The use of the past tense in other sections is not meant to imply that what was true in 1912 is necessarily no longer so; indeed a major task will be to determine to what extent "things have changed."

2. M. M. Knight, *Morocco as a French Economic Venture: A Study of Open Door Imperialism* (New York, 1937), p. 9.

3. Quoted by Alan Houghton Broderick in *North Africa* (London, 1943), p. 4.

4. A geography of Morocco has been written by Georges Hardy and Jean Célérier, *Les grandes lignes de la géographie du Maroc* (Paris, 1933). A more recent work is by Fernand Joly and others, *Géographie du Maroc* (Paris, 1949).

5. A black soil known as *tir*, which is excellent for cereals, is found in the Gharb, Chaouia, and Doukkala for a distance of sixty miles along the coast and to a depth of about thirty-five miles. There is also *tir* in the Triffas, a small valley in eastern Morocco to the north of Oujda. *Hamri*, a reddish sandy soil, is also good for cereals. *Rmel*, a sandy soil less fertile than *tir*, occurs along the coast. *Harroucha* is a sandy type which is often rocky and sterile. Finally, there is an alluvial soil of varying proportions of sand and clay which is frequently found in the Gharb. René Rosier, *Les sociétés indigènes agricoles de prévoyance au Maroc* (Paris, 1925), p. 25. That all soils are relatively poor in humus has been noted by Albert Guillaume, *L'évolution économique de la société rurale marocain*, Institut des Hautes Etudes Marocaines, Collection des Centres d'Etudes Juridique, XLVII (Paris, 1955), p. 18.

6. See, among others, M. M. Knight, "Water and the Course of Empire in French North Africa," *Quarterly Journal of Economics*, XLIII (November, 1928), pp. 44–93.

7. The relatively large figures for the northwestern region are deceptive, for not only does rainfall in a given area vary sharply between seasons, it is extremely uneven from one year to the next. And "vegetation and animals do not live by averages but by realities." Augustin Bernard, as quoted by Jean Despois, *L'Afrique du Nord:* vol. I in *L'Afrique blanche française* (Paris, 1949), p. 17.

8. See Edward W. Bovill, *The Golden Trade of the Moors* (London, 1958).

9. For a discussion of the Berber social and political structure, see Robert Montagne, *La vie sociale et la vie politique des Berbères* (Paris, 1930) and *Les Berbères et le Makhzen dans le sud du Maroc* (Paris, 1930).

10. Despois, *L'Afrique du Nord*, p. xiv.

11. Eugène Aubin, *Le Maroc d'aujourd'hui* (Paris, 1908), p. 47.

12. The coastal city of Casablanca, which had been under French control since 1907, was rapidly gaining in importance.

13. André Chouraqui, *Les Juifs d'Afrique du Nord* (Paris, 1952), p. 218.

14. Allal al Fassi, a leader and ideologist of the Istiqlal Party, has argued that because the Arabs took Morocco by force, Islamic law decrees that all land belongs to the collectivity. See the weekly *Al Istiqlal*, June 22, 1957, p. 9. Needless to say, this position, if officially adopted, would have far-reaching ramifications for the land tenure situation.

15. Often the tenant was in debt from the beginning, when the owner advanced him subsistence until the first harvest. One writer regards this advance as the essential element of the contract. Jean Roussillon, "Problèmes de la main-d'oeuvre de colonisation au Maroc" (Thesis, Ecole Nationale d'Administration, Section Economique et Financière, 1948), p. 6.

16. Ludovic de Campon, *Un empire qui croule: le Maroc contemporain* (Paris, 1886), p. 106.

17. R. Demonrosty, "Le Maroc économique," *Le Bulletin Colonial* (November, 1932), p. 4.

18. For a detailed discussion of movement by the Middle Atlas tribes, see Jean Célérier, "La transhumance dans le Moyen-Atlas," *Hespéris*, VII (1st quarter, 1927), pp. 53–68; and "L'économie montagnarde dans le Moyen-Atlas," *Revue de Géographie Marocaine* (January, 1939), pp. 57–67.

19. It was possible to establish the degree to which a tribe was sedentary or nomadic by noting the type of housing that predominated in the area. Thus, between the house and the tent, lay the brush hut *(mechta)*, which was not easily moved and therefore relatively permanent, and the conical thatched hut *(nouala)*, which was light and compact and could be transported short distances.

20. The plow was used in the lowlands, and the hoe in the mountains, where the plots of cultivated ground were too small for a larger implement. These two were the fundamental tools of Moroccan agriculture.

21. Despois, *L'Afrique du Nord*, p. 54.

22. An exhaustive study of the institution of the *agadir* and the role it played in Berber society is found in Robert Montagne, *Un magasin collectif de l'Anti-Atlas* (Paris, 1931). According to Trotter, the tribes of the Gharb, where land was flat, buried their grain in deep holes about two feet across and then camouflaged them with sticks and grass. Philip D. Trotter, *Our Mission to the Court of Marocco in 1880* (Edinburgh, 1881), p. 27.

23. See J. de la Chapelle, "Une cité de l'Oued Dra sous le protectorat des nomades," *Hespéris*, IX (1st quarter, 1929), pp. 29–42.

24. Recent mineral discoveries may eventually make this statement too strong.

25. See E. Laoust, "Pêcheurs berbères du Sous," *Hespéris*, III (2nd quarter, 1923), pp. 237–264.

26. In the nineteenth century, Rabat (which Sultan Yacoub al Mansour had chosen as his seat of government seven centuries before, but which had never become a first-ranking city) was substituted for Meknes.

27. See "Les conditions géographiques du développement de Fès," *Hespéris*, XIX (1st quarter, 1934), pp. 1–19. For a comprehensive treatment of the city as it was before the French arrival, see Roger Le Tourneau, *Fès avant le Protectorat* (Casablanca, 1949).

28. Jean Gaignebet, "Marrakech, grand carrefour des routes marocaines," *Revue de Géographie Marocaine*, VII (4th quarter, 1928), p. 274.

29. Carleton S. Coon, *Caravan: The Story of the Middle East* (New York, 1951), pp. 247–248.

30. Aubin, *Le Maroc d'aujourdhui*, pp. 204–205.

31. Prosper Ricard, "Les corporations d'artisans au Maroc," *Bulletin du Travail (Maroc)*, (1929), pp. 1–2.

32. Louis Massignon, "Enquête sur les corporations musulmanes d'artisans et de commerçants au Maroc," *Revue du Monde Musulman*, LVIII (1924), p. 70.

33. Marcel Bousser, *Le problème des transports au Maroc* (Paris, 1934), p. 18.

34. The rise and decline of the port of Salé is described by Louis Brunot, *La mer dans les traditions et les industries indigènes à Rabat et à Salé* (Paris, 1920).

35. Aubin, *Le Maroc d'aujourd'hui*, p. 73.

36. *Ibid.*, p. 20.

37. That the German government did not always approve of, and in fact was often embarrassed by, the activities of the Mannesmann Brothers is pointed out by Eugene Staley, "The Mannesmann Mining Interests and the Franco-German Conflict over Morocco," *Journal of Political Economy*, XL (February, 1932), pp. 52–72. Nevertheless, the German government represented the interests of its nationals vigorously several times during the first decade of the twentieth century, most notably in the form of the Kaiser at Tangier and a gunboat at Agadir.

38. Bousser, *Le problème des transports*, p. 16.

39. The figures that will be given have been derived from those found in the following: François Boutin, *L'expansion commerciale du Maroc* (Paris, 1928), pp. 12–13; Jean Donon, *Le régime douanier du Maroc* (Paris, 1920), pp. 62–64, 135; Norman D. Harris, *Europe and Africa* (New York, 1927), p. 280; Stephen H. Roberts, *History of French Colonial Policy, 1870–1925* (London, 1929), p. 549; and *Le commerce extérieur du Maroc, 1912–1954*, Gouvernement Chérifien, Direction du Commerce et de la Marine Marchande (Rabat, 1954), p. 13.

40. It should be noted that British-Moroccan trade, while important to Morocco, had a small part indeed in the pattern of British external commerce. Britain's interest in Morocco resulted primarily from factors other than trade, as we shall see in the next section.

41. It was to crop up in explicit form as late as 1950, when the United States and France carried a dispute over its interpretation to the International Court of Justice at The Hague. A presentation of the treaty history of Morocco was made at this time by Mr. Adrian Fisher, counselor of the Department of State. See *I.C.J. Pleadings, Morocco Case (France v. U.S.A.)*, I, Counter-Memorial of U.S.A. (1951), pp. 258–388.

42. Donon, *Le régime douanier*, p. 11. Professor Knight has noted that another Italian city-state, Genoa, had a trading station at Ceuta over which there was a dispute in 1235. *Introduction to Modern Economic History* (Berkeley, 1940), p. 38.

43. See F. R. Flournoy, "Political Relations of Great Britain with Morocco from 1830 to 1841," *Political Science Quarterly*, XLVII (March, 1932), pp. 27–56.

44. The diplomacy prior to the conquest of Tunis is discussed by William L. Langer in "The European Powers and the French Occupation of Tunis," *American Historical Review*, XXXI (October, 1925), pp. 55–78 and (January, 1926), pp. 251–265.

45. While not represented at the conference, Russia was one of the signatories of the resulting convention.

46. Earl Fee Cruickshank, *Morocco at the Parting of the Ways: The Story of Native Protection to 1885* (Philadelphia, 1935), p. 15. For a discussion of the problem of protégés, see also Hugh C. M. Wendel, "The Protégé System in Morocco," *Journal of Modern History*, II (March, 1930), pp. 48–60.

47. See Aubin, *Le Maroc d'aujourd'hui*, p. 210. For another sympathetic estimate of Abd al Aziz, see Walter Harris, *Morocco That Was* (Boston, 1921), pp. 65, 84–85.

48. The background of this agreement, as well as subsequent conflict between France and Italy over the status of Italian nationals in Tunisia, is discussed by C. A. LeNeveu, "France and Italy in North Africa," *Foreign Affairs*, VI (October, 1928), pp. 132–138.

49. Parker T. Moon, *Imperialism and World Politics* (New York, 1929), p. 278.

50. Donon, *Le régime douanier*, p. 86.

CHAPTER II: PACIFICATION, POPULATION AND PLURAL SOCIETY

1. For a more generalized discussion of the role played by the colonial administrator in economic development, see Clark Kerr, *et al.*, *Industrialism and Industrial Man* (Cambridge [Mass.], 1960), p. 50ff.

2. Knight, *Morocco as a French Economic Venture*, pp. 36, 42.

3. *Ibid.*, p. 40.

4. Augustin Bernard, *L'Afrique du Nord pendant la guerre* (Paris, 1926), p. 6. He estimated the Algerian contribution at 173,000 men and the Tunisian at 80,000. The total for North Africa, then, was around 300,000 troops.

5. *Ibid.*, p. 11. The figure for Algeria, according to Bernard, was 119,000; while the Tunisians working in France numbered 30,000. Thus the total number of North Africans in France as workers was close to 200,000 — together with the soldiers, a contribution of a half million.

6. Louis H. G. Lyautey, *Paroles d'action* (Paris, 1948), *passim*.

7. Actually, the shape of things to come could be seen as early as 1930 in the national reaction to the Berber *dahir* (decree with the force of law issued in the name of the sovereign) of that year. The French proposed to re-establish Berber customary law, thus replacing the *sharia* in those tribes which had adopted the latter. On this incident, see Mouslim Barbari, *Tempête sur le Maroc, ou les erreurs d'une politique berbère* (Paris, 1931).

8. Jacques Breil, "Quelques aspects de la situation démographique au Maroc," *Bulletin Economique et Social du Maroc*, IX (October, 1947), p. 135. Breil broke the total down into 37,000 in Algeria, four-fifths of them in the Department of Oran, and 12,000 in France, three-quarters of them in the Department of the Seine.

9. Quoted by Louis Chevalier in *Le problème démographique nord-africain*, Institut National d'Etudes Démographiques, Travaux et Documents, no. 6 (Paris, 1947), p. 35.

10. V. Halpérin, "Structure et perspectives de la population juive en Afrique du Nord," *Politique Etrangère*, 17th year (March, 1952), p. 476. For

post-independence developments in Jewish emigration, see Chapter VI, pp. 167–168.

11. We have already seen that it was estimated at 8 per cent of the total Moroccan Jewry by 1952.

12. See G.-H. Bousquet, "L'Islam et la limitation des naissances," *Population*, 5th year (January–March, 1950), pp. 121–128.

13. For the results of the first census since independence and for a revision of the growth data, see Chapter VI, pp. 168–169.

14. ". . . generally in the overseas territories, the Europeans are either a crushing majority, or else an insignificant minority. In the first case, the native problem can be neglected; in the second, it is much easier to resolve. The coexistence of the two groups makes the work of France in North Africa exceptionally difficult." Bernard, *L'Afrique du Nord*, p. xvii.

15. See Claude Bourdet, "Les maîtres de l'Afrique du Nord," *Les Temps Modernes*, 7th year (June, 1952), p. 2256.

16. After the return of King Mohammed V to the throne in the fall of 1955, the Jews were granted Moroccan citizenship.

17. If the French authorities really believed that, unlike the Arabs, the Berbers were faithful to France, the belief was shattered by the Berber attack on Oued Zem in the spring of 1955. The tribe involved had been considered one of the staunchest supporters of French policy.

CHAPTER III: THE EVOLUTION OF AGRICULTURE

1. By and large, the Muslims performed the functions of the old economy, the Europeans those of the new. The Jews, while falling between the other two segments of the population in the social sense, were in most cases allied with one or the other in the economic sense. Those in the middle were not sufficiently numerous to alter materially the broad lines of the Moroccan economy.

2. Under the protectorate, no *dahir* was issued without the approval of the Resident-General. In fact most *dahirs* were initiated by the French authorities and later were signed by the sovereign.

3. "In 1934, the cost of opposing a claim was 530 francs, excessive when it is noted that much of the litigation was concerned with only a few hectares of poor land worth perhaps 100 francs per hectare." Tahar Essafi, *Au secours du fellah* (Marrakech, 1934), pp. 42–43.

4. For a discussion of French land policy in Algeria, see René-Eugène Passeron, *Les grandes sociétés et la colonisation dans l'Afrique du Nord* (Algiers, 1925).

5. By 1948, titles to 3 million hectares of collective lands had been cleared, leaving another 2 million to go. Yves Barennes, *La modernisation rurale au Maroc*, Institut des Hautes Etudes Marocaines, Collection des Centres d'Etudes Juridiques, XXVI (Paris, 1948), p. 35. Writing in 1958, Cowan estimated that 5/12 of the cultivated land was registered. L. Gray Cowan, *The Economic Development of Morocco* (Santa Monica, 1958), p. 19.

6. A. Bondis, *La colonisation au Maroc: l'action des autorités de contrôle* (Rabat, 1928), pp. 17, 23.

7. Latron cites the case of four fractions of the Beni M'tir, located in the rich lands of the *dir* (foothills) to the south of Meknes, who were forced to give up their lands without compensation. A. Latron, "Problème foncier et

bled marocain," *L'Afrique Française*, XLVIII (February, 1938), p. 125. As Célérier has pointed out, the remaining lands of the tribe were "melkized" and given over to the chiefs, who quickly sold them off. Jean Célérier, "La modernisation du paysanat marocain," *Revue de Géographie Marocain* (January, 1947), p. 10.

8. For examples of abuses, see Knight, *Morocco as a French Economic Venture*, pp. 67–68; and Bourdet, "Les maîtres de l'Afrique du Nord," p. 2254.

9. The phrase is Célérier's, "Chez les Berbères du Maroc: de la collectivité patriarcale à la coopérative," *Annales d'Histoire Economique et Sociale*, 8th year (May, 1936), p. 219.

10. Henri Fazy, *Agriculture marocaine et protectorat* (Paris, 1948), p. 62.

11. M. M. Knight, "Economic Space for Europeans in French North Africa," *Economic Development and Cultural Change* (February, 1953), p. 365.

12. Bernard, *L'Afrique du Nord pendant la guerre*, p. 76.

13. "Morocco '54," *Encyclopédie Mensuelle d'Outre-Mer*, Special Issue (Paris, 1954), p. 105.

14. Albert Waterston, *Planning in Morocco* (Baltimore, 1962), p. 4. According to a local newspaper, which claimed that its estimates were based on official figures, 28 per cent of the value of all agricultural land and 29 per cent of the value of all agricultural land, buildings, equipment, and livestock were represented by European holdings. *Le Petit Casablancais*, March 24, 1956, p. 1.

15. We do have a figure for collective lands of 45,000 hectares in 1959, of which three-quarters were leased in perpetuity. Concerning the disposition of these lands, see Chapter VI, p. 178.

16. André Page, "Regards sur l'économie marocaine," *Revue d'Economie Politique* (March–April, 1954), p. 27.

17. Although colonization had been limited almost entirely to the northwest, other parts of Morocco also made a contribution to the urban proletariat. Population growth in the narrow mountain valleys and the desert oases made life in these areas increasingly precarious and migration imperative.

18. P. Surugué, "Quelques aspects de la question du paysanat marocain," *La France Méditerranéenne et Africaine* (2nd quarter, 1938), p. 88.

19. F. Olivier, "Répartition des tribus et de la propriété dans la banlieue de Meknès," *Bulletin Economique du Maroc*, IV (July, 1937), pp. 275–276.

20. M. Darré, "L'économie montagnarde chez les Ait Youssi de l'Amekla," *Revue de Géographie Marocaine*, XVIII (January, 1939), pp. 68–78. Gabriel Esquer has pointed to the development of a similar situation in the Mitidja plain of Algeria. See *Histoire de l'Algérie* (Paris, 1950), p. 58.

21. Jean Guillon, "Du collectif à l'individuel dans une terre marocaine" (Thesis, Ecole Nationale d'Administration, Section Economique et Financière, 1951), pp. 1–22.

22. "Morocco '54," pp. 103, 106.

23. *Ibid.*, p. 106.

24. See Chapter I, pp. 26–27.

25. Jacques Jouannet, *L'évolution de la fiscalité marocaine depuis l'instauration du Protectorat*, Institut des Hautes Etudes Marocaines, Collection des Centres d'Etudes Juridiques, XXXVIII (Paris, 1953), I, pp. 26–27.

26. The 1913 law established three such categories. The number was increased to five in 1915 and to nine in 1952.

27. For a more detailed description and an analysis of the *tertib*, see Jouannet, *L'évolution de la fiscalité*, pp. 22–42, 72–77. This author points out that the tax levied on irrigated truck crops (most of which were grown by Europeans) appeared to be very low in comparison with the levies on other cultivated crops.

28. *Annuaire statistique de la zone française du Maroc*, 1952, Gouvernement Chérifien, Service Central des Statistiques (Rabat, 1952), p. 366.

29. The other direct tax levied on those engaged in agriculture was the *touiza* (corvée). Prior to 1927, Europeans were exempt. For Moroccans, the period of annual service exacted varied according to needs, and only those living in the Chaouia and the region of Oujda were permitted to meet their obligation with money rather than labor. After 1927, Europeans discharged their duties with money. Moroccans were allowed to substitute money for work only at the discretion of the authorities. The annual levy was set at four days per year, but often developed to be more. See Jouannet, *L'évolution de la fiscalité*, pp. 51–52, 77–78. The "proceeds" from this tax, including both labor and money, were valued at 970 million francs in 1952. *Annuaire statistique, 1952*, p. 366.

30. This information, not available in official publications, was supplied by a reliable source who asked to remain anonymous.

31. *La conjoncture économique marocaine, année 1953*, Gouvernement Chérifien, Service Central des Statistiques (Rabat, 1953), p. xiv.

32. P. Garcin, *La politique des contingents dans les relations franco-marocaines*, Institut des Hautes Etudes Marocaines, Collection des Centres d'Etudes Juridiques (Paris, 1937), p. 71.

33. *Lexique de l'économie marocaine, édition 1953*, Gouvernement Chérifien, Direction du Commerce et de la Marine Marchande (Casablanca, 1954), p. 38.

34. Chevalier, *Le problème démographique nord-africain*, p. 67.

35. Relatively speaking, however, the Moroccans were probably better off in this respect than the Algerians or the Tunisians. René Dumont has pointed out that the spread between European and native yields broadens as one moves from west to east across North Africa. See "Evolution récente et perspectives de l'agriculture nord-africaine," *L'Observation Economique*, Special Study no. 3 (May, 1949), p. 5.

36. André Sayous, "L'agriculture française et la concurrence de l'Afrique du Nord," *Revue Economique Internationale*, I (July, 1929), p. 31.

37. Garcin, *La politique des contingents*, p. 54.

38. All of these arguments were recorded by Sayous, "L'agriculture française," pp. 8–42.

39. Marcel Amphoux, "L'évolution de l'agriculture européenne au Maroc," *Annales de Géographie*, 42nd year (March, 1933), p. 177.

40. In 1935, the Moroccans produced 702,000 quintals on 208,000 hectares; the Europeans, 972,000 quintals on 135,000 hectares. Garcin, *La politique des contingents*, p. 193.

41. *Ibid.*, p. 182.

42. All wheat was requisitioned by the government during the war, at prices fixed by the *Office du Blé*. It soon developed that the *Office* was sus-

ceptible to political pressures, with the result that the *colon* received a better price for his crop than did the Moroccan. See Edouard Pic, "Les problèmes de la coopération chérifienne" (Thesis, Ecole Nationale d'Administration, Section Economique et Financière, 1949), p. 32.

43. As a *quid pro quo*, Morocco agreed to buy more of the high-priced sugar grown within the French Union. The negotiations for the quota were reported in *Le Petit Casablancais*, July 10, 1954, p. 3. Much of what follows appeared in subsequent issues of this newspaper.

44. *Annuaire statistique, 1952,* p. 152.

45. Less numerous but important for traction and transport are camels and donkeys.

46. Michel Benoist, "La mise en valeur des hauts-plateaux du Maroc Oriental" (Thesis, Ecole Nationale d'Administration, Section Economique et Financière, 1950), p. 8.

47. Figures on surfaces and yields for olives were taken from *Annuaire statistique, 1952,* pp. 135, 148, 151.

48. *Lexique de l'économie marocaine, édition 1953,* p. 14.

49. See *Annuaire statistique, 1952,* pp. 148, 151.

50. *Ibid.,* pp. 135, 149.

51. *Lexique de l'économie marocaine, édition 1953,* p. 12.

52. *Ibid.,* pp. 59, 96, 159.

53. *Annuaire statistique, 1952,* pp. 138–139.

54. See Amphoux, "L'évolution de l'agriculture," p. 180.

55. Pierre Damade, *La vigne et le vin au Maroc* (Paris, 1936), p. 4.

56. The estimate of consumption comes from Damade, *ibid.,* p. 60. Production figures are taken from *Annuaire statistique, 1952,* p. 135.

57. Moroccan vineyards were the last in North Africa to be invaded by this insect. It had come to Algeria in the first decade of the century and to Tunisia just before the Second World War. See Francis Raymond Peyronnet, *Le vignoble nord-africain* (Paris, 1950), p. 13.

58. The pegging of the Moroccan franc to the French franc in 1920 meant that the former was to share all the vicissitudes of the latter. However, Morocco remained a low-cost country — although an expensive one for France to subsidize — so long as imports came in freely in accordance with the Act of Algeciras. Costs rose rapidly after wheat imports were banned in 1928.

59. *Deuxième plan de modernisation et d'équipement, Maroc,* République Française, Commissariat Général au Plan de Modernisation et d'Equipement (Paris, 1954), pp. 4–5.

60. Fernand Joly, "L'agriculture céréalière au Maroc," *Bulletin Economique et Social du Maroc,* VIII (January, 1946), p. 213.

61. In some cases, barley yields actually fell with the adoption of improved methods. *La conjoncture économique marocaine* (June–July, 1955), p. 4.

62. The doum was not a total liability, however. Its presence on the slopes served to check erosion.

63. Dumont estimates that 1,500,000 hectares of cereal land in North Africa lie below this line. "Evolution récente," p. 6. The 200-millimeter rainfall (8 in.) conventionally regarded as the minimum necessary for successful dry farming is much too low here.

64. The movement of whole tribes that had formerly occurred during years of famine was no longer found, however. The bulk of the tribal mem-

bers, held in place by the force of arms, had to rely on remittances from emigrants to assure the margin of subsistence.

65. See, for example, René Schaefer, *Drame et chances de l'Afrique du Nord* (Paris, 1953), p. 122.

66. The heavy inflow of investment during the twenties did bring a shortage of agricultural labor between 1928 and 1930, i.e., the price of labor rose. Pressures exerted by those interested in a cheap labor supply resulted in a temporary ban on emigration to France, where many Moroccans, especially the Chleuh, had been drawn by relatively high wages. The inelasticity of the supply curve of labor in the downward direction was apparent during the depression of the thirties. See, among others, Roussillon, "Problèmes de la main-d'oeuvre," p. 6.

67. *Ibid.*, p. 39. By February 1, 1956, the minimum wage had been raised to 300 francs. *Le Bulletin Officiel*, February 3, 1956, p. 106.

68. Pic, "Les problèmes de la coopération," p. 2.

69. Pages 344–345.

70. The total resources of the *S.O.M.A.P.* amounted to around 75 francs per member in 1930. Assets per farmer of the European credit agencies were a thousand times greater. Knight, *Morocco as a French Economic Venture*, p. 72.

71. See note 30 above.

72. "Morocco '54," p. 109.

73. The Council of Government was a consultative body formed of three colleges — the representatives of the Chambers of Agriculture, of the Chambers of Commerce and Industry, and of consumers. There were separate sections of the colleges for Europeans and Moroccans.

74. *Le Petit Casablancais*, August 20, 1955, p. 1.

75. "Morocco '54," p. 112.

76. Pic, "Les problèmes de la coopération," p. 18. See also René Dumont, *Etude des modalités d'action du paysanat*, Société d'Etudes Economiques, Sociales, et Statistiques, Cahiers de la Modernisation Rurale, no. 3 (Rabat, 1948), pp. 15–16.

77. *Deuxième plan de modernisation et d'équipement*, p. 83. Dumont, in a 1949 mimeographed report circulated privately in official circles, estimated that 30,000 to 40,000 hectares could be under irrigation in the area. "Projet de rapport à M. le Commissaire Général Jean Monnet sur l'accroissement de la production agricole en Afrique du Nord," p. 18. This section leans heavily on the observations of Dumont found in the above report and in "Les données agricoles du problème," in Charles Celier, *et al.*, *Industrialisation de l'Afrique du Nord* (Paris, 1952), pp. 48–74.

78. The charge for water alone was 3,000 francs per hectare in 1949, as compared with 300 francs for water from the Al Kansera dam. Dumont, "Projet de rapport," p. 9.

79. Only 55,000 hectares, out of a possible 460,000 hectares, were irrigated by all the dams in Morocco in mid-1955. *Le Petit Casablancais*, June 25, 1955, p. 4.

80. Dumont, "Projet de rapport," p. 9.

81. It should be pointed out, however, that rural engineers doubt the advantages of steel plows for those Moroccans cultivating rocky hillsides.

CHAPTER IV: NEW INDUSTRY IN AN OLD SETTING

1. For a comparison of the tax burdens on business in France and in Morocco, see Jean Chardonnet, "L'expansion industrielle du Maroc," *Bulletin de la Société Royale de Géographie d'Egypte*, XXIV (November, 1951), p. 168.

2. Under the pseudonym of E. Jussiaume, Eirik Labonne, later a Resident-General of Morocco, wrote a well-known treatise on the competitive relationships between France and North Africa. He contended that the North African and French economies should be made complementary. However, comparative costs were not to be the basis for adjustment; rather it was the North African economy which was to accommodate the French. See *Réflexions sur l'économie africaine* (Paris, 1932).

3. The same author also points out that 90 per cent of the private capital in Morocco was French, with the remainder largely in Belgian, British, and American hands. See Cowan, *The Economic Development of Morocco*, pp. 44–45.

4. *Ibid.*, p. 45.

5. *Le Petit Casablancais*, April 13, 1957, p. 1.

6. Moulay Hafid, who came into power after the Act of Algeciras was signed, granted extensive mining rights in the Sous to the Mannesmann Brothers in exchange for support of his 1908 coup. The Mannesmanns had also negotiated rights over a vast area in the Riff from Raisuli, a chronic trouble-maker for the government. While the French were assuming the military burdens in Morocco, the Germans were threatening to usurp the rewards. Franco-German diplomacy centered at one point around the conflicting claims of the Mannesmanns and the *Union des Mines*. See Staley, "The Mannesmann Mining Interests," pp. 52–72.

7. In 1949, the cost of a permit was still low — only 3,000 francs. Paul Mauchaussé, "La participation de l'état à l'activité minière au Maroc Français," in Charles Celier, *et al.*, *L'industrialisation de l'Afrique du Nord*, p. 164.

8. René Hoffherr, *L'économie marocaine*, Institut des Hautes Etudes Marocaines, Collection des Centres d'Etudes Juridiques, III (Paris, 1932), p. 201.

9. According to one author, the *B.R.P.M.* came into existence as the result of the discovery by a Belgian firm of large anthracite coal deposits at Djerada, south of Oujda. *B.R.P.M.* participation in the mine prevented the benefits from accruing solely to a foreign firm. Georges Spillmann, *L'Afrique du Nord et la France* (Paris, 1947), p. 129.

10. The only foreign company engaged in coal or oil production in Morocco was the Belgian firm which, as part of a consortium including the *B.R.P.M.*, was exploiting the coal deposits at Djerada before the law governing the granting of permits was promulgated. (See footnote 9, above.) In fact, there were only two other mines of any significance in Morocco in which foreign interests were found. One of these, the lead mine at Touissit, not far from Djerada, was wholly foreign owned.

11. See "Les mines marocaines," *Réalités Marocaines* (January, 1953), p. 32.

12. The principal iron deposits were found in the Spanish zone near Nador. Annual production there reached one million tons, all of which was exported through the presidio of Melilla.

13. The Bou Azzer mine was exempted from state ownership in 1929 by the declaration of Thami al Glaoui, the late Pacha of Marrakech, that Berber

customary law conflicted with the mining laws in this case. The concession was then granted by the Pacha to the predecessors of Omnium, in return for a participatory interest. See the editorial of Claude Bourdet in *France-Observateur*, August 11, 1955, pp. 6–7.

14. However, the Walter Group was a joint owner with *Pennaroya* of the lead refinery at Oued al Heimer. It is also interesting to note that a 5 per cent share in the Walter Group was owned jointly by the American Newmont Mining Corporation and the St. Joseph Lead Company.

15. It would take many pages to explore all the interlocking directorates that were a significant feature of Moroccan industrial development. We have confined ourselves here merely to suggesting some of the lines of control which stretched from Morocco to financial interests in Paris — particularly to the *Banque de Paris*, which emerged under the protectorate as the major financier of the country.

16. For a different view, see Chapter VI, p. 197.

17. The largest phosphate exploitation, Khouribga, was connected with Casablanca by rail, while another line linked Youssefiah to the port of Safi. Coal was transported from Djerada by rail to the Algerian port of Nemours.

18. Georges Spillmann, "Les ressources énergétiques et minières de l'Afrique du Nord," in Charles Celier, *et al.*, *L'industrialisation de l'Afrique du Nord*, p. 39.

19. "Les mines marocaines," p. 13. Of course, shipments for that year were considerably increased owing to greater world demand generated by the Korean war.

20. *Ibid.*, p. 11.

21. *Lexique de l'économie marocaine, édition 1953*, p. 114.

22. Knight, *Morocco as a French Economic Venture*, pp. 52–53.

23. See Table 3, p. 65.

24. Even in this case, the traditional *couscous* (a semolina the production of which was a secondary activity of the flour mills), rather than white bread flour, accounted for a heavy proportion of sales to Moroccans.

25. See Chapter III, pp. 98–101.

26. The only exception was a small quota of flour from the Spanish zone. See Chapter III, p. 89.

27. *Annuaire statistique, 1952*, p. 238.

28. These were in addition to consumption taxes, which had been established in 1915 and which were applicable to all sugar, whether produced locally or not.

29. For others, see René Hoffherr, "Le marché économique du Maroc et son investigation rationelle," *L'Afrique Française*, XLII (May, 1932), p. 259.

30. *I.C.J. Pleadings, Morocco Case (France v. U.S.A.)*, II, Rejoinder of U.S.A. (1952), p. 247.

31. It rose, however, to 190,000 tons in the next year. *Le Petit Casablancais*, January 8, 1955, p. 3.

32. *Ibid.*, June 5, 1954, p. 6.

33. *Ibid.*, June 12, 1954, p. 3.

34. The controversy between France and the United States, and the resulting ruling by the International Court, extended far beyond the regulation of exchanges. However, we shall confine ourselves here to the import re-

strictions and their relationship to the textile industry, and then only to the briefest outline of events leading to the court action.

35. At this time, actions taken by the protectorate government were applicable to Americans living in Morocco only if approved by the United States. The exercise of this right of approval or disapproval supposedly found legal justification in the most-favored-nation provision of the 1836 treaty with Morocco before the protectorate. The right was to be denied the United States, however, by the decision of the World Court in 1952.

36. Evidence submitted by American counsel at the World Court suggests that the French were in fact less concerned with the leak in the dike than with the welfare of French businessmen in Morocco. See *I.C.J. Pleadings*, I, Counter-Memorial of U.S.A., p. 312.

37. The provision stated that no aid would go to any nation which conducted the foreign affairs of another nation but did not respect the treaties concluded by the latter. The two nations were, of course, France and Morocco; and the treaties were those concerning the rights of United States nationals.

38. See *I.C.J. Reports, Case Concerning the Rights of Nationals of the United States of America in Morocco*, Judgment of August 27 (1952), p. 185. Among its other pronouncements, however, the Court ruled that the United States did not have the right to determine whether or not its nationals were to be subject to Moroccan laws.

39. *Le Petit Casablancais*, February 12, 1955, p. 1.

40. *Ibid.*, April 2, 1955, p. 1.

41. *Ibid.*, p. 1.

42. Cowan, *The Economic Development of Morocco*, p. 36.

43. Jacques Lucius, "L'évolution économique récente du Maroc," in Charles Celier, *et al.*, *L'industrialisation de l'Afrique du Nord*, p. 265.

44. Géraud de la Borie de la Batut, "L'industrie de la sardine à Safi" (Thesis, Ecole Nationale d'Administration, Section Economique et Financière, 1951), p. 1.

45. *Maroc-Presse*, January 6, 1954, p. 4. The tonnages are calculated by the author on the basis of 50 cases per metric ton.

46. *Ibid.*, February 2, 1954, p. 3. Other important outlets for Moroccan fish products included Indochina, Germany, French West Africa, and the United States.

47. The French prohibited outright imports of Japanese *babouches*, which had been selling at 6 francs per pair, in 1934. However, the Japanese continued to sell rubber shoes at 3 or 4 francs per pair, or about one-quarter the price of the local shoes. Georges Lucas, *Fès dans le Maroc moderne* (Paris, 1937), p. 110. For other observations on the crisis of the handicraft trades in the thirties, see Jean Mothes, "Considérations sur les divers aspects du problème de l'artisanat marocain," *Bulletin Economique et Social du Maroc*, VII (July, 1945), pp. 29–35; and Prosper Ricard, "Pour une première étape dans la modernisation de l'artisanat marocain," *Bulletin Economique et Social du Maroc*, VIII (October, 1946), pp. 368–373.

48. Guy Baumont, "L'avenir des corporations artisanales au Maroc: l'exemple de Meknès" (Thesis, Ecole Nationale d'Administration, Section Economique et Financière, 1949), p. 22.

49. Massignon, "Enquête sur les corporations musulmanes," pp. 74–75.

50. The teeming Moroccan quarters of Casablanca furnished the nationalist movement with the bulk of its manpower; the Fassi supplied its philosophical content.

51. Jean Dresch, "La prolétarisation des masses indigènes en Afrique du Nord," *Chemins du Monde* (October, 1948), p. 68. For a comprehensive study of the origins of the migrants, see Robert Montagne, *Naissance du prolétariat marocain*, Cahiers d'Afrique et d'Asie, III (Paris, 1952).

52. G. Marquez, writing in the thirties of Tangier, estimated that the Chleuh owned 200 grocery stores in the area, the operation of each being rotated among three or four members of a family. "Les épiciers Chleuhs et leur diffusion dans les villes du Maroc," *Bulletin Economique du Maroc*, II (July, 1935), p. 231. The pattern was found in other occupations, too. A waiter's job in a restaurant, for example, might have been shared by several members of a family.

53. *Le Bulletin Officiel* (February 3, 1956), p. 106.

54. R. Baron, *et al.*, "Conditions d'habitation des émigrants indigènes à Rabat," *Revue Africaine*, LXXIX (3rd and 4th quarters, 1936), pp. 889–890.

55. André Adam, "Le 'bidonville' de Ben Msik à Casablanca," *Annales de l'Institut d'Etudes Orientales*, VIII (1949–50), p. 63.

56. *Ibid.*, p. 80. While a 500-franc rental represented only around a sixth of the monthly minimum wage at that time, Adam found that expenditures for food consumed virtually all the rest of the worker's income.

57. Baron, *et al.*, "Conditions d'habitation," p. 883.

58. Adam, quoting UNICEF figures, noted that skin tests for tuberculosis given to the Muslim children of Casablanca in 1950 produced positive reactions in proportions ranging from 36 per cent in the Ben Msik *bidonville* to almost 46 per cent in the old and new *medinas*. "Le 'bidonville'," p. 124.

59. See Robert Montagne, *Révolution au Maroc* (Paris, 1953), p. 273.

60. Over-all, it was calculated that three-quarters of the Moroccan population lived on a yearly income ranging between 150,000 and 180,000 francs ($350 and $450) per family. Cowan, *The Economic Development of Morocco*, p. 68.

61. Page, "Regards sur l'économie marocaine," p. 29.

62. Waterston, *Planning in Morocco*, p. viii.

63. See Chapter II, pp. 67–69. For a detailed study of the Jews in North Africa, see Chouraqui, *Les Juifs d'Afrique du Nord*.

64. Another was an increasing flow of funds for resettlement in Israel as the tide of Moroccan nationalism has arisen.

65. Halpérin, "Structure et perspectives," p. 472.

66. Three times as many migrated to Algeria, but they were employed principally as agricultural workers. Breil, "Quelques aspects de la situation démographique," p. 135.

67. See Jean Gondal, *Destin de l'Afrique* (Paris, 1933), p. 294.

68. Tuberculosis was particularly prevalent. According to Augustin Bernard, the Kabyles of Algeria called this disease "the French sickness." *La main-d'oeuvre dans l'Afrique du Nord* (Paris, 1930), pp. 14–15.

CHAPTER V: THE DEVELOPMENT OF TRANSPORT, TRADE, AND PUBLIC FINANCE

1. Even the free transportation of some Bastille Day celebrants from Casablanca to Rabat in 1912 brought German diplomatic protests.

2. Bousser, *Le problème des transports*, p. 24. In 1934, the trip from Casa-

blanca to Rabat required less than two hours, and the passenger fare was 20 francs. In 1914, five hours were needed, and the cost was 300 francs at their 1934 value. Bousser, "Note sur le coût des transports au Maroc," *Bulletin Économique du Maroc*, I (January, 1934), p. 205.

3. Bousser, *Le problème des transports*, p. 39.

4. Some of the proponents of the often discussed but never built Mediterranean–Niger railroad looked upon the line south from Oujda as the first section of a north–south imperial link.

5. *Annuaire statistique, 1952*, p. 282.

6. Improvements of the port of Nemours were financed by the revenues from the 2.5 per cent surtax on products entering Morocco at Oujda.

7. "Morocco '54," p. 189.

8. Bousser, *Le problème des transports*, p. 88.

9. André Sayous, "La réglementation du transport en commun des voyageurs par route au Maroc Français," *Revue Economique Internationale*, V (September, 1933), p. 15.

10. As an example of the seriousness of this competition from the *C.T.M.*'s viewpoint, the rate charged by this company for the 29-kilometer trip from Fez to Sefrou was 5 francs before the appearance of Valenciana in 1932, and only 50 centimes afterwards. Bousser, *Le problème des transports*, p. 112.

11. *Annuaire statistique, 1952*, p. 285.

12. For details, see Marvin W. Mikesell, "The Role of Tribal Markets in Morocco," *The Geographical Review* (October, 1938).

13. Of approximately 64,000 pleasure cars in Morocco at the end of 1952, roughly 9,000 belonged to Moroccans. Trucks and busses numbered around 35,000, of which 7,500 were owned by Moroccans. *Annuaire statistique, 1952*, p. 275.

14. For the background of the development of the port of Casablanca, see Fernand Joly, "Casablanca, éléments pour une étude de géographie urbaine," *Les Cahiers d'Outre-Mer*, I (April–June, 1948), pp. 119–148; and Jean Célérier, "Les conditions géographiques du développement de Casablanca," *Revue de Géographie Marocaine*, XVIII (May, 1939), pp. 131–153.

15. *Statistiques du mouvement commercial et maritime du Maroc, année 1953*, Gouvernement Chérifien, Direction du Commerce et de la Marine Marchande (Casablanca, 1954), p. 14.

16. See *Statistiques du mouvement commercial et maritime, 1953*, p. 10.

17. *Ibid.*, p. 9.

18. *La conjoncture économique marocaine, 1953*, p. 28.

19. *Ibid.*, pp. 19, 21.

20. Waterston, *Planning in Morocco*, p. 51.

21. Cowan, *The Economic Development of Morocco*, p. 43.

22. United Nations, *Special Study on Economic Conditions in Non-Self-Governing Territories*, Summary and Analyses of Information Transmitted to the Secretary-General During 1954 (New York, 1955), pp. 194–195.

23. See Chapter III, pp. 83–85.

CHAPTER VI: EPILOGUE AND PROLOGUE

1. For an inter-disciplinary treatise on decolonization, see Gilbert Blardone, et al., *Initiation aux problèmes d'outre-mer: colonisation, décolonisation, sous-développement* (Lyon, 1959).

2. Unlike economic independence which is an ideal state, integration is

an on-going process which is directed toward achievement of this ideal. It is continuous because relevant conditions, both domestic and international, are constantly changing, i.e., parameters which demand new orientations for the integration process. This interpretation is similar to, but not identical with, Myrdal's view of integration. See Gunnar Myrdal, *An International Economy: Problems and Prospects* (New York, 1956).

3. For the political, see Douglas E. Ashford, *Political Change in Morocco* (Princeton, 1961); and Robert Rézette, *Les partis politiques marocains* (Paris, 1955). For the social aspects, see the work of Jean and Simonne Lacouture, *Le Maroc à l'épreuve* (Paris, 1958).

4. The continued presence of French troops on Moroccan soil was also for some time a complicating factor. Negotiations for their withdrawal were long and protracted. The same situation prevailed in the matter of American bases and the Spanish garrisons in the north.

5. See *The New York Times*, August 21, 1961, pp. 1, 6; Nevill Barbour, ed., *A Survey of North West Africa* (New York, 1959), p. 196; Jean Dresch in *Al Istiqlal*, March 2, 1957, p. 9.

6. The tendency toward centralization in French governance undoubtedly helps to account for the tight monopoly in the public service since the tendency was carried to overseas territories. Tight control requires tight monopoly. Relatively little authority was officially delegated from Paris to Rabat, although it was often usurped at the latter place, and even less was delegated from Rabat to the local level. The British, on the other hand, had a long tradition of building effective government from the local level up, a tradition which helps to account for the relatively large numbers of competent local officials to be found in ex-British colonies. I am indebted to Professor M. M. Knight for this observation. For a discussion of the British approach in action, see Ursula K. Hicks, *Development from Below: Local Government and Finance in Developing Countries of the Commonwealth* (New York, 1961).

7. *The Economist* (London), February 27, 1960, p. 181.

8. The occasion also offered a chance to "rationalize" Moroccan administration by abolishing many jobs which even casual inspection would show to be unnecessary. Elimination of jobs is probably too much to ask, however, in a country where unemployment is high and chronic and where the numerous party faithful expect rewards.

9. The riots were touched off by the arrest of five Algerian leaders when their plane, en route from Rabat to Tunis, was diverted to Algiers by the French authorities. A further incentive to leave Morocco, in French eyes, is the prospect of rearing children in an alien cultural milieu.

10. *La Vie Economique*, October 7, 1960, p. 1. This is the new name for *Le Petit Casablancais*, which has been cited many times in the previous pages.

11. *Ibid.*, January 1, 1960, p. 1. Not only has there been a reduction in numbers but also a tendency toward redistribution to the northwest. Cities such as Fez, Marrakech, and Essaouira have lost greater percentages of their European populations than have Casablanca and Rabat.

12. *Ibid.*, July 1, 1960, p. 3.

13. A Moroccan Jew has made an eloquent plea for his co-religionists to assimilate with the Muslim Moroccan majority and to build the country together. See Carlos de Nesry, *Les Israélites marocains à l'heure du choix*

(Tangier, 1959). If his plea is heeded by both elements, a long step in the process of social integration will have been taken.

14. *Al Istiqlal*, April 18, 1959, p. 4. Apparently open emigration has resumed following the liberalization of passport issuance to Jews. Heretofore, Jews found it almost impossible to obtain passports. See *The New York Times*, December 9, 1961, p. 10.

15. *Le Petit Casablancais*, June 5, 1959, p. 1. The withdrawal of foreign troops also threatens its adverse effect on employment. For example, approximately 8,000 Moroccans were employed on the American bases which were closed in 1963. In addition, Americans have poured some $40 million annually into the Moroccan economy. See *The Economist* (London), January 30, 1960, p. 433.

16. *La Vie Economique*, February 12, 1960, p. 1.

17. *Ibid.*, June 9, 1961, p. 3.

18. *Statistiques et études économiques et démographiques*, Royaume du Maroc, Ministère de l'Economie Nationale et des Finances, Service Central des Statistiques (Rabat, 1960), pp. 3–13; *La Vie Economique*, June 2, 1961, p. 1.

19. International Monetary Fund, "International Financial News Survey," February 14, 1958, p. 256. For details of the agreement see *Le Monde*, January 9–15, 1958, p. 1.

20. A study of retail prices in Tetouan and Casablanca showed that prices in the latter place were higher by more than 10 per cent for four-fifths of the articles included, and by more than 12 per cent for one-half. See *Le Petit Casablancais*, October 25, 1957, p. 3.

21. One manifestation of discontent based on lack of mutual understanding was a revolt in the Riff in 1958 by tribes protesting the acts of administrators sent from Rabat. Action by the Royal Army and negotiation by the Crown Prince, now King Hassan II, were required to restore order. In the matter of resources, the Riff does have the biggest and best iron ore deposits in Morocco at Nador. For Moroccan plans concerning these, see Chapter VI, p. 197, note 76.

22. For some detail see a letter from Charles F. Gallagher, "The Royal City of Tangier," *American Universities Field Staff Reports*, July, 1957. A more complete history of the city, and especially of the period when it was under international administration, has been written by Graham Stuart, *The International City of Tangier* (Stanford, 1955).

23. Some restrictions on currency for local use was contained in the Governor's announcement that effective January 1, 1958, only the Moroccan franc would be accepted in making payments to the government, public corporations, and other public bodies. Hitherto, the peseta had been the principal medium of exchange, but any currency was acceptable. See United States Department of Commerce, *Economic Developments in Morocco, 1957*, World Trade Information Service, Part I, nos. 58–59, p. 4.

24. So-called free transit accounts were exempt from exchange controls. The owners of these accounts were allowed to use them to deal in goods which passed through Tangier en route to other countries. See *Le Bulletin Officiel*, April 15, 1960.

25. *La Vie Economique*, August 26, 1960, p. 1. During the period between the announcement and the abrogation, 600 corporations were dissolved, and

50 additional ones were transferred to other countries, among them some of the most important in the city. *Ibid.*, April 1, 1960, p. 1.

26. *Ibid.*, September 16, 1960, p. 4. A year later, however, the economy was still stagnating. See *The Economist*, September 16, 1961, p. 1072. Since the Crown Prince has become King, he has made Tangier his summer capital in an effort to aid the ailing city. See *The New York Times*, July 29, 1962, p. 7.

27. For a discussion of the difficulties involved, see Waterston, *Planning in Morocco*. For a "model" of the Moroccan economy as it existed in 1954–1955, see the relevant section in the United Nations study, *Structure and Growth of Selected African Economies* (New York, 1958), pp. 80–147.

28. Morocco received its tariff freedom with the British and Spanish renunciations of the provisions in their 1856 and 1861 treaties, respectively, which had fixed import duties at 10 per cent, provisions which had been extended by most-favored-nation treatment to all countries. The tariff schedule adopted in June, 1957, ranged from zero for certain raw materials to 50 per cent for goods which would compete with certain Moroccan products. See Administration des Douanes et Impôts Indirects, *Tarif des droits de douane* (Rabat, 1957). Morocco also concluded several bilateral trade agreements, some of minor importance whose terms have remained unfulfilled. A crucial agreement is that with Mainland China, now Morocco's main supplier of tea. Due to the great importance of tea in the import accounts, the government makes special efforts to meet the terms of this agreement. For details of the 1957 arrangement, see *Al Istiqlal*, November 2, 1957, p. 4.

29. See Chapter V, p. 157.

30. Embassy of Morocco, *Economic News from Morocco* (Washington), January 1960, p. 6; *La Vie Economique*, January 13, 1961, p. 1. According to another source, Europeans accounted for 60 per cent of Moroccan agricultural exports over-all, although they held only 6 per cent of the land. See *Al Istiqlal*, October 25, 1958, p. 3.

31. Access in the future may be difficult, if not impossible. Since the *décrochage*, there is no assurance that the franc and the dirham will move together. Changes in the relative values of the two currencies could raise the prices of Moroccan products in France.

32. See Chapter III, p. 81.

33. See *Le Petit Casablancais*, August 7, 1959, p. 3.

34. To control land transfers in the other direction, a decree has provided for prior government approval of acquisitions of agricultural land by non-Moroccans. See *Le Bulletin Officiel*, November 17, 1959. Thus the *status quo ante* the 1906 Act of Algeciras, where Article 60 allowed Europeans to buy land in Morocco without government assent, has been restored.

35. *Al Istiqlal*, February 7, 1959, p. 8.

36. *Le Bulletin Officiel*, July 10, 1959.

37. New rent schedules were long overdue. The average annual rent was 170 francs per hectare, a figure which inflation had reduced to the equivalent of less than 40 cents, and there were "numerous cases" where the annual rent was 5 francs. See *La Vigie Marocaine*, July 18, 1959, p. 2.

38. For details of the *tertib*, see Chapter III, pp. 82–85.

39. *Al Istiqlal*, April 18, 1959, p. 4. Other complaints included the increase from 10 to 25 per cent of tax of the "centimes additionnels" which went to

the principal lending agency for Moroccan farmers, *La Société Marocaine de Prévoyance (S.O.M.A.P.)*, and the continued existence of the prestations, 1,100 francs in 1958 from "rich and poor alike," this at a time when the urban equivalent, the habitation tax, had been abolished.

40. *Le Petit Casablancais*, April 10, 1959, p. 1.

41. *Le Bulletin Officiel*, August 29, 1958; October 21, 1959.

42. *La Vie Economique*, June 23, 1961, p. 4. It should be noted that the "trou," through the action of the multiplier, would result, other things equal, in a reduction of the gross national product greater than 50 billion francs.

43. *Ibid.*, June 16, 1961, p. 3. The example suggests why the monetary problems associated with a desperate agricultural situation in a largely agricultural country are an economist's nightmare. It is little wonder that he would much prefer the "simple" monetary problems involved in inflation at full output and employment.

44. Prices were computed from figures cited in International Monetary Fund, "International Financial News Survey," August 25, 1961, p. 261; and *La Vie Economique*, August 26, 1960, p. 1.

45. The figures for 1961 were not available at the time of writing, but it is safe to say that the drought will have reduced the totals far below those of 1960.

46. The figures were derived from data published in *La Vie Economique*, June 24, 1960, p. 4.

47. *Ibid.*

48. *Ibid.*

49. *Ibid.* In 1958 tomato exports had accounted for about 6 per cent of total exports by value.

50. See Chapter III, p. 97 for the background on the running controversy between Algerian and Moroccan growers.

51. From an interview reported in *La Vie Economique*, October 14, 1960, p. 4.

52. *Ibid.*

53. Actually some of presently cultivated land should revert to trees and grass if erosion is to be checked. In fact, the Moroccan government has continued the soil conservation program, calling for such reversion, which was begun by the French in 1951. The 1958 budget, for example, scheduled an expenditure of $2.2 million, part to be supplied by the U.S. International Cooperation Administration. See U.S. Department of Agriculture, Foreign Agricultural Service, *Morocco's Agricultural Policies and Proposals*, Foreign Agricultural Circular, September 29, 1958, p. 7.

54. For background on the *Secteurs*, see Chapter III, pp. 109–111.

55. *Le Petit Casablancais*, October 30, 1959, p. 4.

56. M. F. Clerc, *Bulletin Economique et Social du Maroc*, No. 82 (October, 1959). The figures were calculated on the basis of a "normal" price for hard wheat of 3,500 francs per quintal from land not benefiting from Operation Plowing, but with an increment of 200 francs for land under the program to allow for increased quality.

57. *La Vie Economique*, December 1, 1961, p. 4.

58. From a report by the Minister of Public Works which appeared in *La Vie Economique*, August 11, 1961, p. 1. The major areas are the Gharb (Sidi Slimane), Abda-Doukkala, Tadla, Haouz, and Triffas.

59. Rather than repeat the previous discussion concerning the deficiencies and the wisdom of completing the projects, the reader is referred to Chapter III, pp. 112–114.

60. *Al Fellah*, November 1, 1960, p. 1.

61. In 1957, sugar in all forms represented 12 per cent of all imports by value. This figure was calculated from data appearing in the *Annuaire statistique du Maroc, 1957*, Royaume du Maroc, Service Central des Statistiques (Rabat, 1957), p. 152ff.

62. Of course, the problem of small size, and often that of productivity, can be overcome by consolidation of parcels and the formation of cooperatives, since both help to increase the efficiency of funds in use and thereby to reduce risk.

63. The argument does not take into consideration the possibility of better alternative uses of credit outside agriculture.

64. The statement does not apply to Europeans. Separate credit lines were characteristic of the dual agriculture. The *colons* were provided early in the protectorate with all facilities, including long term, while Moroccans had only limited access to credit — and much later. See Chapter III, pp. 107–109.

65. For other deficiencies, see Piersuis in *La Vie Economique,* February 12, 1960, p. 1.

66. Details can be found in *Le Bulletin Officiel,* December 15, 1961.

67. By 1960, industrial production had risen by 16 per cent over 1953, while mineral production had gone up by 50 per cent during the same period. The increase in the industrial sector, however, came largely from the greater utilization of old plant allowed by protective barriers, rather than from the new. The impact of the increase in the mining sector was considerably greater on the export accounts than on the national product, since mineral production accounted for approximately one-third of exports by value but only 8 per cent of the national product. See *La Vie Economique,* August 8, 1961, p. 3.

68. The declining importance of the European and Jewish elements of the population helps to simplify the process of market identification since there is less need for isolating market segments on the basis of the plural society. On the other side of the coin, however, is the reduced size of potential demand as higher income receivers leave the market. Consumer homogeneity at a low level obviously excludes many products from the market.

69. *The New York Times,* December 28, 1961, p. 3; *La Vie Economique,* December 29, 1961, p. 4. There is also talk of extending the requirement to individual taxpayers. How an individual would qualify for a rebate is not clear.

70. International Monetary Fund, "International Financial News Survey," July 21, 1961, p. 220.

71. For background on the cartel, see Chapter IV, pp. 124–125.

72. Another mainstay of the protectorate era, fish canning, has been in the doldrums owing to the loss of off-shore boats which their European owners moved elsewhere and to the reported reduction of the fish population. It can be suspected too that stiff competition from lower-cost Portuguese canners may also be involved.

73. The principal item on the import side is tea, which represents over 60 per cent of all tea imports. The government nationalized tea importing in

1959 and has since constructed a tea-processing plant where the approximately 13,000 tons annually consumed by Moroccans are treated.

74. Consumption totaled 300,000 tires in 1955, the last year of the protectorate. The drop reflects the heavy emigration of Europeans who owned the majority of the motor vehicles at that time. See *La Vie Economique*, May 5, 1961, p. 1.

75. In the matter of ownership, one author, writing about India, identifies three combinations: mixed enterprise is composed of government and its nationals; composite enterprise includes government and one or more foreigners; while joint enterprise brings together nationals and foreigners. See Daniel L. Spencer, *India — Mixed Enterprise and Western Business* (The Hague, 1959), p. 67ff. In Morocco, composite enterprise appears to be the most popular combination in the expanding industrial sector, as indeed it was during the protectorate, particularly in mining, where private French interests joined with the government in several ventures.

76. Profits and losses are used here in the "real" sense, i.e., are regarded from the social point of view. A transportation facility may yield money profits for stockholders owing, for example, to government subsidy. In many, although not all, cases, it can be shown that the subsidy represents real losses to society as income is redistributed from taxpayers to stockholders. In these instances, the facility, as capitalized, is a social liability rather than an asset.

77. Of course one must make allowance for the fact that large sections of the railroad, e.g., Casablanca–Marrakech and Fez–Oujda, were built for the non-economic purpose of troop transport rather than for freight, and returns from profitable portions, mainly the ore-carrying ones, were insufficient to cover the losses incurred on the military lines. For details, see Chapter V, pp. 148–151.

78. In the matter of ports themselves, the tragic earthquake at Agadir offers an opportunity, although an expensive one, to start afresh with facilities commensurate with Moroccan plans for the hinterland. Extensive improvements are also envisaged for Tangier and Safi, the latter in connection with the development of a chemical industry.

79. The operation of the port of Casablanca is also a concession to the French-owned *Manutention Marocaine*. Since independence, the port has been burdened by a long series of labor troubles which, along with a general decline in efficiency, has raised ship turn-around times and thus freight rates.

80. Just once during the six post-independence years has a rough balance been achieved; this was in 1959, but the result was only brought about by a sharp curtailment of capital goods imports through government regulation and a devaluation of the currency. A balance was also struck during one year of World War II when imports in general fell off greatly owing to wartime shortages.

81. *La Revue Fiduciaire Marocaine*, April 20, 1962; Banque du Maroc, *Rapport annuel sur l'exercice 1961* (Rabat, 1962), *passim*.

82. International Monetary Fund, "International Financial News Survey," September 22, 1961, p. 293.

83. *Ibid.*, July 6, 1962, p. 210.

84. *Le Petit Casablancais*, February 6, 1959, p. 1.

85. For a discussion of the desirability of associate status for Morocco, see *Maroc Informations*, June 17–18, 1962, p. 1.

86. See *The New York Times*, July 6, 1962, p. 3 and July 8, 1962, p. 4; *Le Monde*, July 8, 1962, p. 1.

87. On the contrary, some would argue that Morocco probably has all the capital needed right now, given "absorptive capacity." The idea of absorptive capacity is essentially based on opportunity cost, a crucial notion in pure economic theory having to do with efficient allocation of scarce capital among competing investment possibilities. It is difficult, however, to see its relevance to the political economy of foreign aid where the future of mankind is at stake. The calculus must be different when the investor is rich and the object of investment, not a building or machine, but a human being who is desperately poor. There are as yet no meaningful criteria to measure capital productivity in this kind of environment. Absorptive capacity is not only meaningless but downright dangerous, since it can lead to inaction on the part of the affluent.

88. The beginning of a Five-Year Plan, calling for an expenditure of $1.5 billion, was delayed by political events, and even now its significance remains a question. One might suspect that the Plan represents no more than an "inventory of desires" owing to the loose drafting of its provisions and to the lack of adequate financing. An even more ambitious undertaking, the so-called *Promotion Nationale*, which was to "mobilize national energies" through a vast program of public works, does not appear to have gotten off the ground. See *The New York Times*, October 29, 1961, p. 21; January 21, 1962, p. 9.